Uncovering God's Mysterious Ways

Alton J. Garvey

3/27/2004

Alton Gansky

Uncovering God's Mysterious Ways

BROADMAN
&HOLMAN
PUBLISHERS

NASHVILLE, TENNESSEE

Published by Broadman & Holman Publishers,
Nashville, Tennessee

Dewey Decimal Classification: 231.7
Subject Heading: GOD \ PROVIDENCE AND GOVERNMENT OF GOD

Unless otherwise stated all Scripture citation is from the New American Standard Bible, © the Lockman Foundation, 1960, 1962, 1963, 1968, 1971, 1972, 1973, 1975, 1977, 1995; used by permission. Verses marked NKJV are from the New King James Version, © 1979, 1980, 1982, Thomas Nelson, Inc., Publishers.

Photographs Credits
15: Scott Langston
26 and 63: Nancy Arnold
44: David Rogers
57: Bob Schatz
78, 125, 184, 221: Ken Touchton
88, 109, 130, 145, 214, 246: Thomas V. Brisco
162: Southwestern Baptist Theological Seminary, A. Webb Roberts Library
177 and 223: Scofield Collection, Dargan Research Library
193: Bill Latta

1 2 3 4 5 6 7 8 9 10 07 06 05 04 03

I dedicate this book to the fine people at High Desert Baptist Church in Phelan, California, who have allowed me the opportunity of more than thirteen years of service. May God continue to bless them in the years ahead, and may their hunger for God's Word continue to grow.

Contents

Acknowledgments

No book is the sole result of the writer's efforts. This is especially true for books of this kind. Any contemporary writer who undertakes to write about the Bible and what it contains must stand on the shoulders of great students and scholars who have plowed the field before him. All students of the Bible, whether scholars who walk the halls of seminaries and graduate schools or Sunday school teachers who work diligently to teach children the great truths of God, are dependent upon the unheralded people who construct histories, language studies, commentaries, and theologies, all in an effort to deepen our understanding of God's revelation.

I am no different. People both recent and distant in time have made much of what follows possible because of their thousands of hours of work. I am thankful to God for such diligent men and women.

I would also like to thank the wonderful people at Broadman & Holman Publishers for their support and expertise. I especially wish to thank my editor, Gary Terashita, for his patience and professional approach to this project and the one that preceded it. The world is a better place because of the dedication of these men and women.

I would also like to thank my wife for her unending support and willingness to read the first draft, make suggestions, and ask questions. All this she has done without complaint.

My son, Aaron, is also deserving of thanks for his help with research and with the manuscript. It was good to see that English degree put to work.

Of course, my greatest appreciation goes to our Lord and Savior Jesus Christ, the heart and center of the Scriptures. I praise God for providing us with such an interesting faith and fascinating Bible.

Introduction

Several times every week, I stand before a group of people eager to study God's Word. Before I bring my lesson, I open the floor to questions. There are no boundaries during this Q & A time. I do this because I believe church is the place to have questions answered. Invariably a few hands go up, and the questions begin. Most inquiries start with, "What does it mean . . . ?" or "Why did God . . . ?"

Over the years I've learned that there is a great hunger to know not only what God has done but why He has done it. Every week someone brings a question that has caused them to scratch their heads and wonder about divine motivation and purpose. That's the wonderful thing about Bible study: answers found; new questions discovered. That is the way it should be.

While some people have portrayed the Bible as old, dusty, and out of date, Bible students like you have found it a place of intellectual and spiritual adventure. There is great joy in plumbing the depths of the Scriptures. The deeper we look the greater depth we see.

When I was a child, my family was vacationing in the South. A relative took us to a place where a small lake was located. It was in a limestone depression. Uncle Bob said, "That's a bottomless pit, boy. Nobody has ever discovered how deep it is. They've sent divers down there to find out, but no matter how far down they go, they can't find the bottom." In retrospect, I think old Uncle Bob was having some fun at my expense. Ever the practical child, I asked why someone didn't tie a rock to a long rope and throw it in. When the rock stopped sinking, they could pull up the rope and measure the distance. For some reason the conversation ended at that point.

1

I didn't believe in bottomless pits then, and I don't now. However, the Bible seems to be the one thing on this planet that has an unfathomable depth. Paul felt the same way. He wrote to the believers in Rome saying, "Oh, the depth of the riches both of the wisdom and knowledge of God! How unsearchable are His judgments and unfathomable His ways!"[1]

That's the exciting part. There is more between the covers of the Bible than we can understand in a single lifetime. So intricately woven, so finely tuned, the Bible holds mysteries that have endured through the ages, each one a testimony to God's inspiration of the Scriptures.

What follows is a sampling of the mysterious ways in which God has worked. Some topics are stunning; others, puzzling. Some seem simple at first glance, only to prove themselves as complex as a Swiss watch.

In each case, I've tried to offer explanations. When explanations were not available, I have offered some reasonable supposition. In a few cases, I could offer little more than an examination of the text, then step back and scratch my head along with everyone else.

God works in mysterious ways but ways that always have a purpose, a goal in mind. Careful, prayerful study leads to great understanding, and it's a thrilling journey.

This book follows its companion, *Uncovering the Bible's Greatest Mysteries*. In that work, we looked at the mysterious things, places, and people of the Bible. In this work, we look at the unexpected ways in which God has worked His will. God can be amazing, shocking, surprising, but He is never boring. In each case, we learn that God has worked with a purpose. His work enriches us.

In the eighteenth century, a man named William Cowper struggled with depression. So great was his depression that he attempted suicide several times. He made efforts to poison himself, drown himself, hang himself, and impale himself on a knife. He failed at every turn. Despite his battles with mental illness, his creative skill blossomed. Helped by Christian friends, he took up poetry, writing some of the faith's great hymns, including "There Is a Fountain Filled with Blood." It is a song about Christ's sacrifice.

---

[1]Romans 11:33.

The cross of Christ continues to cast its shadow on humanity.

After reading a portion of Romans, Cowper penned a poem that contains a line that is now a popular English saying: "God moves in mysterious ways."

> God moves in a mysterious way
> His wonders to perform;
> He plants His footsteps in the sea,
> And rides upon the storm.
>
> Deep in unfathomable mines
> Of never-failing skill
> He treasures up his bright designs,
> And works His sovereign will.
>
> Ye fearful saints, fresh courage take,
> The clouds ye so much dread
> Are big with mercy, and shall break
> In blessings on your head.
>
> Judge not the Lord by feeble sense,
> But trust Him for His grace:
> Behind a frowning providence
> He hides a smiling face.

His purposes will ripen fast
Unfolding every hour;
The bud may have a bitter taste
But sweet will be the flower.

Blind unbelief is sure to err,
And scan His work in vain;
God is His own interpreter
And He will make it plain.
—William Cowper (1731–1800)

The first two lines and the last two lines sum up the intent of this book. We endeavor to discover "God's mysterious ways, His wonders to perform," but we are keenly aware that "God is His own interpreter and He will make it plain."

It is my hope and prayer that this book will open new doors of interest in the Bible and further your journey into the amazing world of the Scriptures.

Mysterious
Punishments

Eventually it crosses the mind of every Christian. It may flood the brain while watching the evening news or unfolding the morning paper. It may come after hearing of a tragedy befalling a friend or family member. The realization is bitter in the mind and sour in the soul: The world is an evil place filled with wicked people, stomach-upending crimes of violence, and unfathomable treachery. Moreover, as the images flash on our televisions, we wonder how it is that God can tolerate such behavior from His creation. We are prone to ask, "Where is the justice of God? Why does He delay?"

When we read the Bible, we quickly discover that God can judge quickly. Ironically, many of these accounts cause us to ask a different set of questions: "Why was God's judgment so rapid? Why was His punishment so severe?"

It's an odd sensation to feel that God is too slow to act in some cases and too quick in others. Careless reading of Scripture has led some critics to accuse God of being fickle, reactionary, and even cruel. Longtime believers have wrestled with the whys and wherefores of such accounts. The Bible holds accounts of people besieged by snakes, reports of the ground opening up and swallowing hundreds of complainers, and even a man stoned to death for gathering firewood on the wrong day of the week. Such accounts can cause even the most faithful people to scratch their heads in wonder.

CHAPTER ONE

A Couple's Deadly Choice
Acts 4:32–5:11

The New Testament Book of Acts paints one unsettling account of unexpected punishment. It is a story of conspiratorial deceit and sudden death. The fifth chapter of the New Testament's only history book gives the puzzling details, but the story really begins a few verses before.

The arrival of the first church had rocked Jerusalem on its heels. In less than two months, Jesus made His triumphal entry up the mountain and into the Holy City. He rode on a donkey while crowds of supporters shouted praise. Within hours, the masses left, Judas betrayed Jesus, and a mob arrested Him. Religious leaders and others tried Him illegally several times, and then nailed Him to a cross. On Sunday morning, He rose from the dead and over the next forty days made twelve appearances to His startled followers. He then ascended into heaven before several startled witnesses.

Ten days later, on the day of Pentecost, the Holy Spirit descended upon Jesus' disciples, changing the frightened band of believers into dynamos of faith. Their preaching led thousands to faith, including three thousand in a single day.[1] And they continued growing daily[2] until their number swelled to more than five thousand men (because only men were numbered, the actual count for the congregations could be two to three times that number).

Such remarkable success brings remarkable problems. What does one do with several thousand newly converted souls? And the work was just beginning. Many of the new believers had financial needs, perhaps brought on by their travels and their desire to stay in the city to learn more about Jesus. Away from home and the usual sources of support, they developed pressing needs. Since some had come from as far away as Italy, Egypt, and Mesopotamia, they could not easily ask for help from friends and family.[3] Help had to come from nearby, and the only source for relief was from the world's first Christian church.

Aid came from within the congregation. So unified was this group that they are described as having "one heart and soul."[4] The local

---

[1]Acts 2:41. [2]Acts 2:47. [3]Acts 2:9–11. [4]Acts 4:32.

believers began selling property and homes, sharing the proceeds with the needy in the new congregation. This freed the apostles to continue their preaching about the resurrection of Christ. So successful was the sharing that "not a needy person"[5] remained.

Those first Christians recognized the need and responded sacrificially. The people laid the proceeds at "the apostles' feet" (Acts 4:35). This is an interesting phrase. It appears three times in this account. Nowhere else in the New Testament does anyone lay anything at the feet of an apostle; nowhere else is the corporate act of selling property and sharing the proceeds reenacted.

The great first-century church planter Paul several times encouraged Christians to help one another financially, but he never suggested that the churches he founded follow the example of the Jerusalem congregation.[6] The same can be said of the apostle Peter, who was present in Jerusalem at the time the sacrificial selling occurred. This was not Christian socialism, nor was it meant to be a practice for all churches. It was a determined and voluntary act of love in an unusual situation.

It is also the key to understanding what happened next.

Acts 4 introduces a man by the name of Joseph but better known in the New Testament as Barnabas. The name *Barnabas* means "son of encouragement" or "son of consolation"—not a bad nickname. Like many others, he sold his property and gave the proceeds to the church for dispersal to the needy congregation.

It is no accident that Barnabas is included in this account. As with all Scripture, there is a lesson here. Barnabas's gallant act sets up what follows. Barnabas did what he did simply, honestly, and for noble reasons. The next two people we meet couldn't be more different.

The story of Ananias and Sapphira is the first uncomplimentary statement that Luke (the human author of Acts) makes about the young congregation. The account stands out in the New Testament like a blob of black paint on a white canvas. It is impossible to ignore. It is also often misunderstood. The report is of a husband and wife who, like Barnabas and others, sold property and gave the proceeds to the church. Unlike

---

[5] Acts 4:34. [6] See 1 Corinthians 16:2 and 2 Corinthians 8:11–15 for examples.

Barnabas, who was praised for his generosity, these two died—suddenly and unexpectedly.

We know very little about Ananias and Sapphira. Their names, however, are interestingly ironic. *Ananias* is the Greek version of the Hebrew *Hananiah,* which means "Jehovah has been gracious." His wife Sapphira's name means "beautiful" in Aramaic. Two people with lovely names committed an ugly act—an act that, in God's eyes, was worthy of instant death.

Ananias conspired with his wife to sell a piece of property and hold some of the proceeds back while pretending to have given it all. The mystery of this action is almost overwhelming and begs the question, "Why?" Why sell the property? Why lie about the sale price and the amount given? They were under no compulsion to sell or to give the money. The fact that other property owners did so did not obligate them to follow suit. No apostle demanded the action. It was not part of church doctrine. What was theirs was theirs, and they were free to do with their property as they saw fit. But they formed a two-person conspiracy intent on misrepresenting their gift.

Not mentioned is the price or the percentage of the sale that was "set aside," nor does it matter. This mysterious incident isn't about real estate deals or finances; it's about much more.

We can only imagine the conversation between Ananias and his wife. The passage indicates that the idea sprung to life with Ananias, who decided to keep a portion of the money for himself. The Greek word used here means to "misappropriate" or to "embezzle."[7] Paul uses the word in Titus 2:10, where the New American Standard Bible translates it as "pilfering." This is where things get interesting. A man cannot pilfer from himself, nor can he embezzle his own money. Those terms can only be applied to a person who misuses, steals, conceals, or "cooks the books" of someone else's finances. If we take the Bible literally here (and we should), then we must assume that at some point the proceeds of the sale ceased to be Ananias's.

---

[7]*Nosphizo.*

When could this have happened? Most likely, it occurred when Ananias publicly declared that the proceeds of the sale were dedicated to God. At that point, the property ceased to belong to Ananias. The ancient Jews had a word for something exclusively offered to God: *corban*. It is mentioned only once in the New Testament and in an unflattering way.[8] Jesus accused the ultraconservative Pharisees of misusing the concept. Parents who were in need of help from their children were being turned away with the words, "Whatever I have that would help you is Corban." This meant that it was given to God and not to be shared with others. It had become a way of avoiding responsibility to parents. Jesus had no patience with such behavior. This account shows that the people of Ananias's day had a practice of declaring certain things corban (given exclusively to God).

Had Ananias declared his property corban? If so, then the property no longer belonged to him but to God. Ananias, however, thought he could work both ends of the deal. Declare his property corban, give some to the church for the needy and receive their admiration, and still keep some for other purposes. If Ananias did indeed declare his property corban (Scripture doesn't say), it would explain the use of the term *kept back* (better translated as "pilfer").

Ananias was not alone in his scheming. He did so with the "full knowledge" (collusion) of his wife.[9] The passage tells us nothing of their motive or their plans for the money. Nor do we know why they bothered to give any of the proceeds at all. What does seem obvious is that their gift was intended to achieve something for themselves, not to help the needy.

The dictionary lists Ananias as "an early Christian struck dead for lying."[10] There's more to this spiritual crime than that. If God struck every liar dead, there would be very few people walking the earth. Ananias and Sapphira did more than lie about the dollar amount; they dismissed God entirely. Their actions reveal the nature and extent of their belief. Their view of God must have been dismal to think that they could

---

[8]Mark 7:11. [9]*synoida:* "to share knowledge with." [10]*Merriam-Webster's Collegiate Dictionary,* 10th ed., 1993.

so easily fool Him. Their honor for Christ and the church He died for must have been miniscule if they would entertain the idea of showing such disrespect.

Still, there is more to the story. We get clues from the questions Peter asked: "Ananias, why has Satan filled your heart to lie to the Holy Spirit and to keep back some of the price of the land?" (Acts 5:3).

It's a remarkable question. First, it tells us that Peter knew of the conspiracy. How did he know? Certainly, Ananias didn't tell him. No one else could know—not even the man who purchased the property. It was a secret between husband and wife, yet Peter was fully aware of it. In some unrevealed manner, God filled Peter in on the intrigue.

Not only that, Peter mentioned a third person in the scheme: Satan. The name *Satan* means "adversary." Ananias learned what many others have found to be true: Satan is no one's friend. And not only was Satan involved but he had filled Ananias's heart. The word for *filled* is the same word that is used in Ephesians 5:18 where the Christian is commanded to be "filled with the Spirit." It carries the idea of a container that is close to overflowing.

The biblical idea of filling means to choose our influence. Situations, events, and the people around us influence all of us. We choose what influences we will make our own. So it was with Ananias, who made a choice between the Holy Spirit and Satan. It is this fact that helps us understand the judgment that befell him and his wife.

Peter made the point clear: Ananias had allowed Satan controlling interest in his life, and this led to his lying to the Spirit. Perhaps Ananias thought he was pulling a fast one over on Peter and the other apostles. After all, how could they know what was hidden in his heart? He learned that he could fool people, but he could not deceive God.

The apostle then reminded Ananias that the property was his to sell or keep; the money was his to give or hold. There was nothing in the situation to compel him to do what he did except undisclosed selfish motives.

The accusation was as shocking as it was true, and Ananias died. Literally, he "fell down and breathed his last" (Acts 5:5). What killed Ananias cannot be determined from the text. Some interpreters have suggested that the shock of discovery (especially since it was impossible for anyone to know what he had done) killed him. Perhaps. When we consider that his wife would die in the same fashion three hours later, it seems unlikely that shock was the only cause of death. It is true, however, that the passage is mute on the specifics. It doesn't say that Peter caused the death, nor does it say that God took the man's life. Ananias just died. Stroke or coronary seizure or some other biological catastrophe took his life, and Ananias fell at Peter's feet—the same place he had laid the partial offering just moments before. Peter would have looked down and seen a dead man lying near or even on the money! Ananias thought he was giving just a portion of what he had, but in a moment he gave his life.

Young men were either standing in the room or nearby. They took Ananias, wrapped him for the grave, and buried him. The people of Peter's day usually buried the dead before sundown. Jews seldom embalmed, and therefore burial was always speedy.

But this is not the end of the story. Sapphira showed up after a three-hour absence. Perhaps she was doing the many duties that fell to women of her day (gathering water; buying food for the evening's meal). Whatever the reason, she was not present to see her husband die. Finding herself standing before Peter, she answered his questions with the same lie that her husband had told. Then the bombshell came: "Why is it that you have agreed together to put the Spirit of the Lord to the test? Behold, the feet of those who have buried your husband are at the door, and they will carry you out as well" (Acts 5:9). Ananias had done his wife no favors.

Many people find this account difficult to believe. What they struggle with is not the historical accuracy of the text, but the extreme punishment for what appears to our age as mild dishonesty. The truth is that it was much more than that.

If Ananias and Sapphira were in court, the prosecutor might begin his portion of the trial by saying something like this: "Members of the jury, the state will prove that Ananias and Sapphira did knowingly and willfully conspire to misrepresent the truth, deceiving the church and its leaders, and did choose a course of action that followed the leadership of Satan while dismissing the presence of the Holy Spirit. They further conspired to lie to God and to test Him in a manner they knew to be sin."

Even so, the punishment seems too harsh for the crime. There must be more—and there is.

Ananias and Sapphira lived in a unique time. They, and all people of their generation, stood on a threshold of transition. Behind them lay an Old Testament lifestyle, and before them beckoned a more personal way to relate to God. It was a special time and a sensitive time. God's rapid judgments are rare, sometimes unusual, but always with a purpose.

In this case, the church was like a newborn baby laid on the steps of the world. Some were willing to take the infant in, while others wished it would just go away.

The couple's death achieved several things. First, it was proof that God took the purity of His church as seriously as He did the behavior of the children of Israel when they followed Moses out of Egypt. This was more than a father overreacting to the misbehavior of a child. The church was in a crucial and sensitive time. Its numbers had swelled at a rate that is difficult to fathom. The church was on hostile ground, birthed in an unfriendly environment, surrounded by enemies willing to lie, conspire, and put to death any who rejected their teaching for that of Christ's. Peter and others faced jail and beatings, not once but many times. Stephen, one of the church's first deacons, would soon be stoned to death. Persecution lay around every corner. If the church were to survive, it needed to know that God was with them in the dark moments as well as the sunshine.

The church also had to be unified and internally strong. Organizations usually fail from within, like a sinkhole caused by the removal of underground water. If the people of the congregation could not trust one another, if they had to worry about betrayal from within as well as attacks from without, they would never be able to stand.

When God took the lives of Ananias and Sapphira, He did more than show His ability to do so; He removed a cancer that would certainly have spread to others.

Churches in the modern world (at least in most places) are open places. Anyone can attend anytime the doors are open. Ushers do not ask for identification, and the pastor doesn't insist that each attendee come with a known sponsor. But churches in persecuted lands operate differently, often meeting secretly and limiting their members to the clearly born again. The first church was in such a setting. Yet growing from a little more than one hundred people to much greater numbers in such a short time made congregational purity impossible for church leaders. After Ananias and Sapphira died, that process was much easier.

Judgment Against Outsiders
Acts 12:21–23

In Proverbs there is a warning: "Pride goes before destruction, and a haughty spirit before stumbling."[11] That was certainly true for a powerful man named Herod Agrippa I. Herod was the last king of the land and the grandson of Herod the Great (the one with whom the Magi met and the one who had the children of Bethlehem killed). Like his grandfather, he was an enemy of God. It was he who had the apostle James put to death[12] and had Peter thrown into prison.[13]

He was a man of power, riches, and influence; he was also a man who would meet a gruesome end. Not only does the Bible recount his unusual death; it was also recorded by the ancient Jewish historian Josephus.[14] When we take the two accounts together, we find a fascinating story.

At the age of fifty-four in the seventh year of his reign, Herod Agrippa found himself standing before an adoring crowd in the costal town of Caesarea, a beautiful and important city built by his grandfather. Here crowds gathered to celebrate and pay homage to Caesar and to do something else—appease Herod Agrippa, whom they had somehow angered. The Bible mentions two towns as having special need to please the king: Tyre and Sidon. These towns were dependent on grain that came from an area under Agrippa's control. It was to their benefit that Herod restore them to his good graces.

On the second day of the festival, most likely at the city's beautiful theater, Herod Agrippa made an appearance. He was to deliver a speech.

---

[11]Proverbs 16:18. [12]Acts 12:2. [13]Acts 12:3. [14]Flavius Josephus, *Jewish Antiquities*.

Before stepping in front of the crowd, he donned his royal clothing—clothing that, according to Josephus, had silver woven into it.

With the sun rising overhead, the king appeared in his splendor. The rays of sunshine reflected off his garment, giving him an otherworldly appearance. To the crowd he appeared to glow. As he moved, his image sparkled.

Someone cried out, "He is a god! The voice of a god!" Pretty high praise. The crowd picked up on it (remember, grain for food is at stake). Soon they all declared the human king was deity in the flesh. This was not unusual to the Roman and Greek mind. They often attributed godhood to human leaders, but Herod was a Jewish king and should have known better. According to Josephus, he did know better and would later say to his friends, "I whom you call a god, am commanded presently to depart this life; while Providence thus reproves the lying words you just now said to me; and I, who was by you called immortal, am immediately to be hurried away by death."

Herod was suddenly stricken with great pain, something the Bible records as an act by "an angel of the Lord." A few days later he would die, "eaten by worms," according to the Bible (see Acts 12:23). Worms? Yes, it is possible, even likely, that Herod Agrippa had intestinal round worms (nematodes). The affliction causes extreme abdominal pain and intestinal blockage. It was a horrible way to die.

There is an interesting connection here. The passage reads, "And immediately an angel of the Lord struck him" (Acts 12:33). The word used for "struck" is used a few verse before this, but with an entirely different outcome. Earlier in chapter 12 we find Peter in prison, and he was there because Herod had him arrested. An angel who first awakened the sleeping apostle released Peter. The angel jarred Peter awake by striking him on the side. It's the same Greek word used for striking Herod with illness. In the first case, the angel struck Peter so he might receive freedom and life; in the latter, Herod received death. Peter's event occurred in private (although guards were chained to either side of him, as much asleep as the apostle was); Herod's, in public. God is poetic in His justice.

Does the punishment seem harsh? We must remember that Herod Agrippa executed James.[15] He also had the prison guards[16] in charge of Peter's confinement executed after his miraculous escape. He also began a persecution of the church.[17] God executed the executor.

Persecuting the church was only one of Herod's crimes. In fact, the reason recorded in Acts for his death had nothing to do with persecution but with receiving honor that was not his. "And immediately an angel of the Lord struck him because he did not give God the glory."[18] While it was a common practice among Romans to attribute godlike status to special leaders, it was abhorrent to the Jews. Indeed, it was blasphemy. Caesarea was a mixed town of Gentiles and Jews. It is easy to understand why the Gentile crowd might feel comfortable calling Herod a god (especially since they wanted to make peace with him). But it is astonishing to think that Herod Agrippa, a man with Jewish roots who was considered the king of the Jews, would allow such a practice to continue.

It was most likely at a theater similar to the Great Theater of Ephesus that Herod Agrippa committed the sin that led to his death.

---

[15]Acts 12:2. [16]Acts 12:19. [17]Acts 12:1. [18]Acts 12:23.

In an earlier event, and amazingly in the same town, the apostle Peter faced a similar situation. One of the earliest cultural obstacles faced by the first church was learning the gospel was for everyone, not just Jews. This was not an easy transition for a first-century Jew to make. While in the town of Joppa, Peter received a vision and direction from the Holy Spirit to accompany some men to the house of a Roman centurion named Cornelius, who was a "righteous and God-fearing man" (Acts 10:22). He was well respected by the Jews who knew him.

Peter learned that the Gentile Cornelius had received a vision, too, as well as a message from an angel. Under angelic orders, Cornelius sent men to Joppa to retrieve a man named Peter, which he did. When Peter arrived, Cornelius did what he shouldn't have done: he bent his knee before the apostle as a man would bend the knee before God. The Bible records: "When Peter entered, Cornelius met him, and fell at his feet and worshiped him. But Peter raised him up, saying, 'Stand up; I too am just a man.'"[19]

What a difference. Peter was quick to straighten out the confused centurion.

There is more to this account than first meets the eye. In many ways, the Book of Acts contrasts the simple fisherman Peter with the flamboyant, egotistical king Herod Agrippa. Both were struck, Peter positively, Herod fatally; both had people worship them in the city of Caesarea; both dealt with an angel (to Peter's benefit; to Herod's demise).

An even more graphic portrayal of people wrongfully worshiping other people is in Acts 14:8–18. Paul and Barnabas were in Lystra (a city in what is now modern Turkey). Seeing a lame man of faith, they performed a miracle of healing. The town went crazy and declared, "The gods have become like men and have come down to us."[20] They began to call Barnabas Zeus (the Greek god of the sky) and refer to Paul as Hermes (the Greek god of messages). Soon the pagan priests arrived ready to make offerings to Paul and Barnabas. This was more than the two could take. They tore their clothes to show remorse and rushed into the crowd screaming, "Men, why are you doing these things? We are also men of the same nature as you, and preach the gospel to you that you

---

[19]Acts 10:25–26. [20]Acts 14:11.

should turn from these vain things to a living God" (Acts 14:15). They had trouble restraining the crowd from making sacrificial offerings to them. Some people might relish such attention, but Paul and Barnabas knew better. Such worship and honor belong to God alone. They did what Herod Agrippa should have done.

Didn't See It Coming
Acts 13

Some miracles come in the form of judgment. All of the miracles of Jesus were beneficial to those around Him (with the possible exception of His cursing the fig tree). Some New Testament miracles, however, are just the opposite; instead of bringing relief, they bring punishment. One such case involves a man who decided to stand in opposition to the gospel.

Acts 13 tells the story of Paul and Barnabas's first missionary trip. Sailing to the large island of Cyprus some sixty miles from shore, they began teaching in the synagogues. They traveled the length of the island until they came to Paphos, where they ran into an interesting character by the name of Elymas Bar-Jesus. His name means, "Wise man, son of Jesus." Jesus was a popular name and is the Greek pronunciation of the Hebrew *Joshua*. Elymas's father bore the name Jesus. (There are five men in the Bible named Jesus.) The Bible describes him as a "false prophet," literally a "pseudo-prophet" (see Acts 13:6).

The Roman leader of the island was the proconsul Sergius Paulus. He summoned Paul and Barnabas to come and share their message. Elymas had other ideas. Perhaps he didn't like what he was hearing; perhaps the proconsul was showing signs of being persuaded by the two missionaries; or perhaps the false prophet thought he was about to be replaced. He spoke up in an attempt to counter the message. The word in verse 8 is translated "opposed,"[21] meaning that he argued against the presentation, but the word carries more meaning than that. It means "to twist, to turn, to make crooked." He was doing more than saying, "I don't agree." Using the first-century equivalent of verbal jujitsu, he tried to turn the gospel into something it wasn't.

---

[21]*Diastrepho.*

Paul's response highlights Elymas's behavior. The apostle, a former persecutor of the church himself and one known to have a quick temper, lashed out at Elymas: "You who are full of all deceit and fraud, you son of the devil, you enemy of all righteousness, will you not cease to make crooked the straight ways of the Lord? Now, behold, the hand of the Lord is upon you, and you will be blind and not see the sun for a time."[22]

It's impossible to overlook the cutting words Paul used: "deceit," "fraud," and "enemy of all righteousness." He even called the man the "son of the devil." These are not words without thought, spewed in a torrent of anger. These accurate descriptions tell us the real nature of the false prophet. The previous verse tells us the Holy Spirit filled Paul before he uttered these words. This was not retaliation; it was revelation. Calling Elymas "the son of the devil" was a play on words to contrast with "son of Jesus."

But Elymas was going to endure more than some hot words. Paul announced that the Lord's hand was upon Elymas and that he would be blinded for a time. Ironically, Paul endured blindness himself at his conversion experience on the road to Damascus.[23]

Immediately Elymas began to seek someone to lead him by the hand. The word *seek* is in the imperfect tense, meaning that the false prophet sought help and no one would give it. He had just become the object of God's wrath, and no one wanted to touch him.

The punishment fit the crime. His blind eyes now matched his blind thinking and his desire to keep others in the dark. Still, his blindness was temporary, lasting "for a time."[24] Like Paul, his sight would return. He would have a chance to redeem himself.

What of the proconsul? "Then the proconsul believed when he saw what had happened, being amazed at the teaching of the Lord."[25] He believed (literally "he had faith"), but notice why he believed. Seeing what happened to Elymas was persuasive, but he was also "amazed" at the teaching of the Lord. Sergius Paulus became a believer, not out of fear but out of conviction.

---

[22]Acts 13:10–11. [23]Acts 9. [24]Acts 13:11. [25]Acts 13:12.

Is there a purpose to all this?

Many harsh punishments are described in the Bible. Some, like the ones above, deal with people. Others deal with nations. The events are recorded without apology and with graphic descriptions. The plagues against Egypt end with the death of the firstborn children of the Egyptians.[26] Fire from heaven destroyed Sodom, Gomorrah, and the other cities of the plain.[27] A man named Korah opposed God and Moses, and the ground opened, swallowing him and his followers.[28] Of course, the biggest punishment of all was the flood in Noah's time.[29]

Is this proof that God is too quick to judge? Does He find pleasure in raining down destruction from the sky or devising unpleasant ways for sinful people to die? No. The apostle Peter portrayed God as patient: "The Lord is not slow about His promise, as some count slowness, but is patient toward you, not wishing for any to perish but for all to come to repentance."[30]

One mistake critics make is reading the Bible accounts without awareness of the passage of time. If we read the judgments and punishments that fell upon the children of Israel during their years of wandering in the wilderness, it seems as if there is one judgment upon another. Overlooked is the fact that the judgments delivered came over a period of four decades.

God's judgments are instructive. Using the children of Israel as an example, Paul wrote to the Corinthians, "Nevertheless, with most of them God was not well-pleased; for they were laid low in the wilderness. Now these things happened as examples for us, so that we would not crave evil things as they also craved."[31]

Past punishment is present learning. History is of little use if we do not learn from it. God's swift judgment is rare but real. What is amazing is how rarely extreme judgment happens.

---

[26]Exodus 7–14. [27]Genesis 19:24–25. [28]Numbers 16:31. [29]Genesis 6. [30]2 Peter 3:9. [31]1 Corinthians 10:5–6.

Points to Ponder

1. In each of the examples in this chapter, severe and unexpected judgment fell on those who were obstacles to God's work. How does God deal with those who oppose His work today?

2. Was God too harsh in the past? Is He too lenient today?

3. Why did God take the life of Herod Agrippa for allowing the crowd to honor him as a god when so many others have done the same and have been allowed to live?

4. How big a role did Satan play in the Ananias and Sapphira affair? How big a role does he play in the lives of those who cheat the church today?

5. How does the love of God fit with the wrath of God? Is this a contradiction in God's character?

Mysterious Skies

The sky above us is a fascinating place. On a clear night, away from the light pollution of streetlights and office buildings, stars shine by the thousands. They hover in the dome of blackness, casting their light on us from distances too far away to comprehend. The twinkling flecks of illumination have guided ships at sea and have been the foundation of wonder.

The moon orbits a quarter of one million miles away, shedding its ivory glow on our planet. The fact that men have walked its surface has not stripped away the awe we feel when we allow ourselves to slow down enough to gaze upon its face.

The life-giving sun rises above our horizon each morning like a slow-moving yellow balloon. Without it, life would be impossible. Through photosynthesis the sun energizes the plants that produce the food necessary for the cycle of life to continue. We would be doomed without it.

Some people would have us believe that the delicate dance between earth, sun, and moon is the result of cosmic coincidence; that we are the fortunate benefactors of unreasoning fate and some spectacular luck. But the universe seems more than that. In front of the backdrop of dark space play the proofs of creation. And where there is creation, there must be a Creator.

Astronomer Hugh Ross noted, "There's the mystery of what's really out there, what those specks of light may be, the mystery of how they all got there and of what lies above and beyond. Gazing at the night sky seems to raise profound questions not only about the universe, but also about ourselves."[1]

To wonder about the creation is to wonder about the Creator. It shows us the size and scope of God in concrete terms. Scholars often debate how long ago God called the cosmos into being. Young earth creationists want a ten-thousand-year-old universe; old earth creationists say God did His work four and one-half billion years ago. Both agree on this: Nothing we see on our planet or beyond its atmosphere is here by accident.

The Bible is a book filled with miracles, and many of those miracles deal with the skies above us. When we read those accounts, we see that God did not go on vacation after the sixth day of His creative week. Instead, we see a Creator who still makes clouds rain, forms hail, blinks out light, and generally changes the rules of physics to meet His plans and purposes.

Doubts, Doubts, Everywhere Doubts
Joshua 10

Begin a discussion on miracles in the Bible, and sooner or later someone will ask about the day the sun stood still. Through centuries, it has been one of the most hotly debated accounts in the Scriptures. Could the sun really stand still in the sky? Could someone make a day longer? How is that possible, knowing what we do about how the earth spins on its axis?

Skeptics scoff as we expect them to do, but even generally conservative theologians and Bible scholars struggle with the matter, offering various explanations to knock off the disagreeable edges. Apart from the creation itself, Joshua's long day may be the most spectacular miracle in the Bible. The very thought that the endless progression of rising and setting of the sun could be interrupted goes beyond shocking. For some people, it is too much to believe.

Carl Sagan was a man who left his imprint upon the world. From his many appearances on the "Tonight Show" with Johnny Carson to his

---

[1]Hugh Ross, *The Creator and the Cosmos* (Colorado Springs, Colo.: NavPress, 1993), 9.

many books and his wildly popular *Cosmos* series on PBS, he laid the groundwork for unswerving belief in the principles of science while attempting to erode the foundation of contemporary faith.

In his 1974 book *Broca's Brain,* the astronomer included a chapter entitled "A Sunday Sermon" in which he challenges religious thinking in general and Christian thinking specifically, going so far as to say, "As we learn more and more about the universe, there seems less and less for God to do."[2] Dr. Sagan was not a friend of faith.

While arguing against some of the strange theories of Immanuel Velikovsky,[3] Sagan notes that if somehow the sun were stopped in its tracks—even if it were stopped slowly over the course of a day—the oceans would reach the boiling point of water, something not mentioned in history.[4]

Others have worried over such things. In 1898, the popular writer H. G. Wells penned a short story entitled "The Man Who Could Work Miracles." In the tale, a man unexpectedly learns that he can work miracles. On the advice of a minister, he decides to stop the earth's rotation to lengthen his miracle-working day. He is successful, but he misses a crucial detail. Everything not secured to the ground goes flying off at incredible speeds. It was, in Wells's unique style, a backhand to the story of the long day under Joshua.

It is easy to understand the reluctance of some people to believe the story of Joshua and the long day. That, however, doesn't mean it's a myth. Answers lie in the details of the story.

Mysterious Ammunition and a Slow Sun

Joshua 9 and 10 tell the story of an awkward allegiance between the children of Israel, now led by Moses' successor Joshua, and the leaders of Gibeon. Gibeon was a great Canaanite city in its day, and it was filled with mighty men.[5] In spite of their mighty and marvelous walled city,

---

[2]Carl Sagan, *Broca's Brain* (New York: Random House, 1979), 286. [3]In his book *Worlds in Collision,* Velikovsky argues that a comet ejected by the planet Jupiter was responsible for the plagues of Egypt and Joshua's long day. His theories are generally considered inaccurate. [4]Sagan, *Broca's Brain,* 100. See also his appendix 2. [5]Joshua 10:2.

they knew they were in trouble. Word had reached them that Joshua had destroyed the cities of Jericho and Ai. Ai was just a little more than six miles away. Gibeon was next on the list. They knew that God was on Joshua's side. The proof lay in the ruins of Jericho and Ai. Fear drove them to undertake a devious diplomatic effort. Pretending to be distant travelers (they even dressed in old clothes and worn-out sandals), they entice Joshua and his leaders into a covenant—a covenant sealed with an oath before "the LORD, the God of Israel."[6]

Joshua and the others had made a big mistake: They did not consult God.[7] Making their decision without prayerful consideration bound them in an agreement they felt compelled to honor. In our society, such an agreement would be overturned in court, since it was obtained through lies and deceit. But Joshua faced a moral and spiritual dilemma. They had taken an oath in the Lord's name. Not just any name, but in the name of God. To break the covenant with the Gibeonites was to break a covenant with God. They had made their decision and would have to live with it—and fight because of it.

Gibeon was just one Canaanite city among many. These cities kept a close eye on their neighbors. Their survival depended on knowing what was happening around them. The Gibeonite leaders did what they did out of fear, knowing they were the next logical target. They struck a deal (albeit a deceitful one) to protect themselves from Joshua and his troops. That made the Gibeonites happy, but it annoyed the other cities in the area. The kings of five southern cities waged war against Gibeon. Warren Wiersbe wrote, "The poor Gibeonites had made peace with the invaders and were now at war with their former allies!"[8] Five cities were on the move against Gibeon: Eglon, Lachish, Hebron, Jarmuth, and Jerusalem (then still in Canaanite control).

Joshua, because of his unwise commitment, was obligated to come to their aid. That begins not one but a set of miracles. Joshua calls his soldiers to order and then marches them, under cover of darkness, about twenty miles up a four-thousand-foot grade. To do this in a single night

---

[6]Joshua 9:19. [7]Joshua 9:14. [8]Warren W. Wiersbe, *Be Strong* (Wheaton, Ill.: Victor Books, 1996).

must have been exhausting. An average, healthy man can walk at three miles an hour on flat ground. An extremely fit marathoner can finish the twenty-six-mile, 385-yard race in a little more than two hours. But to march a large army twenty miles up a rugged hill with only the moon for light is phenomenal. The first word the soldiers must have heard from Joshua's mouth was the ancient equivalent of "double-time!"

Arriving on the scene was just the beginning of the difficulties they faced. After a night of grueling travel, they still had a battle to fight. There was only one way for them to win—God would have to intervene.

Intervention came in a series of miracles.

Miracle 1: God Speaks

When Joshua arrived, he saw the war was already underway. Gibeon was under siege by the armies of the five cities. Standing with him were his exhausted troops. It would seem hopeless to any other leader, but Joshua knew where his strength lay. "The LORD said to Joshua, 'Do not fear them, for I have given them into your hands; not one of them shall stand before you.'"[9]

This was all Joshua needed. He began his surprise attack as the sun was beginning its climb in the sky.

Miracle 2: Confusion

"And the LORD confounded them before Israel."[10] There is no mention of how God did this. Whatever way He did it, it worked very well. The word *confounded* means "to confuse, to terrify."[11] It also carries the idea of making noise. Perhaps Joshua and his men attacked with loud screams; perhaps a supernatural storm appeared. In any case, it led to the destruction of the attacking armies. In their confusion, they fled the scene, running down a narrow pass.

Miracle 3: Heavenly Ammunition

"As they fled from before Israel, while they were at the descent of Beth-horon, the LORD threw large stones from heaven on them as far as

---

[9]Joshua 10:8. [10]Joshua 10:10. [11]*hamam* = "to move noisily, to vex, to confuse, etc."

Azekah, and they died; there were more who died from the hailstones than those whom the sons of Israel killed with the sword."[12]

The offending armies quickly learned that they could run, but they could not hide. Those who remained fell to the swords of Joshua and his men. Deadly hailstones pelted those who ran. This was no freak storm. We should be impressed not just with those whom the stones struck but with those whom they missed. Nature is not selective. A tornado cares nothing about the character of people whose homes it destroys. It just does what the laws of physics and meteorology tell it to do. When God is dictating nature, it is a different matter. God can and has controlled the weather, including hail. Directed weather is mightier than any army, then or now.

Hail is frozen rain. In a complex cycle, raindrops are moved through thunderclouds (cumulonimbus) where they repeatedly encounter super-cooled water (water that is still liquid despite being below its freezing point). Layer upon layer of ice builds up until the hail falls to the ground.

Although this sunset took place over the Mediterranean Sea, it was the same sun that stood still in the sky during Joshua's day.

---

[12]Joshua 10:11.

At times, hailstones can weigh more than two pounds. Hailstones in Bangladesh killed ninety-two people on April 14, 1986. Weather can be a powerful weapon.[13]

This is not the only time the Bible mentions hail. It was one of the plagues used against Egypt[14] and as divine judgment in the books of Haggai[15] and Isaiah.[16] How many people died that day because of the hail is unknown, but it was substantial.

Miracle 4: A Slow-Moving Sun

Here is where scholarly opinion divides. What the Bible describes is too hard for some people to accept. Oddly, most scholars who write on this subject spend little time discussing the possibility of the divinely directed hail that assaulted and killed only the enemy while leaving the righteous untouched. But a sun that stands still, or at the very least slows to a crawl, is too much for some to swallow. Many theories circulate to explain away the event as an eclipse (not possible since Joshua sees both the moon and sun in the sky); clouds; a poetic metaphor; or a zeal-induced misunderstanding.

Each of those arguments is interesting, but they fail to satisfy the account given in the Scripture. Perhaps what troubles so many people is not that God did it but our inability to understand *how* He did it.

Joshua was in the heat of battle and ready to pursue the armies that had a short time before been about to massacre the Gibeonites. Apparently, Joshua felt the need for more time, and he made one of the most unusual requests recorded in the Bible: "'O sun, stand still at Gibeon, And O moon in the valley of Aijalon.' So the sun stood still, and the moon stopped, Until the nation avenged themselves of their enemies."[17]

As the sun was rising in the east, the moon hung in the west and Joshua prayed that they would stop their journey. When we add the comments of verse 13, we discover that the sun stopped "in the middle of the sky and did not hasten to go down for about a whole day."

---

[13]For more information on weather in the Bible, see the author's book *Uncovering the Bible's Greatest Mysteries* (Broadman & Holman, 2002). [14]Exodus 9:18–34. [15]Haggai 2:17. [16]Isaiah 28:2, 17. See also Psalms 78:47–48; 105:32; 148:8; Revelation 8:7; 11:19. [17]Joshua 10:12–13.

Shining with neon brightness is the amazing fact that the Bible describes the sun's activities in terms of space and time. It says the sun stood still in the "middle" (the halfway point) of the sky and the moon stopped. These are spatial descriptions indicating not a change in brightness but in location and movement. The text clearly indicates that the sun and moon changed their normal course and behavior for a time.

Understandably, most discussion of this event focuses on the sun, but the text clearly states the moon also stopped. This is where things get tricky.

When we speak of the rising and the setting of the sun, we are speaking in point-of-view terms. That is, we are describing what we see, not what is. Scientists as well as laymen use the terms *sunrise* and *sunset* because that is what it seems the sun is doing. Yet we know what is really happening. Our planet spins on its axis, making one rotation about every twenty-four hours. For the sun to stop literally in the sky, the earth must cease rotating on its axis. But this could not happen suddenly.

The earth spins at about one thousand miles per hour at the equator. If the earth suddenly stopped, great damage would result. Loose objects, including people, would fly through the air, carried by momentum, and come to a messy end. Imagine the tidal waves and the effects on the atmosphere and wind. We see no indication of such a catastrophe. Stalactites still hung unbroken in caves, and history records no events that would match that kind of sudden trouble. Whatever force God used to slow or stop the rotation of the earth, He must have applied to everything on the earth's surface.

This is not beyond reason. If we believe there is a God who is the Creator of the universe and all it contains, He must also be the author of all the natural laws that govern it. The mistake many people make is assuming that the laws of physics fence God in as much as they do us. God has no such limitations.

In addition, if we allow God the power and intelligence to stop the earth's rotation, then we must assume that He is smart enough to avoid the surprising effects of His own actions (unlike H. G. Wells's character in "The Man Who Could Work Miracles"). It is hard to imagine God slapping His forehead and saying, "Oops, why didn't I see that coming?"

But there is more to all of this. The earth spinning on its axis is just one of two pertinent movements that apply to the story. The moon has motion too. It orbits the earth, completing a trip in just twenty-seven days, eight hours, and forty-three minutes. This means the moon is constantly on the move. It appears to move as fast as it does because of the earth's spin. If the earth were to cease its revolving, the moon would still appear to move, although much more slowly.

Why bother with the moon at all? If the goal was to have more daylight for battle, then the moon was an unnecessary element. Why would Joshua ask for both the sun and moon to stop?

Because the real issue here isn't a desperate need for daylight, but a lesson in theology. The Canaanites worshiped many gods, Baal (and his many variations) being the most common. Baal's name means "master" or "lord," and his followers referred to him as the "Rider of Clouds."[18] Statuettes show him with a lightning bolt in his hand. Sometimes called Baal Hadad, he was the god of storms and the bringer of rain. Also included in their group of gods were Yarih, the moon god, and Shemesh, the sun goddess.

The events at Gibeon are a statement and proof that there is only one God and His name is Jehovah. The hail demonstrated that God was superior to Baal Hadad; the sun's odd behavior showed preeminence over Yarih; and the moon's sudden stop proved God's power over Shemesh. Like the plagues of Egypt, God was making a point: False gods have no power, no influence, and no life of their own. They live only in the imaginations of the worshiper, and the worshiper has a better choice.

The real battle was not about possession of ground, not about political allegiances; it was about the reality of God. The hail, the moon, the sun were a very clear message.

How significant was this event? It is mentioned twice more in the Bible. Isaiah 28:21: "For the LORD will rise up as at Mount Perazim, He will be stirred up as in the valley of Gibeon, to do His task, His unusual task, and to work His work, His extraordinary work." Isaiah knew the unexpected God and His mysterious ways. Habakkuk 3:11 says, "Sun

---

[18]Jonathan N. Tubb, *Canaanites* (Norman, Okla.: University of Oklahoma Press, 1999), 74.

and moon stood in their places; they went away at the light of Your arrows, at the radiance of Your gleaming spear."

God achieved much that day—more than meets the eye. As Warren Wiersbe noted, "Instead of having to defeat these five city-states one by one, He would help Joshua conquer them all at one time!"[19] That's the great thing about God. He does more than we ask, achieves more than we imagine, and leaves a message for those of us who follow centuries after the event.

Did it really happen? Did the sun stop in midcourse? Did the moon hang motionless in the sky? Did God confuse the attacking armies and set them to flight by hail? Yes, it happened.

Is it impossible? For any but God, yes. But as Jesus said, "With people this is impossible, but with God all things are possible."[20]

We may never know how God did what He did. Could He have made it just appear that the sun and moon stood still? Yes, but the result is the same. God answered Joshua's prayer with a miracle.

The endangered and beleaguered Gibeonites sent a message to Joshua, "Come save us." Joshua, whose name means "The Lord saves," did just that—with the spectacular intervention of God.

Backing Up Time
2 Kings 20:1–11; Isaiah 38

There is bad news, and then there is really bad news. Seven centuries before Christ lived, there was a king by the name of Hezekiah ("Jehovah is strength"). He was a godly man born to an ungodly king. As soon as he became king, he began to undo the spiritual crimes of his father Ahaz. He reopened the doors of the temple, reactivated the priests and Levites, and did his best to drive idolatry from the land by tearing down sites for idol worship known as "high places." He destroyed cultic icons and toppled pagan altars. He was a man with a mission. But even godly men face trials.

---

[19]Warren W. Wiersbe, *Be Strong,* Joshua 10:1 (Wheaton, Ill.: Victor Books, 1996).
[20]Matthew 19:26.

Hezekiah fell ill. We don't know what disease afflicted him, but we do know two things. First, the illness resulted in a painful boil on the skin. We also know that the condition was lethal. The Bible says that Hezekiah was "mortally ill."

To make matters worse, his country was under attack by Sennacherib, king of Assyria, son of Sargon II. Sennacherib led an army of 200,000 soldiers into Judea and destroyed many cities. He claimed in the Assyrian annals to have taken forty-six strong walled cities and many smaller towns, enslaving 200,156 people as well as countless domestic animals. Sennacherib also said that he had "caged up" Hezekiah in Jerusalem like a bird. While not as strong and driven as his father Sargon II, Sennacherib was not a man to trifle with. Only after Hezekiah paid a large tribute of gold and silver to the attacker, much of it stripped from the gold and silver that adorned the temple, was the siege lifted. Ultimately, 185,000 Assyrian soldiers died by God's direct intervention.[21] Later, back in Nineveh, Sennacherib's two sons, Adrammelech and Sharezer, would assassinate him.

In the midst of this threat from Sennacherib, the great prophet Isaiah approached King Hezekiah with a soul-chilling message: "Thus says the LORD, 'Set your house in order, for you shall die and not live.'"[22] This was harsh news. The phrase "set your house in order" meant "choose your successor." This was one of Hezekiah's problems. Not only was his city and country under attack by a superior force; not only did he have a life-threatening illness; he had no successor. Hezekiah would later have sons but only because God added fifteen years to his life.

One of the great mysteries about this passage is the nature of Hezekiah's disease. We have very little information to go on. All we know is that it was life-threatening and that a boil was involved. The word translated "boil" *(shechiyn)* refers to a skin eruption of some kind and could refer to a type of leprosy, skin ulceration, or abscess. It is a broad term used to describe one of the plagues of Egypt[23] as well as one of the afflictions endured by Job.[24] Such a boil could render a person ceremonially unclean and unable to enter the temple.[25] This is the reason

---

[21]2 Kings 19:35. [22]2 Kings 20:1. [23]Exodus 9:9. [24]Job 2:7. [25]Leviticus 13.

why God's message included these words: "On the third day you shall go up to the house of the LORD."[26] The healing of the boil would be complete, allowing the king free access to the temple once again.

Still, we wonder about the exact nature of the disease. There is a good chance that Hezekiah was suffering from a type of skin cancer. Whatever it was, it was certain to take his life if God did not intervene.

However, the Lord did intervene, and Hezekiah received His promise of fifteen years of additional life. The king's prayer was simple, direct, emotional, and effective. Before Isaiah could finish walking through the palace courtyard, he received another message from God, a message that he was to deliver immediately to Hezekiah. The prophet made a U-turn and delivered the good news.

Still, Hezekiah wanted a sign. This was to be expected, and no one is critical of him for making it. It was customary to ask for a sign from a prophet.[27] This is not evidence of doubt on Hezekiah's part. Indeed, he may have been asking for the benefit of his leaders and others around him.

He received the sign, a sign so mysterious that debate has swarmed around it ever since. A shadow moves normally in the opposite direction in nature. Isaiah gave Hezekiah a choice. He could ask for the shadow to continue to move forward (presumably at a faster rate) or to backtrack. Hezekiah chose the more dramatic.

There is much discussion about what actually happened. The clear part is that a shadow, in response to Isaiah's prayer, changed direction. The question arises over what object cast the shadow. Many people think it was a sundial, but the shadow probably moved along a set of steps. The word translated in some versions as "dial" or "sundial" is the Hebrew word for *step* (from *maalah*). The prophet and the king were looking at a set of stairs on the palace grounds.

The shadow moved ten steps. That's a long distance for a shadow. If the tread of each step were just six inches in length, then the shadow moved backwards five feet, certainly more than could be expected from an optical illusion or a magic trick. It was enough to convince King Hezekiah that the prophet was speaking for God.

---

[26]2 Kings 20:5. [27]Gideon does a similar thing in Judges 6:17, 37, 39.

How is such a thing possible? It's not. That's the definition of a miracle—the impossible done anyway. Still, we can't help wondering what God did to make a shadow do the impossible. The temptation is to say that the earth reversed its spin. Since all things are possible with God, that remains an option, but another approach would work just as well.

It seems that this miracle was a local event and was confined to a particular point on the globe. In fact, it is entirely possible that only the shadow on the steps moved. If we had been standing shoulder-to-shoulder with Hezekiah and Isaiah, we might have seen the shadow move backwards while all other shadows followed their normal course.

Of course, a shadow is nothing of itself. When we look at our shadow on the ground, we are not seeing "something"; we are gazing on "less than something." Seated next to a window on a plane, a traveler can see the aircraft's shadow move along the surface. It travels at the same speed as the jet, touching dirt and trees, houses and buildings, lakes and oceans with no affect on any of them. That's because a shadow represents the blockage of light. A solid object keeps direct light from falling to the ground and therefore that area appears darker. To change a shadow's direction, the location of the light source must change.

God may have changed the way light fell upon the stairs. In the Book of Revelation is a revealing verse: "And there will no longer be any night; and they will not have need of the light of a lamp nor the light of the sun, because the Lord God will illumine them; and they will reign forever and ever."[28] God is light. The apostle John states as much in one of his letters, "This is the message we have heard from Him and announce to you, that God is Light, and in Him there is no darkness at all."[29]

God is the author of all physics. The number of ways in which He may have caused the shadow to move is beyond our ability to count. Certainly, changing the way the light stuck the steps is one of them.

---

[28]Revelation 22:5. [29]1 John 1:5.

Still, it may go even beyond that. In recent years, it has become popular to speak of extra dimensions in our universe, each created by God. We are confined to our familiar three spatial dimensions and one time dimension. But many people believe there are more dimensions beyond our experience. The astronomer and Christian apologist Hugh Ross notes, "God must be operating in a minimum of eleven dimensions of space and time (or their practical equivalent)."[30] Regarding Hezekiah's shadow, Ross says, "Miracles such as the backward movement of the shadow on Hezekiah's sundial also describe extra-dimensional phenomena."

What techniques God used to perform this miracle will remain a mystery. The "how" remains a secret, but we are told the historical fact. It did occur. It is not just a matter of faith, but of reason. It is logical to believe in a thinking, all-powerful God who works in dimensions and times that we cannot fathom. What is illogical is to believe that God is not capable of controlling His own creation.

Many years ago, the great preacher R. G. Lee said in his book *Lord, I Believe*: "And my belief urges me to believe that God is equal to any demand, and all the more so if a moral reason lies behind it. Lord, I believe."[31]

So should we.

Points to Ponder

1. Why do you suppose so many people have difficulty believing the account of Joshua's long day?

2. Do you think the sun and moon just appeared to stop in the sky or that the earth somehow ceased its rotation? Does it make a difference?

3. Isaiah allowed King Hezekiah to choose the direction the shadow would move. Why did he do that?

4. The Bible speaks of many astronomical oddities such as the moon turning to blood (Revelation 6:12), stars falling from the sky (Revelation

---

[30] Hugh Ross, *Beyond the Cosmos* (Colorado Springs, Colo.: NavPress, 1996), 32.
[31] Robert G. Lee, *Lord, I Believe* (Nashville, Broadman Press, 1927), 100.

8:10), and the sun darkening during the crucifixion (Luke 23:44–45). Why does the Bible focus on such strange occurrences? How would you explain these events?

5. So often the Bible describes *what* happened, *why* it happened, but not *how* it happened. Is there a reason for this?

Mysterious
People

While I was growing up, science was one of my consistent interests. It remains so today. The idea that there might be other intelligent beings in the universe fascinated me. Thoughts of planets populated by the kinds of beings I was seeing on television and reading about in comic books filled my mind. It was because of this interest that I devoured a book by Walter Sullivan, the science editor of the *New York Times*. His 1964 book *We Are Not Alone*[1] remains one of the finest works on the topic.

Sullivan concludes his book with the words: "The universe that lies about us, visible only in the privacy, the intimacy of night, is incomprehensibly vast. Yet the conclusion that life exists across the vastness seems inescapable. We cannot yet be sure whether or not it lies within reach, but in any case we are a part of it all; we are not alone."[2]

The debate about extraterrestrial life ("off-earth" life) will continue for decades to come and may never be resolved in this life. The late Carl Sagan and Isaac Asimov as well as scores of others have written popular and scholarly works to show that humankind has neighbors.

Sullivan and the others are right, but perhaps not in the way they were thinking. The Bible describes another realm filled with intelligent life.

---

[1] Walter Sullivan, *We Are Not Alone* (New York: McGraw-Hill Company, 1964). [2] Ibid., 291.

CHAPTER THREE

We Are Not Alone

There are nearly three hundred references in the Bible to intelligent, nonhuman creatures that appear in thirty-four of the Bible's sixty-six books. Generally referred to as angels, these beings possess the same qualities that distinguish humans from animals: intellect, emotion, and will (volition).

From the first appearance to the last, these reasoning life-forms have shown themselves able to think and reason, feel and express emotion, and make decisions on their own. This defines them as intelligent life—life with personality and purpose.

But these creatures do not live on some distant planet. They are far closer than that. They are able to appear in our realm seemingly with no effort, yet we are unable to enter theirs. In every way, they seem superior in strength and intelligence. They have purpose, communicate easily, and are able to do things that mystify mere humans.

They are as ancient as creation itself, and like us, they are the result of God's direct creative act. "For by Him all things were created, both in the heavens and on earth, *visible and invisible,* whether thrones or dominions or rulers or authorities—all things have been created through Him and for Him."[3] These are the apostle Paul's words to the church at Colossae (now in modern Turkey). Amazing words: God created not only the visible but also the invisible. Of course, Paul wrote this from a human point of view. What is invisible to us is home to these beings.

From Genesis to Revelation, we see the occasional, unique, and sometimes dramatic intervention of angels. They amaze us with their messages, sudden appearances, and stunning form.

Not What Most Think

Unfortunately, our view of angels is often the product of Renaissance paintings and television shows. Who can forget the lovable angel Clarence who rescued Jimmy Stewart in Frank Cappa's classic movie *It's a Wonderful Life?* In television and movies, beautiful women or kind old men play angels. Couple that with the erroneous image from

---

[3]Colossians 1:16 (emphasis added).

Renaissance paintings showing angels as bare-bottomed babies like the ubiquitous Valentine's Cupid, and the world ends up with a confused idea of the nature of these special beings.

While it is true that angels (especially those in the Gospels) appear very human, they are still different enough to warrant biblical comment. Often described as men in white, these angels deliver messages directly from God to chosen people. Oddly, men and women respond differently to the sudden appearance of one of these beings: the men faint; the women ask questions. While not universal, there are enough occurrences to wonder what the men find so frightening.

Some angels are indeed bizarre in appearance, at least by human standards. Isaiah, Ezekiel, and the apostle John saw creatures unlike anything we expect to see in our world.

The word *angel* itself can be misleading. The word came into the English by way of ancient Greek. *Angelos* from the New Testament came to be "angel" in English. The Hebrew word *malak* and the Greek word *angelos* both mean "messenger." Yet these beings are far more than the celestial equivalent of mailmen. The Bible shows them working in different ways and appearing in different forms. The contemporary idea that all angels have wings is foreign to the Bible. On a few occasions, certain angels appear with wings, but those cases are in the minority.

Way, Way Back

Angels may not be the only sentient beings in the universe. The first mention of nonhuman beings is in Genesis. In Genesis 3, there appears a serpent, but this serpent is unlike anything known today. The word for serpent is *nachash,* and it appears thirty-one times in the Bible, five times in reference to Eden's serpent. Only in this chapter does the creature appear as intelligent. Eden's serpent was something entirely different from a mere snake, at least at first.

He is described as being "more crafty" (subtle, sly, shrewd) than any beast in the field. Unlike other animals, this creature possesses several very human traits, including the ability to think in the abstract, to communicate verbally, to distinguish between good and evil, to plan subterfuge, to carry out a premeditated plan, the ability to reason, argue, debate, and coerce. The first con man in the world was an intelligent creature with evil on its mind.

Who was the *nachash,* the serpent? For centuries, the widely held view was that the serpent was the fallen angel Satan. How that is, no one is able to explain. There is one passage, however, that implies that this is the case: "And the great dragon was thrown down, the serpent of old who is called the devil and Satan, who deceives the whole world; he was thrown down to the earth, and his angels were thrown down with him."[4]

Could "the serpent of old" be a reference to the serpent in the Garden of Eden? Many people think so. John J. Davis speaks for many when he says, "In any event, the snake which tempted Eve was much more than a snake; it was Satan himself, who is the father of deception and lies, and who can appear as an angel of light—attractive, reasonable, and enticing."[5]

While this is the dominant view and one that is very likely right, we are still left with questions. Why would Satan appear as a creature other than himself? Perhaps God had forewarned Adam and Eve about him, but the text makes no mention of such a warning. Other problems exist too.

After his successful temptation of Eve, God punished the serpent, but the punishment was physical. "On your belly you will go."[6] This implies that prior to the curse the serpent wasn't on his belly. God goes on to say, "And I will put enmity between you and the woman, and between your seed and her seed."[7] "Seed" is a biblical euphemism for children. The Hebrew word for "enmity" *(ebah)* means "animosity" or "hatred." Some people understand this to be the cause of man's basic revulsion of snakes. That is not the case.

The passage refers to an enduring struggle between mankind and "descendants" of the serpent. If the serpent was Satan, then this prophecy is a reference to the struggle between satanic forces and the work of Christ. This is what Jesus referred to when He said to the religious leaders of His day, "You are of your father the devil, and you want to do the desires of your father. He was a murderer from the beginning,

---

[4]Revelation 12:9. [5]John J. Davis, *Paradise to Prison: Studies in Genesis* (Grand Rapids, Mich.: Baker Book House, 1975), 87. [6]Genesis 3:14. [7]Genesis 3:15.

and does not stand in the truth because there is no truth in him. Whenever he speaks a lie, he speaks from his own nature, for he is a liar and the father of lies."[8]

This enmity results in mutual wounds. The serpent would have his head "bruised." A better word would be "crushed" or even "overwhelm." Eve's descendant would receive a "lesser wound" inflicted by the serpent to his heel.[9] Called the protoevangelium (the "first good news"), this passage is the first prophecy made to the work of Christ. It will be completed when Jesus comes again.[10] Paul had this passage in mind when he wrote, "The God of peace will soon crush Satan under your feet."[11]

While it is hard to argue against the notion that the serpent and Satan are one, we still wonder why the Bible never directly refers to him as such. Most will suggest that the serpent was influenced, even possessed, by Satan. If that is true, then why did God punish the serpent? Would not the serpent have been a victim? Even Paul, when he spoke of the event in 2 Corinthians 11:3, did not refer to Satan but referred only to the serpent: "But I am afraid that, as the serpent deceived Eve by his craftiness, your minds will be led astray from the simplicity and purity of devotion to Christ."[12] Why just mention the serpent if Satan was the real culprit behind the deception?

The point for this chapter, however, is that the serpent was a being of nonhuman intelligence. Even if Satan possessed the creature, then he is the being of nonhuman intelligence in question. At any rate, we see that there are other beings, other intelligences at work besides humans.

Cherubim

Moving forward a few verses, we get our first introduction to angels. Genesis 3:24 says, "So He drove the man out; and at the east of the garden of Eden He stationed the cherubim and the flaming sword which turned every direction to guard the way to the tree of life."

---

[8]John 8:44. [9]The word for "heel" is in the masculine. [10]See Revelation 20.
[11]Romans 16:20. [12]From more information on the serpent, see the author's book *Uncovering the Bible's Greatest Mysteries* (Nashville, Tenn.: Broadman & Holman, 2002).

After their sin, God expelled Adam and Eve from the Garden of Eden to distance them from the tree of life. He stationed two or more cherubim as guards. The word *cherubim* is the plural of *cherub*. Today people often describe babies as "little cherubs." This is because many Renaissance painters portrayed angels as wise infants. That image does not come from the Bible. The Bible always shows cherubim as powerful, majestic, and protective. They are usually associated with the throne of God.

Solomon adorned the temple with images of these creatures. God commanded that a veil separate the Holiest Place (often called the Holy of Holies or Most Holy Place) from the larger holy place. The Holiest Place was the thirty-by-thirty-foot room (twenty cubits on every side) in which the people believed God dwelt. It was the resting place for the ark of the covenant. The high priest entered once a year and no more. The holy place spread out in front of the Holiest Place and was a much more active place for the priests. Solomon built the temple more than three thousand years ago, but if we could walk through it today, we would see images of cherubim not only on the veil but also on the doors and walls. They were everywhere. The temple was destroyed in 587 B.C.

The Genesis passage tells us nothing about the cherubim's appearance, only that they protected the tree of life. Some artists have portrayed cherubim as four-legged animals with wings on their backs and a man's head. This is certainly incorrect. Such depictions come from ancient Babylon, but Israel was not Babylon. The Jews of Solomon's day did not equate those mythical beasts with the cherubim of the Bible.

There is an interesting note about the cherubim at the tree of life. The passage states that there were multiple cherubs but only one sword. "He stationed the cherubim and the flaming sword which turned every direction to guard the way to the tree of life" (Genesis 3:24). It appears that the "flaming sword" provided protection apart from that of the cherubim. But, as we will see, there may be another question.

Other passages do describe these beings. In most cases, they appear with wings. Four crafted cherubim were inside the Holiest Place. Two were gold figurines on the mercy seat (the lid of the ark of the covenant). Each of them displayed a single pair of wings that stretched over the mercy seat.

God's command was, "The cherubim shall have their wings spread upward, covering the mercy seat with their wings and facing one another; the faces of the cherubim are to be turned toward the mercy seat."[13] If we were looking at the ark of the covenant, we would see a gold box with a gold top and two winged angels looking down at the lid (the mercy seat) and their wings spread out and forward until their tips touched. The author of Hebrews calls these the "cherubim of glory."[14]

God went on to say, "There I will meet with you; and from above the mercy seat, from between the two cherubim which are upon the ark of the testimony, I will speak to you about all that I will give you in commandment for the sons of Israel."[15] Again, cherubim are associated with the throne and presence of God.

In addition to the cherubim on the ark of the covenant, 1 Kings 6 tells us that two large, gold-covered statues of winged cherubim filled out the Holy of Holies. They were fifteen feet tall with a fifteen-foot wing span. The wing of one cherub touched a wall of the room, as did one wing of the other statue. Their other wings met in the middle, so their combined wing span matched the thirty-foot width of the room.

Why were there so many representations of cherubim in the temple? The answer is simple: cherubim are associated with the throne and worship of God. The temple was a place of worship. It was where the priest made sacrifices for the forgiveness of sin.

This association with the throne of God is seen in one of the strangest and most difficult-to-understand passages of the Bible. The prophet Ezekiel wrote a book that bears his name. He was in exile in Babylonia along with his fellow Jews. There he lived out his life and conducted his ministry. At the age of thirty, the prophet gazed across the water-filled canal called Chebar and saw a storm approaching from the north. That in itself was not unusual or frightening, but what traveled with the storm was.

Using detailed but difficult language, the prophet described a stunning vision. The word *vision* is important. The Bible shows God communicating in various ways with his servants. With Adam, Eve, and others,

---

[13]Exodus 25:20. [14]Hebrews 9:5. [15]Exodus 25:22.

Painted relief of a bull from the famous Ishtar Gate of Babylon, at one time considered the political seat of southern Mesopotamia, which is the region called Babylonia where Ezekiel had the visions recorded in the prophecies that bear his name.

it was face to face; at other times, God appeared in the form of smoke or fire; and still other times He spoke audibly without any physical presence at all. He has spoken from a mountain, a bush, as a person, from above the ark of the covenant, through the casting of lots, and through the mysterious Urim and Thummim.[16]

God has also spoken through dreams and visions. While dreams and visions may seem to be the same, there are differences. What Ezekiel (and others prophets like Isaiah) experienced, they experienced while awake. Dreams conveyed messages, but a vision went a step farther. Much of the message in a vision existed not just in the spoken word but also in the symbolic sights. In a vision, the recipient becomes a participant in the action. He is on stage, not in the audience.

---

[16]A discussion of these can be found in the author's book, *Uncovering the Bible's Greatest Mysteries* (Nashville, Tenn.: Broadman & Holman, 2002).

A vision also provides a spiritual insight that comes from a special, spiritual consciousness. There is a strong sense of "place," of being somewhere different. Ezekiel described rising up "between earth and heaven."[17] The apostle John, who wrote the Book of Revelation, recorded Jesus saying, "Come up here, and I will show you what must take place after these things."[18] Again, there is a change in location.

While visions are a powerful tool of revelation, we can only understand them in the context of symbolism. Much of what a prophet sees in a vision is representative of a greater truth but may not be a literal depiction.

For example, the statues, artwork, and engravings of the cherubim show humanoid creatures with a pair of wings. That's how they appeared on the ark of the covenant and the fifteen-foot-high cherubim statues in the Holy of Holies. Ezekiel, however, saw different cherubim. In Ezekiel 1 and 10, the prophet saw creatures that had four faces: that of a man, eagle, bull (ox), and a lion. As strange as that is, the prophet went on to describe them as having four wings with a human hand under each. They had straight legs and bovine-like feet. They rode on a device that was hard to fathom, a device with a wheel within a wheel.

Why are these cherubim so different from those described in the temple? The simple answer is because Ezekiel saw these creatures in a vision and their appearance may not be literal. Terms like "resembling" and "something like" fill the chapters. Ezekiel was describing what may be indescribable. Also, Ezekiel described seeing God on a throne. The prophet described Him as having the "appearance of a man" (Ezekiel 1:26), that His appearance above the waist was like heated, shiny metal; below the waist was like fire; and that there was radiance about Him.

Is this what God looks like? In John 4, Jesus told the woman at the well that "God is spirit, and those who worship Him must worship in spirit and truth."[19] The apostle John said, "No one has seen God at any time; the only begotten God who is in the bosom of the Father, He has explained Him."[20] Paul described God as being invisible.[21] Paul brought

---

[17]Ezekiel 8:3. [18]Revelation 4:1. [19]John 4:24. [20]John 1:18. [21]1 Timothy 1:17.

the point home in his letter to Timothy: "[He] alone possesses immortality and dwells in unapproachable light, whom no man has seen or can see."[22] So Ezekiel was seeing a manifestation of God as many other people have done (Moses, Abraham, Jacob, etc.).

That is not to say the Bible is not being literal here. Ezekiel described exactly what he saw, but visions are a symbolic communication of truth. The symbolism is as important as the spoken word. John's Book of Revelation is the prime example of this.

In fact, it is in Revelation 4 that we meet the cherubim again. In his vision (the longest in the Bible), John stood before a crystal sea and saw "living creatures" in the act of praise.[23] Their description is familiar, yet distinctly different. Unlike Ezekiel, John saw beings with one face, not four. Still, the faces were the same as those Ezekiel saw. One had the face of a lion, the other that of a calf; another's face was like a man; and the last a flying eagle. The creatures were "full of eyes around and within." In Ezekiel's vision, the wheels had the eyes. John's cherubim had six wings, meaning three pairs.

Are these discrepancies? No. The true form of the cherubim is mostly that of a humanoid with wings, like those depicted in the Holy of Holies.

Another Old Testament prophet saw creatures very much like the cherubim. Isaiah 6 records the prophet's vision and the message he was to deliver. Like Ezekiel, Isaiah had an amazing vision. In 739 B.C., the prophet saw the Lord "sitting on a throne, lofty and exalted."[24] He went on to describe God as wearing a long robe that filled the temple (most likely the Holy of Holies).[25] But God was not alone. Isaiah saw seraphim.

Their name means "burning ones." This phrase is derived from the Hebrew word *seraph*. Are these creatures different from the cherubim? As with John's vision, their description is both similar and different from that of Ezekiel's cherubim and those depicted on the ark of the covenant. Isaiah saw beings that had three pairs of wings. This matches what John saw. Isaiah stated that the seraphim covered their faces with one set of

---

[22]1 Timothy 6:16. [23]Revelation 4:6–8. [24]Isaiah 6:1. [25]Jesus mentions the event in John 12:41.

wings and their feet with another pair. With the remaining wings they flew.

Why did they cover their face and feet? This too is a vision and therefore filled symbolism. God, for example, is shown on a throne, surrounded by smoke and with a robe, whose train filled the temple. All of this shows the Lord to be exalted, powerful, and kingly. Each seraph covered his face, showing his humility in the presence of God. With another pair of wings he covered his feet. There is some debate about what this means, but two interpretations are possible.

First, "cover his feet" may be a euphemism for "hiding his genitals."[26] It might also refer to the Middle Eastern custom of not showing the soles of one's feet while in a social gathering. In any case, the seraphim humbled themselves while glorifying God with the words "Holy, Holy, Holy, is the LORD of hosts, the whole earth is full of His glory."[27]

Overcome with guilt, Isaiah cried out, "Woe is me" (Isaiah 6:5). One of the seraphim took a burning coal and placed it upon the prophet's lips, declaring him guilt free. This is interesting, since we have a "burning one" taking a "burning thing" and using it to symbolize the forgiveness of sin.

Who were these majestic and unusual creatures? The answer is debated, but there is very good reason to believe that they were cherubim. The similarities are impossible to ignore. Like the cherubim, these beings are associated with the throne of God. Isaiah did not describe their faces, but he did tell us that they were winged—winged like those "living beings" seen by the apostle John. Also, like the other references to cherubim, they are associated with fire. They are humanoid in that they have hands, feet, mouths (implied by their speaking), and other human characteristics.

There are differences. Isaiah and John mentioned six wings, Ezekiel described four, and the cherubim on the ark of the covenant and in the Holy of Holies show only one pair. In addition, the seraphim were "above" the throne (although some translators prefer to render the preposition as "around"). If seraphim and cherubim are the same beings,

---

[26]See similar references in Exodus 4:25 and Isaiah 7:20. [27]Isaiah 6:3.

then why are there differences? We come back to the basic understanding of visions. Visions are symbolic representations of truth. Isaiah's vision is highly emblematic. He stood before God in the temple, and this fact is revealing. As we have seen, cherubim are associated with the temple. If, as most interpreters suggest, Isaiah was in the Holy of Holies, he may have seen the four cherubim located there come to life.

If what Isaiah saw were cherubim, then why call them seraphim? Because the word *seraphim* is a description of what Isaiah saw, not a name for the type of being in his vision. They were "burning ones" because that is how they appeared to Isaiah. Several things in Isaiah's vision are associated with fire: smoke and coals.

A chart of cherubim makes things clearer.

Designation	Reference	Number	# wings	Fire	Faces
Cherubim	Genesis 3	Not stated; plural	Not stated	Sword	Not Stated
Cherubim	Ezekiel 1	4	4	Center of device	1
Cherubim	Ezekiel 10	4	4	Between cherubim	1
Temple cherubim	Several	4 in Holy of Holies	2	?	1
Seraphim	Isaiah 6	Not stated	6	Coals	?
Living creatures	Revelation 4	4	6	7 lamps of fire	1

One thing is certain: these beings were intelligent, obedient to God, and magnificent in appearance. They should not be confused with other angels. In the broad meaning of the term, they are angels, but they go beyond that. The Bible makes a distinction. John recorded this verse in Revelation: "And all the angels were standing around the throne and around the elders and the four living creatures; and they fell on their faces before the throne and worshiped God."[28] John distinguished

---

[28]Revelation 7:11.

between angels and the living creatures. In his mind, they were not the same thing.

Part of the problem is our tendency to designate all nonhuman creatures as angels, but the catchall phrase doesn't do justice to God's creation. Cherubim appear to be something different from angels. While it is not wrong to refer to them as angels, we should make some distinction.

The author of Hebrews says, "Are they not all ministering spirits, sent out to render service for the sake of those who will inherit salvation?"[29] Cherubim are associated with the throne of God, angels carrying out some important task for God. They carry the souls of the righteous after death,[30] deliver messages,[31] are God's instruments of judgment,[32] praise the work of God,[33] and are ministers to Christ.[34] We can assume they do much more than we can imagine.

Angels with Names

The Bible names three angels: Michael, Gabriel, and Lucifer.

Michael (whose name means "who is like God?") is mentioned five times in the Bible, first appearing to the prophet Daniel. He is the patron angel of Israel. He is mighty, purposeful, and a warrior who will lead the battle against Satan in the last days.[35] All physical descriptions of him are very human, except he is clearly superior in many respects.

The Bible records Gabriel ("Man of God") as the angel of announcement. Far more than an angelic messenger boy, Gabriel had the honor of revealing God's plan for mankind, first in Daniel when he delivers the prophetic message often called Daniel's seventy weeks,[36] which refers to the coming of Christ as King. He also announced the conception of John the Baptist to a very skeptical Zacharias.[37] Gabriel also brought news of the miraculous conception to Mary, the mother of Jesus. Gabriel is the most famous messenger in creation.

As for Lucifer, we'll deal with him in the next chapter.

---

[29]Hebrews 1:14. [30]Luke 16:22. [31]Daniel 8:16; Matthew 2:13, 20; Acts 5:20; and many others. [32]2 Samuel 24:16; Acts 12:23; and others. [33]Luke 2:13–14; Revelation 5:11–12; and others. [34]Matthew 4:11; Luke 22:43; John 1:51. [35]Revelation 12:7. [36]Daniel 9:24–27. [37]Luke 1:8–20.

Our Bustling Neighborhood

Humankind's desire to know that there is life beyond humans may stem from the subconscious knowledge that such is the case. Unseen by our eyes is a world that is as mysterious as it is intriguing, a world populated by living, reasoning beings that defy full description. In spite of our limited contact with these beings, the Bible reveals many things about them. Still mystery remains, but there is joy in that. God's creation is too wonderful to comprehend, but some day we will see with eyes that are open to horizons far beyond our experience.

Points to Ponder

1. Why is there such a strong desire on the part of humans to believe that there is life in the universe other than human?

2. This chapter focused on cherubim as an example of nonhuman intelligence, but the Bible speaks many times of other beings called angels. Why do you suppose God included them in the Scriptures?

3. Angels have become very popular in recent years. But paintings, toys, television shows, and movies never show angels as they are described in the Bible. Why is that?

4. The only place where cherubim are mentioned without the throne of God is in the Garden of Eden. Is there some significance in that?

5. God stationed cherubim in the Garden of Eden to protect the tree of life. Since the plural of the term is used, we know there were more than one cherub, but the text mentions only one fiery sword. Why? What does the sword represent?

Mysterious
Miracles

Miracles demand attention. Whether one believes in them or not, they still demand attention. Skeptics work hard to disprove the miraculous. This is a testimony of the power of a miracle to grip even the minds of unbelievers. The Book of Genesis begins with a miracle. The majority of the books in the Bible contain accounts of events that are possible only by the direct intervention of God's will and power.

Some miracles puzzle even the most ardent believer. They are beyond not only the norm but also are odd in technique and leave us wondering not just "how" God worked the miracle but "why" He did it in the way He did. While answers are often elusive, investigation is always worthwhile.

Fishing for Money
Matthew 17:24–27

One of the strangest miracles in the Bible occurred in the town of Capernaum on the north shore of the Sea of Galilee. The city was important in the ministry of Jesus and served as His headquarters for the surrounding region. Arriving back in town from one of His many excursions into the surrounding district, Jesus was resting in a home. Matthew (who had been a tax collector) records the event. There was a knock on the door and Peter answered. On the doorstep stood some men with a tax question: "Does your teacher not pay the two-drachma tax?" (Matthew 17:24).

The tariff they sought was the temple tax that has its roots in Exodus 30:13–15. It was different from the tax levied by the Romans. The Jews

CHAPTER FOUR

hated that tax since much of it went to support the lavish lifestyle of Roman leaders. The temple tax was what every Jew over the age of twenty paid to support the work of the temple in Jerusalem. The people paid it once a year, six weeks before Passover. Unlike the Roman tax, it was a matter of pride for the people. The temple was the center of the Jewish kingdom, and it was an honor to support it.

Peter was quick to answer, "Yes." Apparently, Peter sent them away, closed the door, and approached Jesus. Before Peter could speak, Jesus posed another question. "What do you think, Simon? From whom do kings of the earth collect customs or poll-tax, from their sons or from strangers?" (Matthew 17:25).

Peter knew the answer. "From strangers," he said. He was right. Kings did not tax their own families. The children were exempt, a fact Jesus pointed out. The implication was clear. The Son of God was not subject to taxes used for the upkeep of His Father's temple. It didn't make sense, and Jesus wanted Peter to understand that.

Still, to avoid offense (literally, "cause them to stumble") Jesus decided to pay the tax for Himself and for Peter, who apparently was behind on the obligation. This is where things get strange. Since Peter sent the tax collectors away without paying them, we can assume that the silver "double-drachma" *(didrachmon)* was more than they had on hand. Most Jews would have paid the half-shekel temple tax with the Greek silver coin.

It is interesting that Jesus' motivation was not obligation but conformity to the practice. Many people would turn against Him, but they wouldn't be able to do so based on His unwillingness to pay the same tax that everyone else was obligated to pay. Jesus would pay the tax, so He instructed Peter how to obtain the money. It wasn't what Peter expected.

If anyone knew about fishing, it was Peter. It had been his family business for many years, but this was different. Fishing in Peter's day utilized nets. It was the most effective and efficient way of bringing in many fish. Jesus told him to fish for one fish—not many, just one. Jesus gave short but specific instructions: "Go to the Sea of Galilee and throw in a line; bring up the first fish that bites the hook." This wasn't to be a day on the lake. Peter was going fishing for a reason: to get the necessary temple tax.

What went on in Peter's mind? How did fishing, taxes, and coins fit together? Peter must have been mystified. In another odd turn of events, Matthew doesn't record the rest of the story. It ends with Jesus' command to Peter. It's proper to assume that Peter did as he was told, but the actual event is unrecorded.

Why would Jesus work this miracle in this strange way? What do a half-shekel and a fish have to do with each other? How does a fish come to have a coin in its mouth? Of all the fish in the Sea of Galilee, how is it that this particular fish would bite on a particular hook tossed into the water by a particular man?

Fish are prominent in the Gospels. They were a valuable part of the diet of the day, but the symbolism went far beyond that. The Jews of Jesus' day would have been familiar with more than twenty types of fish in the lakes and along the Mediterranean coast. Fish play a role in several New Testament miracles, each of them related to abundance.

There are two miracles associated with a miraculous catch of fish. In the first miracle[1] Jesus, pressed by the crowd, got into a boat with His disciples and moved a short distance off shore. After His teaching, He told the disciples to move into deep water for a catch of fish. They protested by saying, "We've fished all night and caught nothing," yet they obliged Jesus. Dropping their nets, they were surprised to find a catch of fish so great they needed help hauling it in, nearly breaking the nets as they did. That single cast of the nets brought in enough fish to fill two boats to the point of sinking.

A similar miracle occurred after Jesus' resurrection but before His ascension.[2] Some of His disciples went fishing and were having no luck. A man (later identified as Jesus) told them to fish off the right-hand side of the boat. It must have sounded ridiculous, but they did it nonetheless, and were astounded to make another remarkable catch of fish. It was proof enough for John to say to Peter, "It is the Lord."

---

[1]Luke 5:1–11. [2]John 21:1–11.

In both of these occurrences, something came from nothing. Jesus asked His disciples to do what seemed ridiculous and illogical. Their faithfulness in carrying out the odd requests brought an unexpected result. The point was simple: Jesus could do what ordinary men could not, and He could provide for the need from nothing.

Two other miracles in which fish played a dominant role occurred on dry land. Twice in Jesus' ministry, He multiplied food for hungry crowds.[3] On the first occasion, Jesus was standing before a group that had followed Him around the shore of the Sea of Galilee. The crowds that followed Jesus had, over the three years of His ministry, grown to large numbers. Captivated by His profound and authoritative teaching, men, women, and children by the thousands would encompass the Savior. Jesus and His disciples had taken a boat—one way to escape the pressing mass of people—and made their way to the town of Bethsaida (ironically, "house of fish") on the northwest shore. However, the crowd was not so easily discouraged. Many followed along the shore; perhaps others joined them along the way. Instead of finding seclusion, Jesus found a crowd of thousands. The Gospels state that five thousand men were present. That count does not include women and children. The number of people present may have been three times that number or more.

Jesus saw that the group was faint with hunger and felt great compassion for them. He decided to do the impossible: feed them. Overwhelmed by the magnitude of work, the disciple Philip said, "Two hundred denarii worth of bread is not sufficient for them, for everyone to receive a little."[4] Since a denarius was equivalent to a day's wages, Philip was saying that eight months' salary couldn't feed a crowd of that size. Andrew brought to Jesus a boy and his lunch. The lunch was fine for a boy, but laughably small for a congregation of fifteen thousand or more. But with Jesus, little is more than enough. Five loaves of bread and two fish fed the thousands.

[3]Matthew 14:15–21; Mark 6:35–44; Luke 9:12–17; John 6:6–13. [4]John 6:7.

Jesus would do the same again with a different crowd.[5] This miracle occurred farther south with a slightly smaller gathering. As in the first case, Jesus multiplied fish and bread to feed a hungry group of followers.

All of the miracles involving fish showed Jesus' ability to take nothing (or very little) and make something more. In the case of the coin in the fish's mouth, Jesus miraculously provided a means of paying the temple tax. Many people have pointed out that this is the only time when Jesus worked a miracle on His own behalf, but this misses the point. Jesus stated, "Take that [the coin] and give it to them for you and Me."[6] Jesus was not paying just His temple tax (as the Son of God, something He was not obligated to do) but also that of Peter. Jesus did not work the miracle for His benefit but for Peter's sake.

The miracle also taught an important lesson. While Jesus was not obligated to pay the tax, He did so anyway. He did so to prevent a stumbling point for others. If Jesus refused to pay the temple tax, His many followers might do the same. It is interesting to note that Jesus was never critical of the tax itself or of those who came to collect it.

The mechanism of the miracle remains hidden and mysterious. We are safe in assuming that Peter faithfully did what Jesus commanded, but exactly what he found is his secret. The dynamics of the miracle are intriguing. How the fish came to have the coin, how Peter knew where to fish, why the fish would bite his particular hook, and why Jesus would choose this unusual procedure are beyond the text. The bottom line remains clear: Jesus is Lord over all creation.

Figuring the Fig Tree
Matthew 21:18

If the coin in the fish's mouth is the oddest miracle performed by Jesus, then the cursing of the fig tree is the most surprising. It is the only miracle Jesus performed that led to the destruction of something rather than to its benefit. It shocked the disciples, and it puzzles the contemporary Christian.

---

[5]Matthew 15:32–38; Mark 8:1–9. [6]Matthew 17:27.

Matthew records the events in detail. It was the last week of Christ's ministry. The cross was just days ahead. The streets and towns around Jerusalem were crowded with the influx of Jews from nearby and distant lands who had come to the city for Passover. As many as half a million people would have been in the vicinity. Jesus and His disciples were staying in a small town a few miles down the road. Most likely, they were staying with their good friends Lazarus, Mary, and Martha.

Jesus was making His way up the road to the city when the strange miracle took place. It was morning. He, like many other pilgrims, was walking the dirt road that led to the Holy City. Matthew records that Jesus was hungry and saw a lone fig tree in full leaf. Expecting fruit, He found none. Then, in an unexpected move, Jesus cursed the tree: "No longer shall there ever be any fruit from you."[7] Immediately the tree withered, its leaves turning dusty brown and falling to the ground. So fast was the transformation that the disciples were "amazed." The word used to describe their response means "to marvel, to wonder." They had seen withered trees before, but not one that withered right before their eyes. Mark adds the phrase "from the roots up,"[8] indicating the tree was completely emaciated (see Mark 11:20).

Why would Jesus do this? To many people it seems a pointless act, an overreaction and even childish. Jesus could have used His power to cause fruit to appear, to strengthen the tree, but instead He issued a curse. Some people have thought this to be a reaction to hunger and frustration. But is it? There is nothing in the accounts of Jesus to indicate that He was subject to striking out when disappointed. Everything Jesus did, He did with purpose. There was function behind His actions. Sometimes the goal was to alleviate the suffering of others; at other times, He used miracles to teach truth.

This bizarre act isn't bizarre at all. As with many things in the Bible, there is a symbolism here, truth tucked away in the events.

---

[7]Matthew 21:19. [8]Mark includes an interval between the cursing of the tree and when the disciples remark about it. Mark also notes that Peter was "reminded" of the tree, indicating that he was recalling the previous day's event.

A fig tree in Bethphage in early May 1994 soon after the local celebration of Easter. To make an unforgettable point, Jesus cursed a fig tree like this one.

While it was still early for most fig trees to be bearing fruit, this particular tree was already in full leaf. Fig trees, unlike many fruit trees, simultaneously produce fruit along with leaves. Jesus and the others would have expected some fruit from a tree so far along, but for some reason it was barren of figs. It displayed itself as fruit-bearing when in reality it was fruitless.

Wouldn't Jesus know that there was no fruit on the tree? The answer lies in the preceding verses.

Chapter 21 of Matthew tells of Jesus' triumphal entry. Riding on a donkey, Jesus received the cheers of a jubilant crowd as they hailed Him as Messiah. Matthew remarks that the whole city was "stirred" and filled with questions about Jesus.

From this dramatic entry, Jesus entered the temple area and saw what He had seen many times before. The temple area was thirty-three acres of magnificence filled with the hustle and bustle of crowds. Owners led animals to priests for sacrifice, and children hovered around doting parents.

But there was something else going on in the temple complex. Booths had been set up to conduct business. Money changers and "animal retailers" plied their trade. Temple business required money changers since Jews who lived abroad needed to convert Roman coins into Jewish coins. There was no crime in this, and had it remained the simple exchange of one coin for another (even with a small fee) it would have been fine. But, as is often the case with humans, it had gotten out of hand. The operators charged exorbitant fees for the process. Likewise, people were required to pay large fees for animals to be used in the sacrifices. Traveling Jews could not take along sacrificial animals with them while they traveled; it made more sense to buy one once they arrived in Jerusalem. The price for such animals skyrocketed.

To make matters worse, they had set up shop in the Court of the Gentiles, a place meant to be an outreach to the world, a place where people could learn about God. Business forced these spiritual inquirers out of a place God intended them to be. Instead of being a place for missionary work, it had become a place of commerce.

For a second time,[9] Jesus demonstrated His feelings about this by overturning the tables of the money changers. This sent them scrambling for the coins as they clattered to the stone floor. He also upended the seats of those who were selling doves for sacrifice. "My house shall be called a house of prayer; but you are making it a robbers' den," Jesus declared.

The action was popular with the crowd of worshipers, especially with the children who shouted, "Hosanna to the Son of David" (Matthew 21:15). These were words reserved for the Messiah. Since Jesus was the Anointed One, He allowed them to continue.

While the crowd applauded Jesus' actions and the children chanted, the chief priests and scribes became "indignant." The word means "stirred up with anger." They were hot. "Do You hear what these children are saying?" Their words imply that Jesus should quieten the young ones. He refused. Instead, He quoted a verse from Psalm 8: "Out of the mouth of infants and nursing babies You have prepared praise for Yourself" (v. 2).

---

[9]The first temple cleansing is described in John 2:13–22.

This psalm carried weight. It was a creation psalm directed to God. The way Jesus used it implied that He was God. Couple that with the fact that the blind and lame came to Him and He healed them. This was convincing proof to everyone except the religious leaders.

What does this have to do with an unfruitful fig tree? Plenty. Everything. The fig tree represented the temple and faulty religious systems of the day. Jesus had long chastised the religious leaders, who had allowed the rich faith to become a showcase for piety. Real worship, at least nationally, had ceased. Instead, there were the elaborate rituals, traditions, and laws, but tradition and resistance to change had severed the connection between God and people.

Faith had become religion—religion is a pale reflection of truth. There were feast days, sacrifices, rituals, and more that had become little more than window dressing. Worship had become what a person watched instead of what he did. Like the fig tree, the affairs of the temple promised something it couldn't deliver. The fig tree looked healthy at a distance, its green leaves waving in the breeze, its trunk straight and strong. But upon closer examination, it was useless. So was the ritual of the day. The white stone and gleaming gold of the temple made it impossible to ignore. It was a beautiful structure, truly one of the wonders of the ancient world. However, in spite of its beauty it was no longer a place of true worship. Somewhere along the line, the worship of God had been lost.

As the fig tree represented the temple specifically, it also represented Israel generally. Twice the Old Testament uses the fig tree as a symbol of Israel. Jesus did the same in a parable that He told.[10] In the story, Jesus described a man who had a fig tree in his vineyard. For several years, he had gone to the tree, only to find that it produced no fruit. Finally, he ordered a worker to cut it down. But the worker objected, asking for one more year to let him dig around it and apply fertilizer. If the tree produced then, the owner would spare the tree; if it didn't, he would have it cut down.

---

[10]Luke 13:6–9.

The image Jesus paints with His words is that of patience. The tree in the parable received another chance, and the worker would do everything necessary to help it grow. God was patient with temple practices, but that patience had an end. The time of digging and fertilizing would soon be over for the temple. The temple represented itself as a place of worship, but it had failed to live up to its image. In 70 A.D. it would be stripped of its gold, its stone walls pulled down, and its wood burned. The temple—like the fig tree—ceased to be.

Did Jesus curse the fig tree because He was angry and disappointed that there were no figs? No, He worked this unusual miracle to make a point: God cares about worship. He doesn't care about ritual, habit, tradition, or entertainment. God wants us to have a personal experience with Him.

Worship is about Him, not us. Heartfelt worship—worship open to all—produces fruit.

Just a Touch

Miracles are amazing events, but they are made more amazing by the manner in which the worker achieves them. A survey of Jesus' thirty-five miracles shows some intriguing behavior. In some cases, Jesus healed with the touch of His hand; in other cases, He didn't raise a finger. His command was enough to get the job done.

In the first recorded miracle of Jesus, He turned water into wine at a wedding in the tiny town of Cana.[11] He did so at His mother Mary's request. A close reading of the passage shows that Jesus gave direction to the servants, but He touched nothing Himself.

In another case, a royal official traveled from his home in Capernaum to Cana seeking Jesus.[12] He had a desperate plea, "Come down and heal my son." All the man's power and wealth could do nothing for the fevered boy. Rather than making the journey, Jesus simply told the man, "Go; your son lives."[13] While the man was making his way back home, he met his servants, and they revealed good news about his son, "Your son lives." And when the official asked at what time the boy

---

[11]John 2:1–11. [12]John 4:46–54. [13]John 4:50.

had recovered, he learned that it was the same time Jesus had told him his son would live.

There are other accounts where Jesus demonstrated His power at a distance. A word from Jesus was enough to get the job done. There were other times, however, when Jesus insisted on a personal touch. What makes that astonishing is His choice of whom to lay hands on. While some contact seems almost incidental—such as Jesus healing Peter's mother-in-law by touching her hand—others are far more significant.

Touching the Untouchable

One of the most devastating diseases in Jesus' day was leprosy. Leprosy was the term used to describe a number of skin diseases. Even houses and fabrics were leprous if certain spots appeared on the material. The human factor of leprosy is the most heartrending. People considered leprosy a judgment of God and, indeed, the Old Testament records several occasions when someone was stricken with the disease as a punishment for his actions.[14] In most cases, people acquired leprosy naturally, not as an affliction sent from God.

The disease was devastating on several levels, not the least of which was isolation from friends, family, and work. To limit contact that might spread the disease, lepers were required to live away from people, often having to "live outside the camp." They couldn't go home; couldn't hug their children; couldn't go to worship; and couldn't hold jobs. Their heads were to remain uncovered, their clothing torn, and they were to cry out, "Unclean! Unclean!" should anyone come near.[15] The illness made lepers some of the most pitiful people on the planet. Society and law stripped them of everything that made life worth living.

People shunned them. To touch a leper rendered a person ceremonially unclean. That's what makes the touch of Jesus so interesting.

Matthew 8:2–4 relates the account of a leper who came to Jesus. "And a leper came to Him and bowed down before Him, and said, 'Lord, if You are willing, You can make me clean.'" There's a lot in those few words. First, the leper approached Jesus. This was an act of faith. It

---

[14]See Numbers 12:1–10; 2 Kings 5:27; 2 Chronicles 26:20–21. [15]Leviticus 13:45.

was also a violation of law. Most people would have recoiled at the man in the tattered clothing and mottled skin. The leper bowed before Jesus. The Bible does not say, but this may have been a painful act.

There must have been a typhoon of turmoil in this man. He was defying tradition, law, and social expectations to approach a man he had heard could perform miracles. Perhaps he had nothing more to lose. His comments reveal his faith: "Lord, if you are willing, You can make me clean." Clean? It's an odd word. He didn't asked to be cured, didn't ask to be healed. That was his intention, of course, but he used the word *clean.*

This is how lepers viewed themselves—as contaminated. It was also how others viewed them. The disease polluted them. The word *clean* or *cleanse* is always associated with leprosy in the Gospels. The reason goes back to the fact that lepers were more than diseased; but they were ceremonially unclean. The man desired physical and spiritual health.

If we stop the action here, we see that the leper put Jesus in an awkward spot. Contact with such a man was dangerous, first because of the contagious nature of the disease but also because lepers were condemned to live only with other lepers.

Then Jesus did the unthinkable. Those around Him must have gasped in astonishment as the Lord reached out His hand and moved it toward the leprous man. Everyone watching knew that the moment Jesus' hand touched the man's skin or garments, He would be defiled. Then no one could touch Jesus until He was declared clean by the priests. The Greek word used here *(hapto)* means "to handle, cling, touch firmly, hold on to" and even "grasp." It was not a light caress. Jesus took hold of the man, perhaps raising him up. We can only guess how long it had been since anyone other than another leper had made physical contact with the outcast.

The Bible describes the act so briefly that we seldom take the time to appreciate what Jesus did. It is a moving, poignant moment. Jesus extended a touch of love that the leper and anyone watching would remember forever.

Jesus replied, "I am willing," and the man was made whole that instant, in full view of Christ's followers. The joy the man felt was profound and the effect immeasurable. One moment he was a desperate man, with nothing to lose; the next he was whole and able to return to family, friends, society, and worship.

It is hard not to ask, "Why?" Why would Jesus bother touching the leper? He could have simply commanded that the illness leave and achieved the same result. On many occasions He had healed people who were far away; certainly He could have done the same with this man. Yet He chose to defy all the prevailing beliefs and to extend a touch of compassion.

There was a great deal said in that simple act. Christ's gesture spoke more than could be uttered in a hundred sermons. No one was beyond His care or too contaminated for His love. What the world rejected, what the world found repulsive, Jesus found worthy of help and dignity.

In the Bible, leprosy is a symbol for sin. Jesus was willing to look upon the man's sin and offer a cleansing solution. No one is so far down the social ladder that Jesus would ignore him. No sin is so heinous that it would make Jesus turn away.

Plain of Esdraelon — One of the several times Christ raised the dead took place in Nain, a village in southwest Galilee that sat on a hillside overlooking this plain.

Nothing in the healing required a touch from Jesus, but He touched anyway. Did that make Jesus ceremonially unclean? No. The healing was instantaneous; there was nothing to contaminate Jesus. The perfect Jesus remained perfect.

How to Stop a Funeral

Three times Jesus raised the dead: Jairus's daughter,[16] His friend Lazarus,[17] and the son of a widow from the town of Nain. In two of those cases, Jesus touched. Luke 7:11–15 recounts the events of the widow and her son.

Jesus had arrived at the gate of Nain, a town about twenty-five miles from Capernaum. As He came near the gate, He saw a crowd approaching. Jesus was also traveling with a large crowd. The two masses of people met on the street. One was heading out of the city, and the other was heading in. Luke gives us the interesting details.

The funeral was for a young man who had died earlier that day. We don't know the time at which he died, but we do know that the Jews buried their dead quickly. Most likely, the man had been dead less than twenty-four hours. He or his mother may have been people of influence since so many citizens of Nain turned out for the funeral.

Luke also tells us that the deceased was the only son of a widow. Without family to provide support and no social security system to care for her in her later years, she could have been facing great difficulty. In the ancient custom, as the body was being taken outside the city for burial, it was accompanied by wailing and crying. As Jesus and His followers approached, He saw the need and "He felt compassion for her." The word *compassion* means to "be moved within," viscerally. The Lord felt physically moved by the sad sight.

Coming alongside the widow, He said, "Do not weep." It must have seemed odd advice to her. Weeping was all she had left. This was more than saying, "There, there, everything will be fine" as we are prone to do. Jesus was about to do something grand.

---

[16]Luke 8:41–42, 49–56. [17]John 11:1–44.

When Jesus raised his good friend Lazarus from the dead, He did so with a straightforward command, "Lazarus, come forth" (John 11:43). Here, however, He walked to the coffin (most likely a plank or stretcher) and touched it. Again, there was no requirement that Jesus have contact with the coffin, and it appears He had no contact with the corpse. But He chose to make a point by laying a hand on the coffin. Naturally, the pallbearers stopped. Then, as with Lazarus, Jesus issued a command to the dead: "Young man, I say to you, arise!"

And he did.

He sat up and began to speak (proof that he was truly alive). There is no mention of what the young man said, but it got the crowd's attention. They were awe-struck and glorified God by saying, "A great prophet has arisen among us! God has visited His people!"

It must have been a sight to see. Jews prepared a body for burial by wrapping it in linen, mummy-style, from under the arms to the feet. The shoulders and head remained unwrapped, and a face napkin covered the head. Suddenly this bound young man sat up on the stretcher and began speaking.

We come back to the question of *why*. Was there some special reason why Jesus touched the coffin? Such an act (as with the leper) would render Him ceremonially unclean for a time, but Jesus didn't hesitate. Of course, He knew what was about to happen, but He could have made it happen without the touch.

Jesus was in the middle of the miracle. While there are some cases in which He healed at a distance, He usually did so with a touch, which demanded the attention of those around Him. The answer rests in the purpose of a miracle. Miracles are works that not only benefit the recipient but also authenticate the worker. As in this case, the miracle brought about an immediate response from the people: "God has visited His people." That is the purpose of miracles, to direct attention to God.

Jesus may have touched the coffin to show His compassion. Usually only family and close friends touched the corpse and did so only to prepare it for burial. Here Jesus did it to involve Himself in the lives of the mother of the young man, as well as the friends of the deceased. That simple touch made Him one of them. This made them want to be part of Him.

Spit

Sometimes Jesus touched with more than hands. On several occasions He touched the afflicted person with spit. With the blind man of Bethsaida (Mark 8:22–25), Jesus took him aside and spit on his eyes. He then asked the man, "Do you see anything?" He did, but not clearly. The blind man described seeing "men like trees walking about." Jesus then touched him again, fully restoring his sight. At first, it seems that this was a private miracle since Christ led the man out of the fishing town. But when his sight partially returned, he described seeing men. There were others there. How many were there, we don't know, but there were more than the two of them.

In another situation Jesus made mud by mixing saliva and dirt (John 9:1–7). Before Him was a man who had been born blind. The presence of the man prompted some philosophical questions among the disciples. "Rabbi, who sinned, this man or his parents, that he would be born blind?" The answer Jesus gave shattered a widely held belief: that physical ailments are the result of sin. "It was neither that this man sinned," Jesus replied, "nor his parents; but it was so that the works of God might be displayed in him." Jesus went on to pronounce, "I am the Light of the World" (see John 9:3–5).

The story takes an odd twist in the way in which Jesus chose to touch the man. He didn't just touch the eyes with His hands; He applied a mud-pack made from His own spittle. This has caused puzzled discussion through the ages. Why mud? The saliva makes some sense, especially to the people of the day who believed that such a practice could heal blindness. The mud, however, seems out of place.

The solution to this mystery is in the events that follow. The Pharisees, a group of legalists who were the enemies of Jesus from the beginning, interrogated the blind man. These religious leaders were upset because Jesus healed on the Sabbath. They looked upon healing as work. They forbade work, no matter how noble, on the seventh day of the week. The formerly blind man answered their questions the best he could, relating the details he knew. But he had never seen Jesus. He told how Jesus put the mud on his eyes and then sent him to the Pool of Siloam. When pressed about who had healed him, the man could only reply that he didn't know. He had not seen Jesus. Why had he not seen Jesus? Jesus had covered his eyes in mud.

The man received the mudpacks and then was led to the Pool of Siloam to wash. Once he washed the mud away, he could see, but he could not find Jesus. Could it be that Jesus, knowing the controversy that would surround the healing, made the mud not to heal the man but to keep him from seeing until Jesus was out of sight? It is very likely. The mud kept the man in the dark for a little while longer, so the Pharisees could not hold him accountable.

After the interrogation by the Pharisees, Jesus sought out the man and identified Himself. He did this not out of fear but to show the Pharisees for what they really were—hypocrites. When presented with a man everyone knew had been born blind, whose parents testified to that fact, the Pharisees refused to believe. All they could see and all that mattered to them was that the man's healing took place on the Sabbath and that was a violation of religious law. Narrow-minded is too broad a term for these men. Jesus told the grateful man He had healed, "For judgment I came into this world, so that those who do not see may see [the blind man], and that those who see may become blind [the Pharisees]" (see John 10:39).

Hands Off

One remarkable miracle of Jesus was a "hands-off" miracle, a miracle in which He didn't touch the afflicted. As with the blind man above, strict Sabbath laws complicated the miracle. Jesus and His disciples had traveled through a grain field. The hungry disciples ate some kernels of grain. The Pharisees saw this. Never ones to pass up an opportunity to be critical, they accused, "Look, Your disciples do what is not lawful to do on a Sabbath" (Matthew 12:2).

Shortly after, Jesus entered one of their synagogues. There was a man there with a withered hand. The word used to describe the condition is "dried up." This was the perfect opportunity for the Pharisees to test

Jesus. In their minds, they had Jesus in a difficult situation. Would Jesus' compassion compel Him to heal on the Sabbath while so many of His detractors were around? Jesus would heal, but not in the way they were thinking. When asked if it was proper to heal on the Sabbath, Jesus said yes, using Scripture to back up His statement. Then He commanded the man to extend his hand. A moment later Jesus healed the man. His hand was suddenly in perfect working order (see Mark 3:1–5).

What makes this so interesting is that Jesus did nothing physical. The man extended his hand, but there is no record of Jesus actually doing anything. He didn't touch the hand; it just became well in Jesus' presence. This infuriated the Pharisees, who planned to destroy Him, but they would not be able to build a case on this alone. Since Jesus did nothing physical, He had not worked. Therefore, He didn't break the Sabbath laws. Remarkably, unbelievably, the Pharisees again overlooked the miracle and remained fixated on their set of artificially enhanced laws.

Often, the most mysterious thing about miracles isn't just the miracle itself, but the manner in which it is accomplished. Details around the miracles, and the message in those details, show the power and creativity of God.

Points to Ponder

1. Why do you suppose Jesus chose to have Peter find the coin in the fish's mouth? What else did He achieve in that act?

2. Does Jesus' cursing of the fig tree seem harsh and out of character? Why did Jesus teach with this type of illustration instead of simply giving a lecture about the failures of the religious system?

3. What other miracles occurred in which Jesus did not touch the person or object?

4. Are there miracles worked by any other person in which touch was not necessary?

5. Does every miracle contain a message beyond the miracle itself?

Mysterious
Requests

Everyone can say that they have been asked do something unpleasant, even unreasonable. It may stem from a situation at work, a business decision, a family concern, or some other area of life. Bible heroes can say the same. On several occasions, biblical characters had to do the impossible, to go against human nature and to do so in the name of God. Each event is brimming with meaning that reveals the sometimes-mysterious nature of God and the nature of those whom He has called.

When God Asks the Impossible
Genesis 22:1–19

The mind is capable of creating and storing images for decades, and in some cases, for life. The stronger, the more shocking, the image, the longer it remains tucked away in our brain cells. The Bible contains images that go beyond surprising—they are shocking to the soul. We find such an image in the middle chapters of Genesis. This image is of one of the greatest men to walk the earth. His name was Abraham. It is the graphic, disturbing image of an elderly man standing on a mountain, his son bound and laid upon the firewood of a stone altar, a sharp knife held to the young man's throat, a knife wielded by a father who loved him more than life.

The story of Abraham is long and involved. It includes his call from the pagan city of Ur in Mesopotamia, his travel to what is now the Holy Land, his desire for a son, and his long wait for the promise of God. He is the father of the Jews and the Arabs. His importance cannot be questioned, nor can his loyalty to God.

God tested his loyalty on a day many centuries ago. Abraham was an old man when he received a promise from God that his wife Sarah would bear a son. He waited many more years for that promise to happen. More years flowed by as the long-awaited son, Isaac, grew into early adulthood. During that time, God was silent.

From time to time, God had spoken to Abraham directly, and the patriarch responded with loyalty and faith. Years passed before God spoke again. When He did, He spoke in terms that fractured the old man's heart. He said, "Take now your son, your only son, whom you love, Isaac, and go to the land of Moriah, and offer him there as a burnt offering on one of the mountains of which I will tell you."[1]

Abraham must have questioned his own sanity. Had he just heard God say to make a human sacrifice of Isaac, the son He had promised and delivered by miracle? Could this be the same God who had called him out of the pagan land, given him a new life, rewarded him with wealth, long life, and the promise that he would be the father of a nation—a linage that would be passed down through Isaac, the very son he was supposed to sacrifice?

How could the pledge of a future nation come about if Abraham (whose name means "father of multitudes") placed Isaac on an altar of stone and wood and sacrificed him? Human sacrifice commanded by God! It was unheard of. It couldn't be, but the words were undeniable, the message undiluted. The searing words of God sank into the aged heart of the patriarch, who, beyond our ability to fathom, agreed to do the deed.

Human sacrifice was common in Abraham's day, both in the land he left and the one that became his new home. Those were the acts of a people who didn't know God, who were unaware of the God of Abraham. Was God asking Abraham to become like them, to relinquish what distinguished him from the heathen? It seemed so.

---

[1]Genesis 22:2.

The passage tells us that God did this to test Abraham. The word *test* translates *nasah*, a Hebrew word used thirty-six times in the Old Testament. Its primary meaning is to test the value of something, like an assayer weighing gold to learn its value. It is an "attempt to learn the true nature of something."[2] It is the same word used to describe the Queen of Sheba's intent to question Solomon to see if his wisdom matched his reputation. It is not a temptation to sin. God does not do that. The New Testament Book of James makes that clear: "Let no one say when he is tempted, 'I am being tempted by God'; for God cannot be tempted by evil, and He Himself does not tempt anyone."[3]

The test here was not to see if Abraham would do evil, but if he would do good. Can human sacrifice ever be good? No. God prohibits such behavior several times in the Old Testament.[4] Abraham may have witnessed such atrocities himself, but it was not part of his nature and certainly not part of God's.

Yet the command, as devastating as it was, had come and Abraham faced a heartrending decision: Would he show his loyalty and commitment to God and sacrifice Isaac, or would he prove his love for his son and refuse?

Abraham left early the next morning. The night must have been the shortest of his life. God had called for the death of Abraham's son, a death to take place on a mountain north of his home, a mountain called Moriah. It was a three-day journey, which he made with two servants and a donkey. Because of his advanced age, Abraham rode the donkey while Isaac and the servants carried the supplies and wood. Abraham left prepared. He took wood for the altar, a knife for the sacrifice, and his son for the offering.

What does a man talk about on such a journey? As they rested from the day's travel, as they ate the evening meal, what did he say to his only son, the one whom he loved? Did Isaac attempt small talk? "We made good distance today, Father," he might have said under the dome of the

---

[2]James Swanson, *Dictionary of Biblical Languages with Semantic Domains: Hebrew (Old Testament)*, HGK5814 (Oak Harbor: Logos Research Systems, Inc., 1997).
[3]James 1:13. [4]Leviticus 18:21; 20:2–5; Deuteronomy 12:31.

stars. Every step, every mile brought Abraham closer to the deed he feared. What did Isaac see in the eyes of his father?

Isaac at this time was an adult. Some scholars think that he may have been around thirty years old. The text uses terms that make us think of a preteen child, but Isaac was considerably older.

Their trip took them to Mt. Moriah, a significant place in both biblical history and contemporary times. It was the future site of Jerusalem. It was there that Solomon would erect the temple in later years. The meaning of *Moriah* is interesting and prophetic. The term means "chosen of Jehovah"—the place picked by God; picked for this event, and for the temple years later.

Arriving at the scene, Abraham ordered his two servants to remain behind with the donkey while he and Isaac went up to the hill to worship (literally, "to bow down"). Then Abraham laid the wood on Isaac's back so he could carry it to the site. At this point, the patriarch made a prophetic point. "Stay here with the donkey, and I and the lad will go over there; and we will worship and return to you" (Genesis 22:5). Interesting. Abraham believed that Isaac would be returning with him.

How could this be? If he planned to kill his own son and burn his body like a sacrificial animal, how could he say that both would return? Either he was lying or his faith was beyond our comprehension. It was the latter. The author of Hebrews speaks of this event: "He considered that God is able to raise people even from the dead, from which he also received him back as a type."[5] Abraham believed one thing above all others: No matter what happened on Mt. Moriah, Isaac was coming home with him, even if God had to raise him from the dead.

Along the way, Isaac asked the obvious question: "Behold, the fire and the wood, but where is the lamb for the burnt offering?" (Genesis 22:7). It was a poignant question, heartrending in every degree. What answer could a loving father give? The question is proof that Isaac had no idea what Abraham intended. The patriarch answered in cryptic faith: "God will provide for Himself the lamb for the burnt offering, my son."[6]

---

[5]Hebrews 11:19. [6]Genesis 22:8.

It is amazing that Isaac didn't question this. We always want to ask, "How?" "How is God going to provide the lamb?" Both Abraham and Isaac understood that God is not required to explain Himself.

The phrase "God will provide for Himself the lamb" immediately snaps the mind of the Bible student to the New Testament and to the riverside scene with John the Baptist pointing at Christ and shouting, "Behold, the Lamb of God who takes away the sin of the world!"[7]

Then they came to "the place" that God had chosen (remember the meaning of the name Moriah). Abraham, with the help of his son, did the most grueling work of his life. He built a stone altar. Every stone must have weighed a ton in Abraham's hands. Every stick must have seemed the size of a tree trunk. They made the altar and arranged the wood carefully. Did Abraham lay the wood in such a fashion that it would be more comfortable for his son? Did he try to engineer the altar to ease any discomfort?

The horrific scene played on. He bound Isaac. Isaac didn't complain. He laid Isaac on the altar. Isaac didn't complain. He pressed the knife to his son's tender throat. Isaac didn't complain.

Never before had God asked a man to do such a thing. Never again would He command a human to do what Abraham was doing. It isn't hard to image the tears running down Abraham's face. Did their eyes meet?

Abraham prepared to draw the knife.

Then a voice came from heaven: "Abraham, Abraham! Do not stretch out your hand against the lad, and do nothing to him; for now I know that you fear God, since you have not withheld your son, your only son, from Me" (Genesis 22:1–12). The words Abraham starved for finally came. Sweet words! Wonderful words!

God, however, wasn't finished. A sacrifice was required, and He provided the animal for it. Abraham looked up and saw a ram with its horns caught in a thicket. The ram became the substitution for Isaac. Abraham named the place Jehovah-jirah, which means, "The LORD will provide."

Through the centuries, thinking men and women have pondered this account. At first, it seems as though God was being cruel, so needy for

---

[7]John 1:29.

worship, so hungry for unflagging obedience that He contrived the worst kind of experiment to test the loyalty of a man who had proven his dedication many times.

Many people have thought God pitiless, petty, and even sadistic. To ask a man to sacrifice the son he loved more than life itself sickens many. And it should. It was a horrible scene. It was cruel. It was painful. It was the most difficult thing God could call any man to do. It angers some, and well it should. It should anger all of us.

It is true that Abraham hovered over his long-awaited son with a knife to Isaac's throat, ready to draw it across the skin, but God stopped him before any physical damage was done. Here's the point. There was no one to stop God from sending His son to a slow and painful death on the cross. We should be furious about this, but not furious with God. We should be furious with the price Jesus had to pay for sin—our sin.

This is where the story takes on meaning. Readers often make the mistake of thinking this is an account about Abraham and Isaac. It is, but only in part. In fact, it is the shadow of the real story about God and Jesus.

Everything in this account is repeated in the life of Christ. The more outraged we become at the unfairness and cruelty of God's request, the more we will understand what it meant to God to send Jesus to the cross for our sake.

Look at the parallels.

First, Isaac is the son whom Abraham loved. This is more than a word used to set the tone of the account; it conveys the idea that father and son were inseparably connected at the heart. Parents understand this emotional-spiritual bond. When a child hurts, the parents often hurt more. Abraham would sooner die than see harm come to his son. Yet God commanded him to end his beloved son's life.

Isaac is Abraham's "only son." Abraham did have another son through his wife's handmaid Hagar. Ishmael, though older and a direct descendent of Abraham, was not the promised child, the covenant child. After Isaac was born, Sarah caught Ishmael mocking Isaac. It was enough of a threat to Sarah that she insisted that both mother and child leave the camp.[8] When their situation became dire, an angel of the Lord brought relief.[9]

One cannot read the terms used to describe Isaac without thinking of several New Testament passages. Perhaps the best-known Bible verse is John 3:16. The phrases God utilizes in describing Isaac are the same as those used in that passage. "For God so loved the world, that He gave His only begotten Son, that whoever believes in Him shall not perish, but have eternal life." Jesus was loved of God and was His only begotten Son. God knew exactly how Abraham felt. His insisting that Abraham go through this heartrending process helps us to understand the sacrifice made by God.

On two occasions, God spoke from heaven and stated His love for Jesus. The first was at Jesus' baptism in the Jordan River. After John the Baptist immersed Jesus and He came headfirst out of the water, "Behold, a voice out of the heavens said, 'This is My beloved Son, in whom I am well-pleased.'"[10] The same words were spoken on the Mount of Transfiguration where Jesus, before the surprised eyes of the disciples, met with Moses and Elijah. From a cloud came the voice of God, "This is My beloved Son, with whom I am well-pleased; listen to Him!"[11]

As much as Abraham loved Isaac, as much as any parent ever loved a child, God loved Jesus more. The cross was as cruel and grueling for God the Father as it was for God the Son.

Another parallel is in the name of the location picked by God. The fact that the Lord commanded Abraham to move to a distant place was no trivial detail; it was part of the plan. Moriah means "chosen place." Chosen how? Chosen why? Centuries later, the site where Abraham "sacrificed" Isaac became the very place where the temple would stand. The ancient Jews believed the temple altar where the priests sacrificed animals was the very spot where Abraham had so carefully arranged the stones and laid the wood for the altar on which he believed his son would die.

A thousand years after the temple was built, Jesus, the only begotten Son of God, would be nailed to a cross near the busy streets of Jerusalem.

---

[8]Genesis 21:9–10. [9]Genesis 21:17–20. [10]Matthew 3:17. [11]Matthew 17:5.

(The crucifixion took place near thoroughfares so that the citizens of the area could see and be warned what awaited those who defied Rome.) God chose Moriah not for what it was but for what it would become and for how history would remember it.

A third connection is found in Genesis 22:6. Abraham took the wood of the burnt offering and laid it on Isaac his son. It is impossible to overlook the parallel. "They took Jesus, therefore, and He went out, bearing His own cross, to the place called the Place of a Skull, which is called in Hebrew, Golgotha."[12] Later, because of the cruel treatment inflicted upon Jesus by the sadistic Roman guards who left Him too weak to finish the journey, the cross of Jesus was passed to Simon of Cyrene.[13] As Isaac carried the wood meant to fuel the pyre of his sacrifice, so Jesus carried the wooden instrument of His death on His back.

The Genesis account also shows that Abraham split the wood to use in the sacrifice. This was something he could have assigned to a servant, but he chose to do it himself. It is impossible to imagine what those moments were like. God is responsible for growing the tree from which the cross came to be. The Book of Hebrews tells us that Abraham assumed a resurrection. Jesus was resurrected as the firstfruits of the dead (see Hebrews 11:17–19).

The connections continue. The trip from Beersheba to Moriah was a journey of three days. The trip separated Isaac from his mother and the others who lived in Abraham's camp. Reflecting that separation is the time Jesus spent in the tomb. As Isaac would symbolically return to the "living" after the "sacrifice," Jesus would literally return to life and those who loved Him.

Abraham stated that God would provide the lamb for the sacrifice. This He did in the form of a ram caught by the horns in a thicket. It is interesting to note that God provided a male animal. The Hebrew term for *ram* describes men who were leaders or otherwise powerful.[14] This is an apt description of Christ. In Revelation, John saw Jesus as a slain lamb.

---

[12]John 19:17. [13]Mark 15:21. [14]Exodus 15:15; 2 Kings 24:15; Ezekiel 17:13; and others.

Another correlation comes into the picture unstated. The passage simply states that Abraham bound his son and laid him on the altar. There is no indication of struggle or reluctance on Isaac's part. He submitted to everything willingly. The image boggles the mind. The apostle Paul said it best in his letter to the Philippians: "Being found in appearance as a man, He humbled Himself by becoming obedient to the point of death, even death on a cross."[15] Jesus went willingly, submitting to the will of the Father as Isaac portrayed He would do thousands of years before.

Jesus made a fascinating statement to the religious leaders: "Your father Abraham rejoiced to see My day, and he saw it and was glad."[16] When did Abraham see Jesus' day? It was that evening on Mt. Moriah when he came to understand that God would provide a sacrifice for the world, for him, and for all others who followed.

Only when we see the links between Abraham and God, between Isaac and Jesus, does the command of God to sacrifice Isaac make sense. God was not being cruel, not being heartless; He was showing us what He went through to bring about our salvation through Christ. It was expensive in emotion, not only for Jesus, but also for God Himself. Abraham was not required to finish the deed. God stopped him before harm could come to Isaac.

There was no one to stop God—and for that we should all be thankful.

An Unusual Diet

There are odd dietary practices around the world. What is delicious for one culture is repulsive to another. There are even societies in which humans have eaten other humans. The Bible contains two mysterious requests in which God told a person to eat the unusual—a book.

Ezekiel received a call from God to serve as a prophet to his rebellious nation. The call came in the form of a dramatic vision. The first few chapters of the book that bears his name record the event. A biblical vision is a divine revelation in which the recipient plays an active part. Rather than

---

[15]Philippians 2:8. [16]John 8:56.

just receiving information, the recipient is involved in conversation and activities. It is also different from a dream in that it occurs in a waking state. Ezekiel and the apostle John received the most intense and lengthy visions in the Bible. Each also received a command to eat a book.

Ezekiel was a prophet to the Jews in exile. King Nebuchadnezzar of Babylon had taken them captive when he overthrew Jerusalem in 597 B.C. Nebuchadnezzar took Ezekiel, along with about ten thousand other Jews from the area, and moved them to Babylon, where they joined other exiled Jews. The rest of Ezekiel's land would fall in the summer of 586 B.C. The assault destroyed the temple and left Jerusalem a plundered shell. It was while in Babylon that Ezekiel received a startling vision of God's throne and the cherubim who guarded it.

In his vision, Ezekiel heard a strange command, "Son of man, eat what you find; eat this scroll, and go, speak to the house of Israel."[17] Eat a scroll? Scrolls were long bands of writing material of various sizes. To protect the delicate writing, scribes rolled the material into a tube shape, the ink facing inward. Some scrolls came from the papyrus plant that grew in Egypt along the Nile

A Torah (Genesis–Deuteronomy) scroll is held in its wooden case at a celebration in Jerusalem. Ancient books were written on scrolls that were unrolled when read.

[17]Ezekiel 3:1.

River. The plant also grew in the Jordan River valley and other areas. The ancient city of Gebal imported so much of the material that people referred to the town as Byblos (from which we get our word *Bible*). Papyrus makers manufactured the paper by laying strips of the plant material horizontally and vertically and then pressed them together with an adhesive. The result was a yellowish writing surface that took ink well and lasted for centuries in dry climates. Some ancient papyrus scrolls were more than one hundred feet long.

Another ancient writing material came from animal skins, usually sheep, goat, or calf. This treated skin, called parchment or vellum, came from young animals and made a finer writing material. Parchment was coarser. Parchment makers would scrape the animal skin clean of hair, wash it, rub it with a pumice stone, and then stretch it. They would then take sections of the material and sew them together into rolls. Throughout history, parchment was the choice for special documents. This is why college diplomas bear the name "sheep skins."

God told Ezekiel his mission in very certain and clear terms. "Son of man, I am sending you to the sons of Israel, to a rebellious people who have rebelled against Me; they and their fathers have transgressed against Me to this very day."[18] God described the sons of Israel as rebellious, transgressors, stubborn, and obstinate children. It was going to be a rough ministry.[19] In fact, God instructed Ezekiel not to fear them or their words, which He compared to thorns, thistles, and sitting "on scorpions."[20]

How does a person prepare for a ministry like that? What kind of sermon would turn people like that around? It had to be a message from God. To deliver that message, Ezekiel had to have it in his own heart and mind. So God told the prophet, "Open your mouth and eat what I am giving you."

Then God stretched out a long scroll. It's hard to imagine what Ezekiel thought at that moment. We don't know if the scroll was vellum or papyrus, both natural products, but we can be sure it didn't look appetizing. The whole thing was more difficult to digest because of the

---

[18]Ezekiel 2:3. [19]Ezekiel 2:3–4. [20]Ezekiel 2:6.

message of doom written on it. Three words describe the message Ezekiel was to take to the people: "lamentations, mourning and woe."[21]

A *lamentation* is a dirge, a song or poem of bereavement. In ancient Middle Eastern custom, loud crying and shouting was part of the grieving process and funeral rites. God was lamenting the rebellion of the nation He loved. It was as if they had died to Him.

The message was also one of mourning. *Mourning* in this verse means "to groan, sigh, and moan." It is the picture of a deep sadness oozing to the surface and expressing what words cannot. *Woe* is the eruption of grief, the explosive release of sorrow and pain. It was not a pretty message, but it was one that God gave the prophet to preach "whether they listen or not."[22]

How can a person take such a message to such a people? First, he must be with the message himself, having internalized the revealed word of God.

The scroll received from God by Ezekiel represented that revealed will, and it was more than expected. Ezekiel tells us that the scroll contained writing on the front and back. This is very unusual. Scribes wrote on only one side of parchment, the "hair side" of the material. God had so much to say to His rebellious people that it not only filled the long scroll but ran over to the other side.

If the message was so long, then why did God not hand Ezekiel multiple scrolls? Perhaps it was because multiple rolls were unwieldy to handle, but it goes beyond that. It means there was one God who was giving one message to one people through one prophet.

To internalize this message of woe, God told Ezekiel to eat the scroll. The message that was to come out of the prophet's mouth must first enter him. A few verses later, God reiterates the idea: "Son of man, take into your heart all My words which I will speak to you and listen closely."[23]

Ezekiel was obedient to the mysterious request. "So I opened my mouth, and He fed me this scroll."[24] It is interesting that God did the feeding. How this happens isn't described, but it is clear that in the

---

[21]Ezekiel 2:10. [22]Ezekiel 2:7. [23]Ezekiel 3:10. [24]Ezekiel 3:2.

vision, the prophet ate the scroll and it was as "sweet as honey"[25] in his mouth. This is not an unusual description of God's Word. King David said, "The fear of the Lord is clean, enduring forever; the judgments of the Lord are true; they are righteous altogether. They are more desirable than gold, yes, than much fine gold; sweeter also than honey and the drippings of the honeycomb."[26]

Jeremiah the prophet said something similar, "Your words were found and I ate them, and Your words became for me a joy and the delight of my heart."[27]

It seems oxymoronic to think that God's spoken or written judgments could be pleasing and sweet, yet that is how the Bible describes them. God does not judge without cause; He is not fickle or pernicious. He corrects those whom He loves. As the writer of Proverbs said, "For whom the LORD loves He reproves, even as a father corrects the son in whom he delights."[28] Not to correct His people would be apathy on God's part, and one thing God is not is apathetic. Receiving correction from God is a privilege and sign that He loves us.

What God started, Ezekiel was to continue. "He said to me, 'Son of man, feed your stomach and fill your body with this scroll which I am giving you.'"[29] The ultimate responsibility to feast on God's Word rested with the prophet. God provided the needed commands, put them into action by His order, and made His will known on the matter, but Ezekiel had to assume responsibility for the consumption.

Many people today want someone to feed them spiritual information, but the responsibility remains with the individual. To grow in grace and knowledge, God's Word must be "consumed." This occurs only when we are willing to invest the effort to fill our hearts and minds with what God has provided. Spoon-fed Christians are inherently weak; believers who feast on the Word of God are empowered to make a difference in the world.

The longest revelatory vision in the Bible is the Book of Revelation. Many Christians make the mistake of referring to the book as "Revelations." It's a simple and common mistake, but it is important to

---

[25]Ezekiel 3:3. [26]Psalm 19:9–10. [27]Jeremiah 15:16. [28]Proverbs 3:12. [29]Ezekiel 3:3.

note that the book records one revelation, not many revelations. There are many segments to what the apostle John experienced on the rocky island of Patmos, but it is still a single divine unveiling of things to come.

John, caught up into heaven, saw many amazing and frightening things. These things included a great judgment to come—the Great Tribulation. During his vision, he wrote down what he saw and heard. The book is an open field of cryptic comments, symbolic items, and unusual sights. Much of the book remains a mystery to this day.

As in all biblical visions, John was involved in the experience. He was not in the audience; he was one of the actors, and as such, he took certain actions. In one such event, a "strong angel" descended to earth and set his right foot on the sea and his left foot on the dry land. The angel held a small book in his hand. What John saw was a tiny scroll that had been open to full view (see Revelation 10:1).

A voice from heaven told the apostle to take the book from the angel, and he obeyed. As John took the tiny scroll, the angel told him, "Take it and eat it; it will make your stomach bitter, but in your mouth it will be sweet as honey" (Revelation 10:9). Again, sweetness is associated with a scroll, but this time there is a promise of bitterness. The scroll was good going down, but it was sour in the apostle's stomach.

No one knows with certainty what was on the scroll. There has been much speculation, but we simply don't know. The two effects of sweetness and bitterness imply that this "little book" contained the Word of God but it also contained judgment. The Bible is that way. Many wonderful passages deal with comfort, love, and peace. In it, we can find encouragement, strength, and wisdom. But the Bible is an honest book. It speaks of sin and the punishment of sin. It describes a beautiful afterlife, but it also unapologetically describes hell. It portrays forgiveness but also warns of the price of sin. It shows the wonderful miracles of Jesus, but it pulls no punches in describing His betrayal, beatings, and crucifixion.

The Bible is an honest book, designed by God to speak to generations of humans by giving them the knowledge they need. That knowledge includes the warm and comfortable verses as well as those that warn us of misbehavior.

Anyone who spends time with the Bible quickly learns that it is as frank as it is true; as honest as it is direct; and as specific as it is general. This makes it powerful and enduring.

Food is often a metaphor for the Word of God. Jesus taught us, "Man shall not live on bread alone, but on every word that proceeds out of the mouth of God."[30] The apostle Paul, when describing the weak spiritual standing of the church at Corinth, wrote, "I gave you milk to drink, not solid food; for you were not yet able to receive it."[31] The apostle Peter spoke of the "pure milk of the word" and said that through it we grow in our salvation.[32]

The idea is consistent and the command is clear: The Word of God needs to be "ingested" into our lives. From it we learn God's will, find strength for the day, are corrected in our misdeeds, and learn more about the God who made sure that we have every opportunity to know as much about Him as possible.

In God's mysterious ways, He has shown us that making His Word a part of our lives is important, even crucial.

Points to Ponder

1. How does the rest of the world see the story of Abraham's "sacrifice" of Isaac? Do you think most Christians understand the message portrayed by the act?

2. Does knowing that Abraham and Isaac typify the sacrifice made by God and Jesus make the story any easier to understand?

3. If Abraham had come to you for advice, what would you have told him?

4. The Bible describes God's Word as "sweet." What makes it so "sweet"?

5. Do you think the modern church emphasizes Bible study enough?

---

[30]Matthew 4:4; Deuteronomy 8:3. [31]1 Corinthians 3:2. [32]1 Peter 2:2.

Mysterious
Evil

It doesn't take much to convince people that evil exists in the world. A few nights watching the evening news on television is enough to convince even the most ardent skeptic. The fears of today were unheard of a generation ago. Child abduction, violent crimes against children, nations turning chemical warheads against its own citizens, armed students in schools, newer and more dangerous drugs flooding the streets, corporate scandal, and much more are evidence of evil. And that's just what humans do to one another.

The Bible speaks of evil on several levels. It is clear about humankind's sin and its responsibility for it. But it also shows that there is more than just general, impersonal evil in the world. There are malevolent beings.

The Western world is fascinated with such topics. Books of horror line the shelves of the bookstores, movies about great violence and uncontrollable monsters rake in money at the theaters. Why is there such a fascination with evil? Perhaps it's because of the innate knowledge in each of us that evil is a reality.

The Bible shows evil as being resident in intelligent, nonhuman creatures. These beings, while not responsible for the world's ills (we humans can make a mess of things all by ourselves), are responsible for much of what we see in history and today.

The topic is huge and has been the subject of many books. Speculation has been broad, even though the facts are few. One thing is certain: In God's mysterious universe, there are evil creatures.

CHAPTER SIX

The devil seems out of place in the twenty-first century. To many, a belief in a malevolent being is antiquated and only for the uneducated and superstitious. Contemporary scholars pooh-pooh the idea of such a creature, and convincing them otherwise is difficult. The theologian Charles Ryrie said, "Like the matter of the existence of angels, the existence of Satan probably could not be proved to the man who refuses to accept the evidence of the Bible on the subject. But if he did he would find ample evidence."[1]

The Bible is not shy about the subject. It teaches a literal, personal, living Satan. Verses about him dot the Old Testament and frequent the New Testament.

Jesus is our most authoritative source, and He mentions Satan by title in the first three Gospels and refers to him in the fourth as the "devil."[2]

The Bible never questions the reality of Satan. It assumes his existence as common knowledge, not needing explanation. Still, details are few and clarification is rare. This should not be surprising. The focal point of the Bible is Jesus, not Satan. What information is given is to show him as the enemy of all things godly and all those in the faith. Despite the limited amount of information the Bible gives, it does give us enough to draw a clear picture of the unholy person.

What We Know

First, we know that Satan is a person. By person, we mean that he has the qualities of personhood, not that he is or ever was human. Every person, human or otherwise, has three characteristics in common: intellect, emotion, and will.

Intellect means the ability to think, to reason, and to contemplate in the abstract. Humans are unique in that we possess the ability to solve problems at a high level. Psychiatrists have tested animals on their ability to solve problems, and some have shown an amazing skill. In one experiment, they locked a chimpanzee in a room. The room was bare except for a few boxes scattered around the floor and the chimp's favorite food

---

[1]Charles Caldwell Ryrie, *A Survey of Bible Doctrine* (Chicago, Ill.: Moody Press, 1972, 1995). [2]Matthew 4:1; 12:26; Mark 3:26; 4:15; Luke 10:18; 22:31; John 8:44; 13:27.

hanging from the ceiling just out of reach. After a time, the chimp figured out that he could stack one box on top of the other, climb up, and snag the food. As ingenious as that was for a chimp, it remains well below the complex reasoning of humans. It is the ability to think in the abstract, to have a sense of the future, which distinguishes human beings from other life on our planet. Satan has an ability that is at least equal to and most likely exceeds that of humans.

For example, Satan used the principles of argument to state his view that Job was loyal to God because He had given Job so much. "Then Satan answered the LORD, 'Does Job fear God for nothing? Have You not made a hedge about him and his house and all that he has, on every side? You have blessed the work of his hands, and his possessions have increased in the land.'"[3] Only a creature who understands human behavior, motive, and has a high level of communication skills can make such statements.

Second, Satan, like humans, is an emotional creature. A survey of all the Bible verses dealing with him reveals that his motivation is some unstated, unexplained goal. He seems to delight in the trouble of others, finds some satisfaction in tormenting Job, and even asks to sift Peter "like wheat."[4]

Third, Satan displays volition or will. "No wonder, for even Satan disguises himself as an angel of light."[5] Disguise requires forethought, planning, and desire. Ephesians 6:11 speaks of "the schemes of the devil." Scheming implies intelligent choice and will.

One mistake people make about Satan is assuming that he is the "opposite" of God. While it is true that God is good and Satan is evil, Satan lacks those qualities that make God, God. Scripture shows the devil to be intelligent, but he is not omniscient; he is seen as powerful, but not omnipotent; he seems able to trot the globe, but he is not omnipresent. By human standards, he is far more powerful and intelligent than we are, but he has limitations. While he is anti-god; he is not the "Anti-god."

---

[3] Job 1:9–10. [4] Luke 22:31. [5] 2 Corinthians 11:14.

Tradition places the tempations of Jesus in this desolate and rugged terrain of the Judean wilderness west of Jericho.

Many questions about Satan remain unanswered in this life. We have some information in the Bible but not details. One thing is certain: Satan is the enemy of anything good and godly. That may sound like an overstatement to some people, but it is closer to being an understatement.

No one would know more about the entity called Satan than Jesus, who spoke from personal experience. He must be our first source of information.

Matthew 4 reports an encounter between Jesus and Satan. Jesus, freshly baptized at the hands of John the Baptist, "was led up by the Spirit into the wilderness to be tempted by the devil" (Matthew 4:1). It's an unusual phrase. The temptation of Christ came about not by chance encounter but by divine plan. In the desolate country hills (a place where many ancient Jews believed demons lived), in the cold of the night and the direct sun of the day, Jesus fasted for forty days and nights. When He was hungry and weary from exposure, "the tempter" did his work. He came at a time when Jesus was physically weak. Apparently, he took the task seriously.

Twice in Scripture Satan is called the tempter, here and in 1 Thessalonians 3:5: "For this reason, when I could endure it no longer, I also sent to find out about your faith, for fear that the tempter might have tempted you, and our labor would be in vain." Temptation is Satan's stock in trade. Matthew records three temptations endured by Jesus, one dealing with His physical hunger, one with His reputation, and one with wealth. At each temptation, Jesus refused the offer and responded with Scripture.

The passage is revealing in several ways. One of the most remarkable details is in the twice-repeated phrase: "The devil took Him" (see Matthew 4:5, 8). In the first case, Satan took Jesus to the pinnacle of the temple, that is, the highest point of the temple. Many people expected the Messiah to arrive on the scene by descending from the sky and coming down to the temple courts. The temptation here was to exchange the suffering Messiah role for the victorious Messiah role. The latter offered less pain. Jesus refused. He had come to teach, love, and die. He would not be persuaded to take an easier course.

The second time, Satan took Jesus to a "very high mountain" and showed Him "all the kingdoms of the world and their glory" (Matthew 4:8). Satan was offering success without painful cost, but Jesus found the price too high. Satan demanded that Jesus worship him. What a picture: Jesus on His knees before Satan! Never. Jesus not only refused, but He also sent him packing. "Then Jesus said to him, 'Go, Satan! For it is written, You shall worship the LORD your God, and serve Him only.'"[6]

How Satan moved from place to place or how long it took is unknown. Scripture is often silent on the *how* of supernatural events, while being clear on the reality of the experience. The passage implies that the movement happened quickly, beyond something that mere humans could do of their own volition.

When dealing with creatures like Satan, angels, demons, and others mentioned in the Bible, it becomes clear that they live, work, and move in a world that is far different from ours. It seems that their world includes ours, but our world does not include theirs.

---

[6]Matthew 4:10.

This chapter of Matthew shows a few of the different names and titles applied to Satan. He is called "the tempter" once, the "devil" three times, and "Satan" once. A study of Satan reveals that he has many names and appellations, as the following chart shows.

New Testament Names of Satan		
Name	Meaning/Application	Reference
Satan	Adversary (Hebrew and Greek)	Matthew 4:10
Devil	Slanderer/Accuser	Matthew 4:1
The evil one	Hurtful, wicked	John 17:15; 1 John 5:19
Great red dragon	Fearsome animal	Revelation 12:3, 7, 9
Serpent of old	Unclean, despised animal	Revelation 12:9
Abbadon	Destruction (Hebrew)	Revelation 9:11
Apollyon	Destroyer (Greek)	Revelation 9:11
Adversary	Opponent/rival/legal contestant	1 Peter 5:8
Beelzebul	Lord of the fly (Baalzebub)	Matthew 12:24
Belial	Worthless or wicked	2 Corinthians 6:15
God of this world	Controls philosophy of world	2 Corinthians 4:4
Ruler of this world	Rules in world system	John 12:31
Prince of the power of the air	Ruler of unbelievers	Ephesians 2:2
Enemy	Foe	Matthew 13:28
Tempter	Solicits people to sin	Matthew 4:3 1 Thessalonians 3:5
Murderer	One who takes life	John 8:44
Liar	One who misrepresents	John 8:44
Accuser	Prosecutor	Revelation 12:10

Despite his many names and titles, Satan is an individual and, like all living things, created by God. For reasons we can only speculate about, he is diametrically opposed to God and His kingdom. Jesus' testimony of Satan reveals not only his reality, but also his nature. In one of the scores of confrontations with religious leaders, Jesus stated, "You are of your father the devil, and you want to do the desires of your father. He was a murderer from the beginning, and does not stand in the truth because there is no truth in him. Whenever he speaks a lie, he speaks from his own nature, for he is a liar and the father of lies."[7]

---

[7]John 8:44.

Murderer, void of truth, avoider of truth, liar by nature and the father of lies—a hard-hitting list! The verse speaks of Satan's desires. The word for *desire* means a longing, a craving, and a passion. Satan lives to lie; it is part of his nature. He has chosen not to "stand" in the truth. The verse states that he has not stood in the truth in the past and implies he will not in the future.

In modern society, these words would be grounds for slander, but Jesus was making clear the nature of the religious leaders who, by default, had made Satan their "father."

The apostle John echoed Jesus when he said, "The one who practices sin is of the devil; for the devil has sinned from the beginning. The Son of God appeared for this purpose, to destroy the works of the devil."[8] The Satan problem is an ancient one.

Jesus also indicated that the work of Christians has an effect on Satan. After sending out seventy of His disciples on a mission, they returned filled with excitement and told the Lord, "Lord, even the demons are subject to us in Your name."[9] They had been empowered by Christ to subdue and cast out demons. It was heady stuff. Jesus rejoiced with them and then added this provocative remark: "I was watching Satan fall from heaven like lightning."[10]

What makes the remark so interesting is the Greek verb translated "watching." It is in the imperfect tense, meaning that Jesus had and was continuing to watch Satan fall. It was an ongoing action. And even more intriguing was that Jesus linked this "falling" to the work of the seventy disciples. This passage is not about Satan's original fall. The point of the passage is to teach us that Christians have power over Satan; it is not the other way around.

The apostle Peter (whom Jesus said Satan wanted to "sift like wheat") taught that the devil could be resisted by firm faith;[11] James offered the encouraging advice to "resist the devil and he will flee from you";[12] Paul spoke of spiritual armor that will allow the believer to "stand firm against the schemes of the devil."[13] He also reminded his

---

[8]1 John 3:8. [9]Luke 10:17. [10]Luke 10:18. [11]1 Peter 5:9. [12]James 4:7. [13]Ephesians 6:11.

readers that God was faithful not to allow any believer to be tempted beyond his or her ability to resist and that He would always provide a way of escape.[14]

What Some Suppose to Be True
Ezekiel 28; Isaiah 14

Two Old Testament passages (Isaiah 14:12–16 and Ezekiel 28) have been frequently cited as referring to Satan's fall from heaven. As far back as Tertullian (A.D. 160–225), the ancient African theologian, scholars began suggesting that much of Isaiah 14 is about some nonhuman person. A few of the verses seem to make this argument work, but the rest of the passage aims directly at the king of Babylon. God comforted his people about the impending captivity by telling them that they would one day take up the "taunt" against the king who oppressed them. The king faced a future of failure, disrespect, and unpleasant death (complete with maggot and worms!). These verses speak of a human leader.

It is verses 12–16 where things seem to make a shift. "How you have fallen from heaven, O star of the morning, son of the dawn!" The King James Version translates "star of the morning" as *Lucifer,* which many people understand to be the proper name of Satan. The Latin name *Lucifer* means "light bearer" and referred to the planet Venus.

The passage speaks of an individual who makes five "I will" statements: (1) "I will ascend to heaven"; (2) "I will raise my throne above the stars of God"; (3) "I will sit on the mount of assembly"; (4) "I will ascend above the heights of the clouds"; (5) "I will make myself like the Most High" (see Isaiah 14:13–14). Each one was an arrogant and grand proclamation.

Many scholars presume these words cannot refer to a human. But not only can they be applied that way; they have. Ancient kings often boasted of the impossible, and many considered themselves gods. In most pagan cultures, people treated their kings as deity in the flesh. The fact that the king of Babylon (most likely the Assyrian/Babylonian king Sennacherib) has said these things of himself does not make the statements true; they

---

[14]1 Corinthians 10:13.

merely reveal his enlarged view of his place in the universe. He might have desired to be a god, but it was well beyond his reach.

Most likely, the Isaiah 14 passage has little to do with Satan. Words from verses 12–14 are intriguing, but they put the rest of the chapter out of place. As John Martin noted: "Though verses 12–14 seem to support the view, little else in the chapter does. Though many hold that verses 12–14 refer to the entrance of sin into the cosmos by Satan's fall, that subject seems a bit forced in this chapter."[15]

Ezekiel 28:1–19 is another passage that seems to show a conflict between God and Satan. The prophet is told by God to "say to the leader of Tyre," then a few verses later, "take up a lamentation over the king of Tyre." The statement to the "leader of Tyre" lasts for ten verses, and he is chastised for arrogance and for claiming to be a god and to sit with gods and greed. God praised him for his great wisdom (a wisdom that exceeds that of the prophet Daniel!) but promised judgment for his sins. That judgment includes attack by ruthless nations, war, rejection, and death. In verse 9, it is clearly stated, "You are a man and not God."

Starting with verse 11, however, things change. A long, descriptive list is given, and the terms used are difficult to apply to any human. The list is amazing.

- You had the seal of perfection.
- Full of wisdom.
- Perfect in beauty.
- Present in Eden, the garden of God.
- Possessed a covering of precious stone and gold.
- Was created.
- Called the "anointed cherub who covers [guards]."
- Placed at the garden by God.
- Present on the mountain of God.
- Walked in the midst of the stones of fire. (The person is described as a cherub, and cherubs are always shown in association with fire and the throne of God.)

---

[15]John Martin, *The Bible Knowledge Commentary: An Exposition of the Scriptures,* John F. Walvoord, ed. (Wheaton, Ill.: Victor Books, 1983–85), Isaiah 14:3.

- Formerly blameless from creation until some event that is not described.
- Found with unrighteousness in him.
- Filled with violence.
- Sinned.
- Heart lifted up (arrogant) because of beauty.
- Self-corrupted wisdom because of splendor.

Then there follows a list of actions taken against the strange being.

- Cast out as profane from the mountain of God (defiled, polluted, desecrated).
- Destroyed (in the sense of being cut off, vanquished) from the midst of the stones of fire.
- Cast to the ground.
- Placed in view of kings (for purposes of scoffing).
- Fire brought from the midst of him.
- Turned into ashes on the earth.

It is difficult to imagine these things said of a human. The most intriguing points come from the description that the subject was "in Eden" and called a "guarding cherub" who was placed there by God Himself (see Ezekiel 28:13–14). What can this mean? Here is mystery.

The traditional view holds that the serpent and Satan are one and the same. Or, at the very least, Satan influenced the serpent to do the tempting. This would certainly answer the question of how Satan came to be in the garden, but it has its problems. The Bible always refers to the serpent as "the serpent," never as Satan. If Satan influenced, possessed, or by some other means caused the creature to deceive Eve, then why (as we asked earlier) is the serpent punished and not Satan? One possibility is that Satan's sin was the temptation itself, but most scholars teach that the Fall took place at a time prior to that.

Part of the problem lies in the missing time line. Much about Satan and the events that brought him to the point where he is today is lost in ancient days. Logic suggests that God created him during the same creation week that brought about the universe and all who dwell in it. "God saw all that He had made, and behold, it was very good."[16] At the end of creation, God declared the universe "good." Satan's rebellion must have come some time after that.

The question remains: How long after creation did sin enter the universe? Several suggestions exist.

First, some suggest that an unrecorded gap exists between Genesis 1:1 and 1:2. This argument rests on the assumption that God would not make anything "formless and void."[17] The assumption is that something must have happened to turn God's beautiful creation into the mess described in verse 2. Could we place Satan's rebellion here? Could that revolt have been so dramatic and violent that it actually altered what God had created?

It is true that "formless and void" were not the goal, but the creative acts were not over. Verse 2 simply means that after that moment of creation, the state of the world was still in need of powerful creative intervention. The idea that a gap exists between those two verses, and that Satan led such a dramatic, violent rebellion that God had to re-create the earth is simply not supported by any other Scripture. While it is an interesting idea, it carries no real weight.

A second idea suggests that the rebellion took place prior to God's creative act as recorded in Genesis 1:1. This idea speaks of a pre-Adamic race who lived in a previous creation. It's a clever idea, but lacks scriptural support. The Bible never mentions a race of humans prior to Adam. In fact, the Scriptures refer to Adam as the "first man."[18] The idea of a race of people prior to Adam and Eve's creation is loaded with problems and theological land mines.

The time line is indistinct. Some time after the creation and before Satan's first appearance in the Book of Job, Satan did something arrogant and unwise that cost him his position and standing before the Lord. Exactly what that was, no one can say. It remains one of God's mysteries.

What we do know is that Satan is real and he is locked in combat against God and His people. If Ezekiel 28 is truly about the fall of Satan, this once beloved, beautiful, and powerful creature succumbed to arrogance

---

[16]Genesis 1:31. [17]Genesis 1:2. [18]1 Corinthians 15:45.

and hatred. The one who was a liar and murderer from the beginning remains so today. He troubles and deceives the nations of the world.[19] This will not end until Christ comes again.

But Satan's work is not confined to nations. Christians and churches remain his enemy. What God loves, Satan certainly hates. With unbelievers, his scheme is to blind them to the truth of the gospel. Paul told the Corinthian church, "In whose case the god of this world has blinded the minds of the unbelieving so that they might not see the light of the gospel of the glory of Christ, who is the image of God."[20]

Why does Satan bother? What does he gain? Scripture is silent on the matter. As the enemy of God, the only success he can have is through the believer. God is out of his reach, beyond his power to affect, but humans are a different matter. God loves the world. He proved that by making the extreme sacrifice to pay for our sin.[21] The only way to hurt God is to hurt that which He loves. Since humankind is the object of His great affection, it makes sense to strike at that sensitive spot.

Satan does more than blind the eyes of unbelievers; he also is the great enemy of the faith. Ananias and his wife Sapphira sold a piece of property and gave a portion of the money to the young church at Jerusalem. It led to their deaths. (See chap. 1, "Mysterious Punishments.") Peter confronted them with an interesting question: "Ananias, why has Satan filled your heart to lie to the Holy Spirit and to keep back some of the price of the land?"[22] Satan's involvement in that sad scene came to the forefront. His attempt to weaken the church with dishonest people failed, but it did reveal something about his nature and methods.

Satan also is the untiring accuser of believers. Revelation 12:10 describes Satan as "he who accuses them before our God day and night." It is interesting to note that Satan has access to God to do this.

He also interferes with the spiritual work of believers. Paul told the church in Thessalonica, "For we wanted to come to you—I, Paul, more than once—and yet Satan hindered us."[23] There is a great deal of detail that we don't know about Satan, but the Bible makes it clear that he is

---

[19]Revelation 20:3. [20]2 Corinthians 4:4. [21]John 3:16. [22]Acts 5:3. [23]1 Thessalonians 2:18.

no friend of humans, especially those who have given their lives to Christ.

The Mystery of Satan's Permission

Two intriguing passages about Satan's activities and limitations often go unnoticed. These two passages show Satan asking permission of God to do evil. The thought of it is unsettling: Satan standing before God and making a request to wreak havoc in someone's life. Once in the New Testament and once in the Old, Satan sought just that kind of permission.

The New Testament passage is short but full of meaning. Jesus is speaking to Peter in Luke 22:31–32 and says, "Simon, Simon, behold, Satan has demanded permission to sift you like wheat; but I have prayed for you, that your faith may not fail; and you, when once you have turned again, strengthen your brothers."

Jesus uttered these words near the end of His earthly ministry. Very little time stood between Him and the cross. Not long after Jesus said this to Peter, He predicted the disciple's denial. At that moment, Peter was filled with courage and was ready to stand with Jesus, no matter what trouble might come. All of that would evaporate very soon. In an effort to help Peter understand the trials that lay ahead, Jesus made the puzzling remark, "Satan has demanded permission to sift you like wheat" (Luke 22:31).

The word *you* in the verse is plural ("you all"). More than Peter is involved. All the disciples were targets. In Jesus' day wheat was sifted in a simple, direct fashion. Wheat grain was heavier that the other material gathered during harvest: loose dirt, chaff, bits of stalk. Farmers used a winnowing fan to toss small amounts of the grain into the air. The breeze would blow the lighter material away while the weightier grain would fall back into the fan. The clean grain could then be stored.

Satan's desire was to put the disciples in the winnowing fan to see which were "chaff" and which were "grain." It wouldn't be long before Peter would deny Christ, and the rest of the disciples would be scattered in the winds of persecution. The winnowing fan was the arrest, trials, and the sentence of death.

What is intriguing is the fact that Satan must ask for the privilege of doing this evil. The word *demanded* is used of the request, but it may be a little too strong. The Greek word comes from *exaiteomai,* meaning to successfully request something of another. Before he could sift, Satan had to ask God for the right to do so. And, surprising to most of us, God apparently gave it.

This is not the first time Satan made such a request. The first two chapters of the Book of Job have Satan coming before God and accusing Job of being faithful only because of the riches he had. Job was the richest man of his day. He had a large family, massive herds, and much more. Satan contended that Job loved God because God had been good to him. "Take all that away," Satan suggested, "and Job will turn against you."

Twice (Job 1:12; 2:6) God granted permission to the accuser to afflict Job. Questions spring up like weeds. Why would God allow this? The answer may not be what we like. God is free to do as He wills. The fact that the account appears in our Bible and serves as a lesson to millions of Bible-believing people shows that a great good came out of all of it. It seems unfair, of course, but life is often unfair. Job became an object lesson of faith that endures endless trials. The lesson of his life has benefited countless numbers of people. Of course, that didn't make it any easier on Job.

Just as amazing is the fact that Satan needed God's permission to carry out the assault on Job's body and faith. Apparently, the ability to affect the weather and afflict the human body was in Satan's power, but he was somehow limited. Without God's release, he could afflict no damage on Job.

That brings new questions. Jesus encountered a woman who had spent eighteen years bent over by an unknown disease, presumably an affliction of the spine. He laid hands on her, healing her immediately. A synagogue official saw the healing and, since it occurred on the Sabbath, became upset and reprimanded the people. Jesus refused to let the man's protest pass. He asked, "And this woman, a daughter of Abraham as she is, whom Satan has bound for eighteen long years, should she not have been released from this bond on the Sabbath day?" (Luke 13:16). Since

Jesus attributed her affliction to Satan, should we assume that God had given him permission to strike her body?

Perhaps not. Job and Peter (all the disciples really) had something in common: they were people of faith. We have no idea what the spiritual state of the woman whom Jesus healed was. Jesus made no remark about her faith. There is a good chance that until the healing, she was a person of social (she was at the synagogue) but not genuine faith.

If this assumption is correct, then we can conclude that Satan must ask permission of God to do anything directly to a believer. That is not to say that he could not tempt or try to deceive a Christian. It means only that he cannot physically afflict any believer without first receiving permission to do so. "Resist the devil and he will flee from you," James tells us.[24] Believers have authority over Satan. The reverse is not true. What control Satan and his minions have in the Christian life is limited to what we surrender to him.

Was it fair for God to grant Satan permission to strike Job with personal and financial devastation, or to "sift" the disciples like wheat? The human point of view is limited, so it is difficult for us to see the fairness in God's consent. We simply don't have the big picture, so our judgments lack information. However, we do know the nature of God. "God is love," the Bible states.[25] He is also just: "The judgments of the LORD are true; they are righteous altogether,"[26] the psalmist tells us. We can be certain that God is not frivolous concerning His children.

Satan, as a creature of free will, prowls the earth seeking whom he may devour, but it appears he has limitations concerning the believer. Still, he remains our adversary, and we are to be on the alert ready to resist him, firm in our faith.[27]

Lord of This World

As we have seen, the Bible refers to Satan by many terms, titles, and names. Some of the most striking show his influence in and power over the world.

---

[24]James 4:7. [25]1 John 4:8. [26]Psalm 19:9. [27]1 Peter 5:8–10.

In 2 Corinthians 4:4, Paul wrote, "In whose case the god of this world has blinded the minds of the unbelieving so that they might not see the light of the gospel of the glory of Christ, who is the image of God." Who is the "god of this world"? It almost seems like an overstatement, but it is right on target. The word translated "god" comes from the Greek *theos* from which we get our word *theology*. It is the same term used for the one, true God, but it also refers to any divine being. The Greeks favored the term for their multiple gods. "World" comes from *aion* and refers to time. We get our English word *eon* from it. The verse could be translated the "god of this age."

Satan is indeed that. Those outside the faith, especially those who have not believed in God, see the world as operating in a near vacuum. In their world, people and animals populate a physical world, and that's it. The Bible teaches that there is much more life than what we see, and that includes the malevolent devil. Since sin entered the world through Adam, Satan has been the "god of this age." It is hard for many people to grasp the fact that by refusing to follow Christ, they are defaulting to the kingdom of Satan. It need not be a conscious choice; it is a simple either/or proposition.

This is borne out by other verses. John made it clear in his first letter: "We know that we are of God, and that the whole world lies in the power of the evil one."[28] It's a clear and sharply drawn contrast. Two kingdoms exist, and we choose the one in which we shall live.

The good news is that Satan has already lost the war—at least functionally. Jesus said, "Now judgment is upon this world; now the ruler of this world will be cast out."[29] The New Testament frequently uses the word *ruler,* which means "chief," "judge," "magistrate," or anyone with power and authority over others. The Bible describes Satan as being such a person, but one whose days are numbered. He will be cast out. Literally *(exballo)*, he will be "thrown away."

While the cross and resurrection defeated Satan, his final punishment remains in the future when he will be "thrown into the lake of fire and brimstone" to be confined and tormented forever.[30]

---

[28]1 John 5:19. [29]John 12:31. [30]Revelation 20:10.

One thing has already occurred: God has judged Satan. "And concerning judgment, because the ruler of this world has been judged."[31] Judgment is a legal determination. Satan's activities have condemned him. While he is still active, his future doom is sealed. Like a murder in court, the gavel has come down and the punishment is around the corner.

Mysteries Remain

A great many questions about Satan remain unanswered. The Bible gives us the big picture, the things we need to know, but not everything we want to know. This is not by accident; it is part of God's design. Our focus is not Satan, but Christ. Still, the questions float on the surface of our minds, refusing to sink and demanding notice.

In the Book of Jude is a verse that reveals: "And angels who did not keep their own domain, but abandoned their proper abode, He has kept in eternal bonds under darkness for the judgment of the great day."[32]

One wonders why these angels are bound while the insidious cherub Satan is free to roam about on the earth and walk "around on it."[33] It is part of God's mysterious ways. From a human perspective, the world would be better without Satan, but his presence works in God's sometimes-mysterious plan.

The good news is that Satan has been defeated. Jesus saw to that on the cross. As the author of Hebrews said, "Therefore, since the children share in flesh and blood, He Himself likewise also partook of the same, that through death He might render powerless him who had the power of death, that is, the devil."[34]

Amen to that!

Points to Ponder

1. The media often portrays Satan differently than the Bible does. Why is that? What image do you have of Satan?

2. Many think Isaiah 14 deals with Satan. This chapter disagrees. Does it make a difference?

---

[31]John 16:11. [32]Jude 6. [33]Job 1:7. [34]Hebrews 2:14.

3. Why do you suppose many of the details about Satan's fall are not in the Bible?

4. Is it surprising to discover that Satan has at times asked for and received permission to afflict certain saints?

5. How much time and thought should be given to Satan and his work?

Mysterious
Intelligences

Those who study the UFO phenomenon sometimes use an abbreviation to describe alien life: EBE. The acronym stands for "extraterrestrial biological entity." The Bible contains evidence not for EBE's but ESE—"extraterrestrial spiritual entities"—extraterrestrial in the sense of nonhuman. These beings are shown to be intelligent, self-aware, interactive, able to communicate, and very harmful. The Bible records seven occurrences where Jesus cast out demons. These exorcisms are dramatic and unforgettable. The apostles would later also cast out demons.

One doesn't have to read very far in the Gospels to encounter the strange and mysterious world of demons. These foreign intelligences plagued many people in Jesus' day, inflicting a wide variety of calamities and afflictions. Sometimes called "evil spirits" (fourteen times), "unclean spirits" (twenty-three times), and at other times "demons" (sixty-eight times), these frightening entities seem more suited to a Stephen King novel than the Bible. But there they are—and they are part of God's mysterious universe.

Demons have been the subject of many books and movies. Who are they? Where did they come from? What drives them? What is their fascination with human beings? Are they active today?

Who Are Demons?

Demons make themselves known in the Gospels very early. Mark 1:2–27 tells the story of Jesus' first recorded encounter with the beings.

Jesus often visited the Galilean city of Capernaum. In many ways, the town became His "northern headquarters." While at a synagogue in the city, Jesus was teaching with such authority that the people were stunned with amazement. They had never heard such teaching before. It was during this teaching that a man with an unclean spirit "cried out" (Mark 1:23). The term *cried out* comes from the Greek *anakrazo*, meaning "to make a loud, guttural sound." It was the word chosen to describe the call of ravens, donkeys, a war cry, and even the grunting of a woman in childbirth.

But there was more than just frightening sounds coming from the man; there was speech: "What business do we have with each other, Jesus of Nazareth? Have You come to destroy us? I know who You are—the Holy One of God!" (Mark 1:24). There is a great deal in those few words. The unclean spirit was aware of Jesus, His hometown, and the fact that He was the Messiah. That was more than any human knew at that point.

This account shows that demons (unclean spirits) are capable of rational thought, are aware of themselves and others, are aware of God's plan, and can sense fear. It also shows that they can possess a human. They can take up habitation in a person and control his actions.

These are strange and frightening beings. Who are these guys? The short answer is: No one really knows. For centuries, the topic has been debated, and not just among Christians and Jews. Almost every culture has folklore about demonic spirits inhabiting humans. Several concepts about their identity exist.

The ancient Greeks and Jews believed that demons were the spirits of the dead—in essence, ghosts. A few early Christian writers as well as the Jewish writers Josephus and Philo held this view. This is contrary to the overall teaching of Scripture.

There is nothing in the Bible to indicate that disembodied spirits of the dead roam the earth. In fact, the opposite is the case. In Luke 16, Jesus relates the account of two men who died. One was rich and the other poor and afflicted with disease. When the rich man (tradition gives him the name Dives) opened his eyes, he found himself in torment. Poor Lazarus, however, was poor no more. He awakened in a place called Abraham's bosom. It was a place of peace, joy, and comfort.

The point of the story is to show that the earthly condition of man means nothing in the next life. The poor believer will fare far better than the rich unbeliever will. It also shows that life continues after death, but not in the form of disembodied spirits haunting the world. Each person has a destination based on what he has done with Christ. Nowhere in the Bible are demons linked to dead humans.

Other people have suggested that God created a race that predates the human race. In this view, something destroyed this pre-Adamic race and their disembodied spirits are present-day demons. Some suggest the destruction is tied to Satan's fall. This idea is intriguing, but it's not scriptural. As Charles Ryrie said, "Though there is nothing antiscriptural about this view, there is nothing scriptural about it either, for the Bible nowhere speaks of the existence of such a race."[1] This view is just one step away from the ghost idea, and it falters for the same reasons.

The most popular belief is that demons are fallen angels. Most scholars teach this, but it also has its problems. The basic assumption is that a group of angels rebelled with Satan and that God punished them by casting the rebels from heaven. These cast-off angels became the demons of the Bible. There is some meat to this argument, and many fine theologians have adopted it. Still, it seems to come short of the biblical description.

Demons are never referred to as angels, fallen or otherwise. Nothing in their words or actions fits with what we know about angels. While many people teach that angels are "spirit beings" (meaning they have no substance to their bodies), the evidence is contrary. Angels are seen wielding swords, touching people, moving objects, and they seem as solid as the humans who see them. This does not mean that their bodies are identical to ours. In every way, they seem superior in form and mind. Why would an angel need to possess an inferior human body?

There is no doubt that fallen angels exist. Second Peter 2:4 reads, "For if God did not spare angels when they sinned, but cast them into

---

[1] Charles Caldwell Ryrie, *A Survey of Bible Doctrine* (Chicago, Ill.: Moody Press, 1972, 1995).

hell[2] and committed them to pits of darkness, reserved for judgment."
Jude 6 adds that these fallen angels will remain in bonds until the final
judgment. These verses create a conundrum. If demons are fallen angels,
then why are they free to roam while God keeps the others safely locked
away and chained?

Also, the demons in the New Testament seem to act in ways vastly
different from what is seen of angels or even Satan. There is no biblical
account of Satan possessing anyone. He has influenced, tempted, attacked
(as in the case of Job) and filled the heart (Judas) but never possessed.

Admittedly, this is an argument from silence. Simply because the
Bible never shows Satan or angels possessing a human doesn't prove that
they couldn't, but it does seem unlikely.

The general view is that there are two classes of fallen angels: free
and bound. The fallen but free angels are demons. While this may be
true, it is at best an awkward fit.

Some interpreters suggest that demons are the disembodied spirits of
the Nephilim. The first few verses of Genesis 6 tell the story of the
Nephilim. According to the account, the "sons of God" (angels) came
down and took human wives. The offspring of that union were the
Nephilim, which many understand to be powerful giants. The Greek
translation of the Old Testament known as the Septuagint[3] translates the
name *gigantes,* from which we get our word *giants.* While this passage is
hotly debated (sometimes too hotly), it seems that the offspring of the
"sons of God" and the "daughters of Adam" were unique enough to
warrant a new name for themselves. Nephilim means "feller," that is,
one who causes others to fall, or who fells (as in attacks) another.

Immediately following that account is the long story of Noah. Genesis
6:9 states that Noah was "blameless." The Hebrew word is *tamim* and
means "without spot or blemish." It described animals that were of high
quality and without defect. Some understand this to mean that Noah was

---

[2]Hell is a mistranslation. The text uses the word *tartarus,* which appears to be a place
different from hell. The word is used only in this verse. [3]The shorthand for Septuagint
(which means "seventy") is LXX and can be seen in many notes in contemporary
English translations. Most of the Old Testament quotes that appear in the New
Testament are from the Septuagint.

untouched, unpolluted by Nephilim. In other words, he was still genetically pure as well as being morally and spiritually upright. The rest of the
world had been genetically contaminated by the wayward sons of God.

All except Noah and his family die in the flood, but what happened
to the Nephilim? They certainly died too. But what of their souls? Is
there a place for such hybrid souls? Some suggest that these disembodied
Nephilim spirits are the same as demons and they possess bodies because
they are incomplete without them. The nature of demons seems to be the
same as the Nephilim, but there is no one-to-one correspondence.

This, like all the other contentions, is beyond proof. The best that we
can do is to see which idea fits best with Scripture. This one is intriguing
and may be correct. Its greatest weakness is that the Bible does not relate
the Nephilim with demons.

So what's the bottom line? Honesty demands that we say we don't
know. Demons are real. Jesus confronted them many times, but the Bible
does not explain their origin.

The most likely case is that demons are undefined creatures that we
know very little about. All the current explanations carry unsolvable
problems with them. Since we have very little information on the topic,
the best we can do is make prayerful speculation. It is doubtful that fallen
angels are the same as demons, but whatever the beings are, however
they originated is beyond the knowledge of humans—for now.

While it is unlikely that the angels that fell with Satan are demons, it
is certain that Satan controls and rules over the demonic world as well
as a fallen angelic kingdom.

After one exorcism of demons by Jesus, the Pharisees made a harsh
accusation against him: "This man casts out demons only by Beelzebul
the ruler of the demons."[4] They used a harsh and insulting term,
Beelzebul. The history of the name is uncertain, but it is most likely from
Baal-zebub, a pagan god worshiped by the Philistines in Ekron. It meant
"lord of the house," or "lord of the loft place." The Jews would not use
the term, so with some clever letter substitution the word became

---

[4]Matthew 12:24.

Beelzebul, "lord of the flies" (perhaps "lord of dung," that is, "the dung god").

What the Pharisees mean as an insult, Jesus turned into a lesson. Deftly, He substituted the word *Beelzebul* for *Satan*. It's interesting that the Jewish Pharisees used a pagan term while Jesus used a Hebrew term. "If Satan casts out Satan, he is divided against himself; how then will his kingdom stand?"[5] In this one line, we learn that Satan is associated with the demons. The Pharisees said that Beelzebul was the prince of demons, but Jesus corrected that.

Doesn't this mean, then, that demons are fallen angels? No. As we've seen, Satan is the "god of this world." As such, he rules over many things. Jesus said the Pharisees were of their "father the devil."[6] That did not make the religious leaders demons, at least not literally.

Satan does rule over the demons and "his angels." In speaking of the great judgment, Jesus set the scene in heaven, then said, "Then He will also say to those on His left, 'Depart from Me, accursed ones, into the eternal fire which has been prepared for the devil and his angels.'"[7] *Angel* is a broad term that simply means "messenger." The way the term appears here refers to a special group of beings, those who fell with him in the rebellion.

What Are Demons Like?

The Bible reveals several characteristics of demons.

First, they are immaterial. They are called spirits. The Greek word is *pneuma,* a term that means "breath, wind, or spirit." Only context tells us how to translate the word. They bear two such titles: "unclean spirits" and "evil spirits." "Unclean" refers to their nature; "evil" refers to their behavior. Unlike angels, no one has seen a demon. They are experienced by the possessed and their actions are witnessed by others, but no physical description appears in the Bible. Angels appear many times in the Bible. Each time the Scriptures describe them in physical terms, including phrases like "standing," "sitting," and "wearing." This is not so for demons.

---

[5]Matthew 12:26. [6]John 8:44. [7]Matthew 25:41.

They possess intelligence, are self-aware, and can carry on conversations. They were conscious of their surroundings and were aware of who Jesus was. They possessed emotion, especially when in the presence of Christ.

Being in a body seems important to them. They even preferred to inhabit pigs rather than to exist in a disembodied state. When Jesus faced the two violent demoniacs in the Gadara tombs, the demons in the men began to beg Him, "If You are going to cast us out, send us into the herd of swine."[8] Jesus agreed. So shocked were the pigs that they rushed down a steep slope into the sea and drowned. One wonders what happened to the demons after that.

Demons, therefore, are entities that think, feel, and reason, making requests and even pleading for mercy. Yet, they are not sympathetic characters. They are vile entities who inflict pain and anguish on those whom they possess.

The synagogue at the site of ancient Capernaum. In the early part of Jesus' ministry, He healed a possessed man in a Capernaum synagogue.

[8]Matthew 8:31.

Jesus gave the only detailed insight into demons. In Matthew 12:43–45, He used the example of a demon-possessed man to represent the sign-seeking generation. He stated that when the "unclean spirit goes out of man, it passes through waterless places." What waterless places? The simplest answer is the wastelands familiar to everyone in Jesus' audience. Or, it could be a euphemism for whatever plane of existence in which evil spirits dwell. It is interesting to note that the ancient Jews believed that demons lived in the desert (waterless) regions of their country.

According to Jesus, the unclean spirit was searching for rest. The Greek word used by Jesus means "to cease from something," such as to cease working and therefore to rest, or to cease from traveling.[9] Another translation is "relief." In other words, the demon traveled through the waterless places seeking some type of relief. The implication is that the entity was troubled in its present state, that it was missing and desiring something.

Taken literally, the passage implies that the demon was discontent, restless, and driven to obtain something that would satisfy its need. That satisfaction came from possessing a physical creature. It is hard to imagine an angel with this kind of need. Jesus went on to say that the demon's search was futile. He was unable to find the relief he so eagerly desired.

Unsatisfied, the demon decided to return to his "house." Jesus used an interesting term here. It is *oikos,* which is the generic term for house or dwelling. There is nothing special in the word, but there is in the fact that the demon referred to the previously possessed person as a place of dwelling, and he used the possessive "my house." This is important because it shows that demons need (or at the very least, strongly desire) a place—or person—of habitation.

"Then it [the demon] says, 'I will return to my house from which I came'" (Matthew 12:44). This simple statement reveals a frightening fact about unclean spirits: They have memory and are able to recognize persons they have possessed before. Jesus didn't tell us how they recognized

---

[9]*Anapausis.*

specific individuals, but the demon in question sought out the man whom he had previously inhabited.

As Jesus continued the reprimand, He added that the demon found the house "unoccupied, swept, and put in order." The man, now free of the demon's influence, seemed to have everything in order. But here the story takes a strange twist: The demon left to obtain the help of other unclean spirits "more wicked than itself, and they go in and live there."

Why would the demon need the help? What was it about the clean and unoccupied state of the man that made the spirit think it needed help? Jesus didn't reveal the motivation in the account, but one fact becomes clear: While having a life swept and in order, the man was still empty. This was Jesus' point in telling the story. Religion could offer some benefit, such as mental and spiritual orderliness, but it could not fill the man. His emptiness left him open and vulnerable to other demons.

Thankfully, the Christian is in a different situation. From the moment of salvation on, the believer is "occupied," but with someone positive and vital: the Holy Spirit. Paul told the Ephesians to "be filled with the Spirit."[10] Christians are the temple of the Holy Spirit,[11] meaning that He (the Spirit) lives in every believer. The apostle Paul, in writing to the church at Rome, reminded them, "However, you are not in the flesh but in the Spirit, if indeed the Spirit of God dwells in you."[12]

What Jesus described was a man suddenly freed from the inhabitation of a demon. He cleaned up his life, but he failed to fill himself with something that would provide protection. That something was in reality a someone—the Holy Spirit.

The demon, now joined by seven others, moved back in, leaving the man in worse shape than before. Here is another trend we see with demon possession: multiple entities. Of the exorcisms performed by Jesus, several deal with a single person with multiple demons.

In the early part of Jesus' ministry, He healed a possessed man in a Capernaum synagogue.[13] The presence of Jesus was a threat to them, and

---

[10]Ephesians 5:18. [11]1 Corinthians 6:19. [12]Romans 8:9. [13]Mark 1:21–27; Luke 4:33–36.

they cried out, "Let us alone! What business do we have with each other, Jesus of Nazareth? Have You come to destroy us?" This account and the others like it introduce us to the odd and sometimes confusing mixing of pronouns. When the verses refer to the man, the singular "he" is used— "and *he* cried out with a loud voice." But when the dialogue is recorded, the plurals "we" and "us" are used.[14] It's bad grammar, but an accurate reflection of the situation. Multiple, intelligent creatures possessed the man.

There appears to be no limit to the number of demons who can take up residence in a person. Mark 5:1–13 recounts a confrontation with a demon-possessed man (Matthew 8:28 tells us there were two men), who is described as violent, strong, and self-destructive. When Jesus arrived on the scene, there was a confrontation similar to the one that took place in the Capernaum synagogue, including the question, "What business do we have with each other, Jesus, Son of the Most High God?" (Mark 5:7). Then they pleaded with Jesus not to torment them. The torment came from Jesus' repeated commands to come out of the man.

Again, there is a confusion of singular and plural words. Jesus said, "Come out of the man, you unclean spirit!" *Spirit* is singular—just one— but the demon's reply is in the plural. When asked "What is your [singular] name," the reply came back, "My [singular] name is Legion, for we [plural] are many." This gives most English thinkers psychic whiplash. And if Legion is to be taken as equivalent to the Roman legion of soldiers, then the number of demons in this poor man may have been as high as six thousand! While there is no reason to believe that is impossible, "Legion" may simply mean "a great many" or it may be arrogance on the part of the demons.

Whatever the actual number, we can say that it was a great many and they were causing unending suffering for the man. Jesus cast them out, allowing them to go into a herd of nearby pigs.

Demons often possess in numbers. Seven demons possessed the great follower of Christ, Mary Magdalene, before Jesus freed her.[15] No one

---

[14]Luke 4:33–34. [15]Luke 8:2.

knows why they possessed in numbers, but it seems to have been common in Jesus' time.

The Demon Effect

No one knows the exact dynamics of demon possession. The Scripture is silent on the mechanism, but it provides a great deal of information on the effects.

Physical effects are the most obvious. This has caused some interpreters to suggest that Jesus was accommodating His teaching to the beliefs of the day when He cast out demons; that though demons don't exist, Jesus went along with the superstition rather than correcting the error. Such statements are far from the truth and don't do justice to the text. The Bible distinguishes between possession and illness: "At that very time He cured many people of diseases and afflictions and evil spirits; and He gave sight to many who were blind."[16] The Jews of Jesus' day did not confuse demon possession with illness. It is true that the word *healed* is often associated with the act of dispelling demons, but it is used in the broadest sense. Demons infested their hosts like viruses infest a body. Healing is an appropriate term.

Of the ten possessions listed on the next page, an equal amount were male and female. All but three were adults, and no ages can be determined from the text. These physical afflictions varied from blindness to convulsions. How such physical manifestation came about from immaterial (as best we can tell) entities is unknown.

In addition to physical affliction, demon-possessed people in New Testament times showed a propensity for disorder, loud vocalizations, and self-destruction. Often the person would convulse when the demon left.

Why?

It is certainly one of God's mysterious ways to allow such creatures to torment the world. Their activities are connected to their prince, Satan. Many wonder why God allows Satan and demons to exist at all.

---

[16]Luke 7:21. See also Luke 8:2; 13:32.

Physical Affliction by Demons				
Event	Gender	Age	Affliction	Reference
Capernaum synagogue	Male	Adult	Unspecified	Mark 1:24 Luke 4:35
Gadara tombs	Male	Adult	Mental anguish, self-abuse, violence, unnatural physical strength	Matthew 8:28–32 Mark 5:2–13 Luke 8:26–33
?	Male	Adult	Mute	Matthew 9:32–33
Tyre/Sidon	Female	Unknown	Unknown	Matthew 15:28; Mark 7:29
Boy at foot of mountain	Male	Unknown	Convulsions	Matthew 17:14–18; Mark 9:25; Luke 9:42
Before Pharisees	Male	Adult	Blind; mute	Matthew 12:22; Luke 11:14
Bent woman	Female	Adult	Doubled over	Luke 13:10–13
Mary Magdalene	Female	Adult	7 demons	Mark 16:9; Luke 8:2
Slave-girl	Female	Youth	Divination	Acts 16:16
Sceva's sons	Male	Adult	Violence	Acts 19:15

Annihilating them would seem to solve many problems, but they remain alive and active and the world is worse for it.

On the other hand, their presence serves as a reminder that there is more to the universe than what we see. In the midst of evil, whether perpetrated by humans, evil spirits, or the fallen cherub Satan, God still reigns supreme. A relationship with Him through Jesus empowers the believer.

While many people have written books and articles listing activities that lead to demon possession, the Scripture gives no such information. Every demon-possessed person in the New Testament arrived before Jesus already possessed and in great need. Jesus made no comment about how they came to be that way. He offered no rebuke to the person, no chastisement—just help and love. There are no pat answers, no lengthy explanations. The facts are just the facts. We must confine our beliefs to what we know. The rest is speculation.

As Moses said, "The Rock! His work is perfect, for all His ways are just; a God of faithfulness and without injustice, righteous and upright is He."[17] God's ways are not man's ways. While we may question the purpose of demons and their freedom to inflict harm to others, we know that God is faithful and just in all things at all times.

A day is coming when demons will see their end. When Jesus cast Legion from the man who lived in the tombs, the demons begged Him not to send them to the abyss. In many ways, demons are frightened creatures, afraid of Christ and His people. The Christian need not fear evil spirits. John the apostle said, "You are from God, little children, and have overcome them; because greater is He who is in you than he who is in the world."[18]

It appears that a time of judgment is coming their way. In one encounter with Jesus, the demons asked a provocative question: "What business do we have with each other, Son of God? Have You come here to torment us before the time?"[19] What time? Revelation speaks of a day when an angel will open the abyss to receive Satan and his angels. At that time, God will cast them into the lake of fire. Could this be the time to which the demons referred?[20] If so, they know their end.

Mysteries abound about demons. What we know is tiny in comparison to the questions we have, but the greatest truth is clear: Christians are not victims in this spiritual war; they are the victors. Christ has made that so.

Points to Ponder

1. So far we have seen a host of nonhuman intelligent beings, including Satan, cherubim, angels, and now demons. Is there room for such beliefs in the twenty-first century?

2. Many people suppose that demons are fallen angels, but there is biblical evidence that this is not the case. Does it make a difference?

---

[17]Deuteronomy 32:4. [18]1 John 4:4. [19]Matthew 8:29. [20]Revelation 20:10. See also Matthew 25:41.

3. During Jesus' ministry there seemed to be a great deal of demonic activity, and this continued through the days of the apostles. Do you think there is less demonic activity today?

4. What do you suppose drives demons to possess the bodies of humans, and why do they carry out such destructive behavior?

5. Why is there so little information in the Bible about the origin and purpose of demons?

Mysterious
Failures

I f God faces challenges, then His greatest challenge must be dealing with people. The Bible is the record of God's interaction with humanity. Sometimes He deals with them in groups, such as nations or tribes; at other times He focuses on the individual.

The problem with people is their propensity to let others down. Even the most noble of humans have a selfish streak. Part of this is for self-preservation, but much of it is rooted in our sin nature. We all fail from time to time. Paul said it clearly, "For all have sinned and fall short of the glory of God."[1] The apostle John was even more blunt: "If we say that we have not sinned, we make Him a liar and His word is not in us."[2]

While we all have our faults, there have been some people who have failed in spectacular ways. Some cause us to wonder what they were thinking, or if they were thinking at all. Others made decisions that were not only shocking but also puzzling, and the way God dealt with them makes the puzzle even more inscrutable.

When we think of mysterious failings, several people pop to mind: David and his sin with Bathsheba; Adam and Eve in the Garden of Eden; Peter's denial of Christ. But no one demonstrates mysterious failing more than Judas Iscariot. Even more mystifying than his betrayal was the length Jesus went to in order to include the man in the circle of His disciples.

---

[1]Romans 3:23. [2]1 John 1:10.

CHAPTER EIGHT

A Peek at the Man

So despicable was Judas Iscariot's action that his very name is now synonymous with treachery and betrayal. It is a great insult for someone to call us a "Judas." Yet there is nothing ominous or evil about the name. Judas is the Greek form of the Hebrew name Judah—a good, strong, respectable Jewish name. The Bible lists several people named Judas, including one of the brothers of Jesus.[3]

The second name of Judas is uncertain and is debated by scholars. Iscariot may mean "man of Kerioth," indicating his family's home. Others, however, think it could be a transliteration of an Aramaic word that means "assassin." The bottom line is that we simply do not know the origin of the term.

Judas was the only disciple not from Galilee. This does not mean that the others treated him as an outsider. There is no indication of that. In fact, by all accounts, he was not only part of the group but he held a significant position. He was the group's treasurer.[4] The disciples felt safe trusting Judas with the money. The disciples never saw beneath the surface, never looked beyond the façade.

The early life of Judas is an enigma. We know nothing of him prior to his call to be a disciple. Indeed, the Bible does not even record his calling; he just appears in the list of the chosen disciples (and his name always appears last). His entrance into the fold of the disciples is as much of a mystery as the rest of his life. We can't help wondering what words Jesus spoke to him. Did He say, "Follow me and I will make you a fisher of men" like He did with the disciples? Did the Savior put a hand on the to-be traitor and extend a personal invitation to enter the fold? Did Judas request to be part of the group, volunteering to join the itinerate lifestyle? No one knows.

We can't help wondering why Judas would want to join? We know that his goals were not in harmony with those of Christ. Many have assumed (and it's a good assumption) that Judas was looking for a conquering Messiah to overthrow Rome and return Israel to its days of freedom. He was not alone in that desire. Shortly before His ascension,

---

[3]Matthew 13:55. [4]John 13:29.

Jesus met with His disciples. Naturally, they were thrilled at His resurrection, but many things still puzzled them. "So when they had come together, they were asking Him, saying, 'Lord, is it at this time You are restoring the kingdom to Israel?'"[5] He told them it was not for them to know the "times or epochs"[6] that the Father had established. Their question, however, highlighted a persistent misconception that Jesus had come to establish an earthly kingdom, dispelling Rome in the process. Certainly, this was in Judas's mind.

Everyone who has read the Gospels has questions about Judas. His behavior is baffling beyond words. How is it that a man can receive a unique and special call from Jesus; spend three years with the Master in itinerate ministry, see amazing miracles, hear indisputable truth, observe the sinless nature of Christ, be himself empowered to work miracles, and then betray the Savior? How is that possible?

There is a mystery greater than that. While the other disciples seem oblivious to Judas's nature and plans (whenever they formed in his mind), Jesus knew that Judas would be the one to betray Him—something He knew from the very beginning.

John 6 records a poignant scene in which, after some difficult, shocking teaching by Jesus, many "disciples" withdrew from following Him. It was as if He were a preacher in a pulpit and the congregation began to exit the building in the middle of the sermon, not wanting to hear the message. Jesus was trimming the discipleship tree.

The focus of the passage switches from the crowd to the small group of disciples. "'But there are some of you who do not believe.' For Jesus knew from the beginning who they were who did not believe, and who it was that would betray Him."[7] The passage continues with Jesus adding, "'Did I Myself not choose you, the twelve, and yet one of you is a devil?' Now He meant Judas the son of Simon Iscariot, for he, one of the twelve, was going to betray Him."[8]

These comments followed several miracles by Jesus, including the feeding of thousands with a few bits of food. In spite of what they had seen, some of the crowd refused to believe. The crowd that followed

---

[5]Acts 1:6. [6]Acts 1:7. [7]John 6:64. [8]John 6:70–71.

Jesus was a mixed group. It was true then, and it is true now. Many of those were the ones fed by the wondrous miracle. They were willing to receive blessing, but they were not willing to invest their hearts and minds in the Savior.

What was generally true for the crowd was specifically true for Judas, a point Jesus made clear. A quote often attributed to Abraham Lincoln is, "You can fool all of the people some of the time; you can fool some of the people all of the time; but you can't fool all of the people all of the time." No one can fool Jesus at anytime.

What is remarkable in this encounter is that Jesus did not point out the traitor. The text is clear that He knew the traitor was Judas, but Jesus kept that information to Himself. One wonders if Jesus knew what Judas did not. Did Judas hear these words and glance at the other disciples, wondering who the devil was, not realizing that it was he who fit the bill?

Unlike the crowd that withdrew (literally, "went away"), Judas remained in place. He arrived on the scene with the twelve disciples, he left with them, and no one but Jesus was wise to the events that would happen. While those who withdrew were "not walking with Him anymore,"[9] Judas continued.

Judas wasn't the only one who turned his back on Jesus. While he receives an enormous amount of criticism—and rightly so—there were many like him. His rejection of Christ's plan was not the first, nor would it be the last. His was just the most graphic and difficult to understand.

Jesus followed all this with a heart-piercing question: "You do not want to go away also, do you?"[10] It is perhaps the saddest question Jesus asked in His ministry. He asked it of the Twelve, and that included Judas. The answer was honest: "Simon Peter answered Him, 'Lord, to whom shall we go? You have words of eternal life. We have believed and have come to know that You are the Holy One of God.'"[11] We can almost see the nodding of heads and hear the mumbled "Amen." Judas was there affirming that commitment. It was then that Jesus laid out the truth that

---

[9]John 6:66. [10]John 6:67. [11]John 6:68–69.

one of them was a devil—a devil that Jesus Himself chose. How ironic that Judas, whose Hebrew name Judah means "praise of God," would have the description "devil" tied forever to his name.

Not Clear on the Principle

In the United States, when we think of traitors, one name comes to mind: Benedict Arnold. But there are some matters about Benedict Arnold that most people don't know.

He fought in the French and Indian War and had commercial success as a druggist. As a militia colonel, Arnold joined with Ethan Allen to take Fort Ticonderoga in New York from the British at the start of the American Revolution in 1775. Military supplies from the fort helped George Washington's ill-equipped American forces, who were besieging Boston. Later the same year, Arnold led a brave but unsuccessful assault on British Québec, and his efforts earned him a promotion to brigadier general. Enemy reinforcements subsequently forced his retreat to Lake Champlain.

On the lake, Arnold was defeated (1776) by a British naval attack, but his delaying tactics thwarted an enemy drive to New York City, which would have divided the colonies. His leadership in the Battle of Ridgefield, Connecticut (April 1777), won him a belated promotion to the rank of major general. During the crucial Saratoga campaigns in New York in the summer and fall of 1777, his relief of Fort Stanwix and his courageous and imaginative battlefield leadership contributed decisively to an American victory.

So what happened? He became disgruntled over slow promotions and fell into financial difficulty. So he sold out to the British. He lost sight of the principles for which he fought.

So did Judas.

The newspaper cartoonist Wiley occasionally pens a comic subtitled "Not Clear on the Principle." He's fond of showing one of his characters making some remark that demonstrates his complete lack of understanding for a situation. The cartoons are about people who seem to miss the point of things. For example, a cartoon might show a man who has been condemned to hell standing before the devil and saying to the prince of darkness: "You know, if you set up a lemonade stand, you could make some real money."

A man does not become a Judas without having several things wrong in his thinking, emotions, and motivations. Judas was never clear on the principle of who Jesus was and what He came to achieve.

The Gospel of Luke demonstrates how much Judas had to overlook and the principles he had to ignore in order to do what he did. "And He called the twelve together, and gave them power and authority over all the demons and to heal diseases. And He sent them out to proclaim the kingdom of God, and to perform healing. . . . When the apostles returned, they gave an account to Him of all that they had done. Taking them with Him, He withdrew by Himself to a city called Bethsaida" (Luke 9:1–2, 10).

The amazing and puzzling thing about Judas was all the things he saw, experienced, and participated in, yet he still missed understanding Jesus.

Jesus sent out the disciples after first giving them power *(dunamos)*. The word, from which we get our word *dynamite,* means to be imbued with spiritual ability. They did not previously possess this power. It was a special gift. It was also power they could not obtain on their own. Jesus gave them a unique gift.

The power was nonhuman, originating in Christ and no one else. In every way, it was a supernatural, uncommon gift.

Jesus gave them something else. He imparted to them authority *(exousian),* which is the "right to exercise power." It was the ability to command demons and disease. This was no small matter. These twelve common men were now twelve extraordinary men before whom demons would tremble and flee and disease would surrender its grip on people.

Their mission was twofold: to proclaim the kingdom of God and to perform healings. They were to focus on the many while never losing site of the individual. The powers that Jesus gave them would enable them to do those very things.

Not only were they empowered, but they were also entrusted—entrusted with tremendous power and responsibility. And Judas was part of all of it. He received the same power, the same authority, the same commission, the same opportunity, and the same blessing. An outsider would not have been able to tell the difference between Judas and any of the other disciples.

They went out just as Jesus commanded. What a sight to see. Mark 6:1–12 reveals that Jesus sent them out in pairs. We have no idea whom Jesus paired with Judas. They went out among the villages. Apparently, they had assignments. It is easy to imagine them walking down the dirt roads, entering a village, finding the demon-possessed and ill, performing miracles, and preaching the kingdom of God in Christ. The healings would gather the crowds; the empowered disciples would preach the message.

They preached the gospel. One can't preach what one doesn't intellectually know, but a preacher can deliver a message he doesn't believe. Judas understood the message. This is amazing. Judas was preaching the word of Christ. Like Benedict Arnold who fought against the British, Judas fought against Satan. He cast out Satan's demons, only later to succumb to the enemy. There were people made well by the power of God because Judas laid hands on them. There's nothing in the Gospels to indicate otherwise. However, it wasn't by Judas that these things happened—Jesus gets the glory here.

Six teams of disciples worked the power and authority they were given. Here's what we need to notice: (1) Judas was empowered like the others; (2) Judas did the work like the others; and (3) Judas preached the same message as the others. Yet he did not let that experience change him. There is the lesson.

Perhaps Judas worked under the "grace by association" principle—the idea that he was in good standing with God because he was numbered among the disciples. Many people believe they have a relationship with God because they go to church—instead of going to church because they have a relationship with God. Jonas Salk does not get into heaven because of his great work on the polio vaccine; Mother Teresa doesn't gain admission to heaven because of her faithful work with the poor in India; Billy Graham doesn't pass into life eternal because of his many evangelistic crusades. These people, like everyone else, receive eternal life based on a personal decision they make for Christ, and nothing else. Judas was not spiritually clean because he was part of the close group of disciples.

In movie making, there is a term called "day for night." By using special filters, the cinema photographer can shoot a scene in broad daylight and have it look as if it occurred at midnight. The viewer sees something different from reality. So it was with Judas and others who suffer from the "Judas Syndrome"—that ability to see things the way they want to see them rather than the way they really are.

Will the Real Judas Please Stand Up

The one thing that reveals the true nature of a person faster than any other is money. One of the many ironies concerning Judas is that he seemed trustworthy enough to earn the position of treasurer. He was the keeper of the coins; he held the money box. The appearance of trustworthiness, however, does not mean it is trust well placed. John 12:1–8 gives us an insight into the real Judas.

The events are set against the backdrop of a small town near Jerusalem known as Bethany. It was in this town that the good friends of Jesus—Mary, Martha, and Lazarus—lived. Before Jesus, just a few miles up the hill in Jerusalem, loomed the sorrowful hours in the upper room where He would institute the Lord's Supper, the Garden of Gethsemane where He would pray with agonizing words, the moment of betrayal, the trials, and then the horrendous agony of the cross.

Jesus was at a dinner held in his honor. Mark reveals that the actual meal was in the home of Simon the Leper. Perhaps it was a larger home than that of the sibling trio. Mary, overwhelmed with devotion and love, anointed Jesus' feet. There was great meaning in this. Jews could not require another Jew, not even a Jewish slave, to wash their feet. It was considered too humiliating. Yet Mary did so with loving spontaneity, and she didn't use water and a towel, but "nard" and her own hair.

The material used was "very costly perfume."[12] Nard, sometimes called spikenard, came from eastern India. It was not a cheap import. The passage lists its value at three hundred denarii. A denarius was a silver Roman coin equivalent to a day's wages. In other words, Mary

---

[12]John 12:3.

The traditional site of the upper room, or Hall of the Coenaculum, in Jerusalem. It was here where Judas, along with the other disciples, met with Christ shortly before His betrayal.

poured a year's salary on Jesus' feet. This was more than most people could save in a lifetime.

This was more than Judas could take. He complained, "Why was this perfume not sold for three hundred denarii and given to poor people?"[13] This questioning was harsh on several counts. First, the comment indicates wastefulness on Mary's part. Judas was implying that Mary had acted foolishly. Second, he made this comment in the hearing of everyone at the dinner. It was a public admonishment and had as its goal the embarrassment of Mary. It also cheapened the act. Mary did something wonderful, and Judas immediately and publicly tore it down. Jesus reversed the tables on Judas, telling him to "let her alone."[14]

Scripture is always honest and upfront. Even more so in this passage, because John records: "Now he [Judas] said this, not because he was concerned about the poor, but because he was a thief, and as he had the money box, he used to pilfer what was put into it."[15]

Three scathing statements in that one verse. One, Judas had no concern for the poor. He was misrepresenting himself and his intentions. Two, he was a thief. The word used for *thief* is *kleptes,* which means "an embezzler, cheat, or thief." We get our English word *kleptomania* from

---

[13]John 12:5. [14]John 12:7. [15]John 12:6.

it. Three, he was stealing from the ministry. It shows Judas's love of money, which may have been one of his motivating factors.

Paul gave straightforward advice to his protégé Timothy and warned him about the problem that money could create. "For the love of money is a root of all sorts of evil, and some by longing for it have wandered away from the faith and pierced themselves with many griefs."[16] Perhaps he had Judas (as well as others) in mind when he wrote this. In describing the kind of men who could be leaders in the church, Paul gave a list of traits to avoid. That list included, "Free from the love of money."[17] Judas knew no such freedom; instead, the love of money bound his mind and heart as if he were imprisoned.

The World's Worst Trade

Few things define us more quickly than the company we keep, especially that company we keep in secret. Judas made a change in allegiance; he took as a friend someone who would lead him to his own demise. The words are brilliant upon the pages of the Bible, brilliant but garish and ugly. They are a string of terms that give a repulsive, frightening image: "And Satan entered into Judas who was called Iscariot, belonging to the number of the twelve."[18]

Satan the adversary entered Judas. Whereas the believer is indwelled by the Holy Spirit, Judas allowed the entrance into his life of the very enemy of God. The word *entered (eiserchomai)* has various meanings but is generally translated as "enter in" or "go in." It is not the same as demon possession. In a legal sense, the word means to "enter court." It also described actors coming on stage. Another good translation would be "to arise." In other words, "Satan arose in Judas."

This is borne out by John 13:2: "During supper, the devil having already put into the heart of Judas Iscariot, the son of Simon, to betray Him." The devil "put in" the heart of Judas the idea of betrayal. Judas was already evil, but Satan prompted the next activity. The phrase *put it* comes from the Greek word *ballo,* a strong word meaning to throw or

---

[16]1 Timothy 6:10. [17]1 Timothy 3:3. [18]Luke 22:3.

propel something, as a person might toss a ball. It can also mean to "pour" as to pour a liquid into a container.

The point is, Judas was not possessed, as some people have suggested. The Bible shows that Jesus, and later the disciples, held Judas accountable for his treachery. *What Judas did was give room to Satan.*

In many ways, Judas made a trade—the worst trade in history. Judas, who had spent the last three years of his life walking with Christ, decided to trade masters, to swap Satan for Jesus. Satan and Judas were two of a kind.

Satan had this kind of influence by default. Judas opened the invitation by holding on to his desires rather than letting go to Jesus; by standing back from Jesus when he should have embraced Him; and by closing his eyes to the clearly demonstrated truth when he should have been watching and accepting.

This led Judas to make another swap, exchanging his relationship with the disciples for one with the religious leaders who wanted Jesus dead. Like those in John 6, Judas "went away." He turned his back on Jesus.

But he did more than exit the upper room. He made his way to the sworn enemies of Jesus and struck a deal—a business deal! Luke 22:4–6 gives the details. It states that the traitor "discussed with the chief priests and officers how he might betray Him to them." *Discussed* is literally "talk together." In this case, it carries the idea of haggling and planning. After this satanically inspired conference, several things came to be.

First, there came joy: "They were glad."[19] Odd that this detail is included, but it's important. It reveals their state of mind.

There was also an agreement in principle: They were to seize Jesus somewhere away from the crowds. The religious leaders didn't know where that might be, but Judas did. He knew the garden where Jesus often prayed.

There was an agreement of money. The Gospel of Matthew pulls no punches: "Then one of the twelve, named Judas Iscariot, went to the chief priests and said, 'What are you willing to give me to betray Him to you?' And they weighed out thirty pieces of silver to him."[20] Thirty pieces of silver. Since the text does not state the type of coin used, the

---

[19]Luke 22:5. [20]Matthew 26:14–15.

value of the transaction is unknown. We do know the coins were silver. This is an important detail. Thirty pieces of silver was the price of a slave (Exodus 21:32). It also fulfilled a prophecy made five hundred years before (Zechariah 11:12).

Judas also exchanged missions. Once he had walked into villages along with the other disciples, performed miracles, and cast out demons. Once he had victory over evil; now he embraced it for thirty coins.

The World's Most Loving Effort

Before Judas struck his deal, Jesus made one last attempt to reach the man: "When Jesus had said this, He became troubled in spirit, and testified and said, 'Truly, truly, I say to you, that one of you will betray Me.' The disciples began looking at one another, at a loss to know of which one He was speaking."[21]

No one other than Jesus knew. At least eleven other people were in that room with Jesus and Judas (probably more), and not one of them suspected what evil was in the traitor's mind and heart. Again, we see Christ's mysterious ways. He didn't call Judas by name. He didn't point a finger. Instead, He dipped a morsel of bread into juice of the cooked lamb that would have been present at the Passover meal and handed it to the betrayer.

There is sadness in the act, a poignant message. A host would dip the bread and hand it to the honored guest at the table. No more dishonorable person could be present, yet Jesus held out this cultural custom to the one He knew had already betrayed Him in heart and was about to betray Him in deed. It was a sign of friendship. It was a symbol of honor. It should have been the other way around.

Judas took it.

Judas ate it.

"After the morsel, Satan then entered into him." *After* the morsel. Judas made the first move of treachery; Satan joined in. Then the words that have echoed down the halls of history: "What you do, do quickly."[22]

---

[21]John 13:21–22. [22] John 13:27.

John 13:30 makes a poetic statement: "So after receiving the morsel he went out immediately, and it was night." This is far more than a statement that the sun had gone down. It speaks to the darkness of Judas's heart. That's all that Satan can bring to a life. That's all that greed can bring to a person's existence. When Judas left Jesus behind, he left behind the only one who could bring light to his shadowy existence.

The Ultimate Failure

The plan was simple. Judas and the religious leaders were the only ones in on it. Initially it was a tight group of conspirators. Judas knew the plan; he had helped devise it, to plot it. It was simple: gather as many people as possible and take Jesus away when there was no crowd around. They would surprise Jesus . . . except no one can surprise the Savior. What they thought they had conceived in darkness and secrecy Jesus knew long before the idea germinated in their minds.

Still, Jesus went to Gethsemane. Still, He prayed. Still, He waited for those who thought they had outsmarted the Son of God.

Judas took the initiative. Every step he took after leaving the upper room and along the path toward the enemies of Jesus was an opportunity to change his mind. Every breath, every passing second was another occasion to stop, to turn around, to ask forgiveness. Judas ignored them all. In his mind, he knew better than Jesus. Judas kept going.

Judas also knew the place where Jesus would be: "Now Judas also, who was betraying Him, knew the place, for Jesus had often met there with His disciples."[23] He had been there on a number of occasions. Judas had watched, maybe even participated in the prayer meetings.

The traitor led a crowd, a mob of dignitaries and soldiers, to the place where Jesus waited. Notice who accompanied him to the site.[24] First, he brought a "Roman cohort." The phrase refers to a group of soldiers that comprised one-tenth of a legion (six thousand men). The conspirators brought a detachment of six hundred Roman soldiers. Their fear had been crowds. Rome had charged the soldiers with keeping the peace. In

---

[23]John 18:2. [24]John 18:3.

some ways, they served as police officers. Here the traitor came with great confidence. Who could stand against six hundred trained soldiers?

With the battalion came "officers from the chief priests and the Pharisees."[25] This included temple guards and representatives of the priests. With them were the long-time opponents of Jesus—the Pharisees. The scene must have been terrifying to the disciples, because this horde came with "lanterns and torches and weapons." Matthew notes that the weapons included "swords and clubs."[26] They came expecting trouble. We can almost hear the sound of their footsteps as the soldiers marched in time, as the temple guards followed behind, torch lights flickering against the ebony night. What was it like to face a throng of armed men in the dark?

It some ways, it is odd. These people didn't always get along. Most of the religious leaders hated the Romans and had several conflicts with their leader, Pontius Pilate. But their hatred for Jesus overcame their animosity for each other, so the crowd surged forward.

A stand of old olive trees in the traditional Garden of Gethsemane. It was in the garden that Judas betrayed Christ with a kiss.

[25]John 18:3. [26]Matthew 26:47.

Judas led them along the path like a bandleader.

Then the betrayal took on a surrealistic tone. Judas didn't point a finger and say, "There He is boys. Get Him." Instead, he marked his betrayal first with a casual greeting. "Hail!" Greetings! (see Matthew 26:49). Like nothing was wrong. The hypocrisy was amazing, and the gall even more so. With more than six hundred men behind him, Judas acted as if he had just encountered Jesus while on an evening stroll.

He also called Him "Rabbi," a term of respect. It meant "teacher," but it is clear that Judas had learned none of the important lessons Jesus taught. Judas had been educated, but he had never learned.

The most difficult thing to stomach is that the betrayal came with a kiss. Why a kiss? Why not a pat on the back or a simple pointing of the finger? We may never know the logic behind that, but it reveals the macabre nature of Judas. The kiss was unnecessary. Two things are amazing: the audacity of Judas to betray Jesus with a kiss, and Jesus' willingness to allow him to do so.

An often-overlooked part of the account (and something as mysterious as anything we've seen so far) is Jesus' reserved response. First, He addressed Judas by name. "Judas, are you betraying the Son of Man with a kiss?"[27] At the same time, He referred to Himself by His favorite designation, "Son of Man." Jesus used this term for Himself about forty times in the Gospels. It emphasizes a part of His nature. Not only is He the Son of God (which shows His deity) and the son of David (which shows Him as Messiah), but He is also the Son of Man (humanity).

Then Jesus made the most unusual reference of all: He called Judas "Friend" (Matthew 26:50). It is an unusual term because it appears only three times in the New Testament. It means "companion" or "clansman," even "cousin." This was not sarcasm. It was a supreme act of love. Judas had left Jesus, but Jesus had not left Judas. Judas attempted to separate himself; Jesus worked to include him. Even at that moment, it was not too late.

Judas stepped aside, and the mob seized Jesus.

The deed was done.

---

[27]Luke 22:48.

The Unanswerable Why

There are many speculations about why Judas did what he did. Speculation is all we have since the Scripture does not speak to the matter. However, we can surmise a few things.

"Then when Judas, who had betrayed Him, saw that He had been condemned, he felt remorse."[28] Judas watched the trial of Jesus before the Sanhedrin. He heard the accusations and watched the beating. He heard the hot words of the accusers as they mocked Jesus, "Prophesy to us, You Christ, who is the one who hit You?"[29] Then there came the plot to put Jesus to death. It was then that Judas felt remorse. Odd that he should feel the emotion at that moment. Why the sudden change? Was it the cruel treatment Jesus received that prompted the ache in Judas's consciousness? Or was it because Judas had a plan that was clearly failing? All of this was a direct result of Judas's actions. He was responsible. While others were involved in Christ's death, it was he—the insider— who set it all in motion.

What prompted this turn of thinking was the realization that the leaders had condemned Jesus to death. This seemed to surprise the traitor. But wasn't that to be expected? Wasn't that part of the plan? It certainly was on the part of the Jewish leaders, but Judas seemed to have something else in mind.

Jesus was not responding the way Judas expected. Jesus took the insults, endured the beatings without lashing back. Did Judas expect Jesus to defend Himself? The scene was the opposite of what Judas expected. No one really knows what Judas anticipated or wanted, but we can make an educated guess.

Remorse invaded Judas. Two Greek words describe the English word *repent*. The first is *metamelomai*, and it means "to care after." It carries with it the idea of regret. A choice made, an action taken, and now the actor regrets the decision. It occurs a handful of times in the New Testament and is never associated with salvation.[30] The other term is *metanoi*, and it means "to think after." The former means "to second

---

[28]Matthew 27:3. [29]Matthew 26:68. [30]Matthew 21:29, 32; 27:3; 2 Corinthians 7:8; Hebrews 7:21.

guess oneself," but the latter means "to make a change." It is used many times in the Bible. It is usually associated with salvation.

So strong was Judas's regret that he attempted to return the money to the chief priests and elders. They wanted nothing to do with it. Judas, in what must be the greatest understatement in the Bible, said, "I have sinned by betraying innocent blood."[31] The leaders were unsympathetic and replied with a unified, "So what?" They refused to touch the blood money.

Then Judas did something interesting. He returned the money anyway by throwing it in the "temple sanctuary"—not where the elders met, but in the temple[32] proper (see Matthew 27:5). In other words, Judas marched to the central place of worship, passed through its various courts, and entered the holy place, a place where only priests went. There, in full view of the Holy of Holies, he tossed the money to the stone pavement.

Why go through all that trouble? Why not walk outside and throw the money to the ground, or drop it at the feet of the leaders? Why walk into the temple? Perhaps he followed behind the leaders, begging them to take back the money, and then threw it after them as they entered the temple's inner court. That's possible, but there may be more to it than that. First, it fulfilled a prophecy[33] but it was also the actions of a desperate, hopeless man. Was he giving the ransom money to God? Or was he showing disdain for the actions of the religious leaders? He couldn't keep the money. He wouldn't need the money. No one would take the money from him.

Judas attempted to cool his hot remorse by refusing to benefit from his actions, but the guilt was too heavy. His treachery left him more alone than any man who had ever lived. His cohorts wanted nothing further to do with him; he had placed himself outside the circle of disciples. Who would want him? He was a pariah. In Judas's mind, there was only one option open to him. He could not live with remorse, nor could he rid himself of it, so Judas went away and hanged himself.

[31]Matthew 27:4. [32]*Naos.* [33]Zechariah 11:12–13.

Judas confessed his sin when he said, "I have sinned by betraying innocent blood," but he confessed to the wrong people. His statement was true, his emotions genuine, but he directed his words to people instead of God. He failed to ask for forgiveness. He was remorseful, but never repentant.

King David said, "For I know my transgressions, and my sin is ever before me."[34] Paul said, "For the wages of sin is death, but the free gift of God is eternal life in Christ Jesus our Lord."[35] For Judas, this statement referred to both physical and spiritual death.

Paul wrote the believers in Corinth, "For the sorrow that is according to the will of God produces a repentance without regret, leading to salvation; but the sorrow of the world produces death."[36]

Judas died guilty.

What's He Doing Here?

Judas's behavior is mystifying, but even more so are the actions of the Savior. When we look at the twelve disciples, we see men from every occupation. Some were fisherman, one was a tax collector, and one may have been a revolutionary.[37] Judas seems out of place. The Bible tells us nothing of his occupation, family, age, or how he came to be in the group, yet we know Jesus called him to participate in the ministry, all the while knowing that he would betray Him.

It seems as if Jesus' life would have been much simpler had He excluded Judas, yet the traitor was mysteriously picked to fulfill Christ's plan. Some have argued that Judas was a dupe, a pawn in God's chess game and therefore not responsible for his actions. Such is not the case. Jesus repeatedly reached out to the troubled man, giving him every opportunity to turn, but he refused.

Christ came to teach, to heal, but ultimately to die on the cross for the sins of all humankind, sins forgiven only through a relationship with Him. Certain events had to happen before that death took place, and

---

[34]Psalm 51:3. [35]Romans 6:23. [36]2 Corinthians 7:10. [37]One of the disciples is called Simon the Zealot. The Zealots were first-century Jewish revolutionaries who refused to pay tribute to Rome and sometimes fought against Roman occupation.

Judas was a key player. Still, he had at all times full control of his actions and choices. He allowed the seed of treachery to sprout; he allowed Satan to enter his heart; he allowed greed to get the best of him; he chose to end his own life.

In his mind, his motives may have been noble. Perhaps he wanted to force Jesus' hand, to put Him in a position where He would have to defend Himself against the corrupt religious leaders and thereby establish Himself as the conquering Messiah. If the corrupt leaders fell, Rome would certainly be next.

But Jesus had a different plan, one Judas could never understand. How amazing that a man so close to Jesus could be so far from Him.

Judas will be forever associated with treachery and betrayal. His very name is synonymous with backstabbing disloyalty. Whatever his hopes and dreams, they were shattered when he decided he knew better than Christ.

Points to Ponder

1. Why do you suppose Jesus never told the other disciples about Judas?

2. Why does the Bible not record Judas's call to be part of the disciples?

3. Do you agree that Judas had a choice until the very last moment?

4. Why do you suppose the other disciples never caught on to Judas's thievery?

5. Judas showed remorse, but not repentance. Why do you think he failed to repent?

Mysterious
Travel

For humans, space and time are unchanging quantities. Einstein taught us that time is relative and space is curved. This is fascinating in theory, but it changes nothing in our day-to-day lives. Seconds tick by with or without our permission. To move from one place to another requires the expenditure of energy and the passing of time. We can never travel so fast that time becomes nonexistent, nor can we simply will ourselves to be elsewhere.

Such are the limitations of humans, but for God, the author of time and the Creator of space, there are no limitations. He has demonstrated this on several occasions with mysterious transportations.

Case 1: By Foot, by Carriage, by Spirit
Acts 8:25–40

Here is one of the strangest stories of the Bible. The events surround a man who doesn't get enough credit for his Christian service. Of the early Christians, he was truly one of the greats. Although he was not (as best we can tell) an original disciple and certainly was not one of the Twelve (although one disciple shares a name with him), the few accounts we have portray a man of vital spiritual energy and godly commitment.

His name was Philip, and he appears on the scene with a bang, a sudden burst of service, then slips from the scene for a silent twenty years. One thing is certain: he experienced one of the oddest things to happen to a person.

A Few Philip Facts

Philip first appears on the scene in Acts 6, when the church selects him and six others as deacons. They do this to solve the growing problem of food distribution among the congregation in the Jerusalem church.

The first church was unique in many ways, and it faced some unexpected problems because of their great and sudden success. A congregation that could be numbered at no more than a couple of hundred suddenly swelled into the thousands, with three thousand people being added in one day—one day! "They were continually devoting themselves to the apostles' teaching and to fellowship, to the breaking of bread and to prayer."[1] Such devotion is remarkable and wonderful. It was also taxing.

Many converts remained in Jerusalem to learn more about Christ. This required vast provisions of food and shelter. Many in the church sold what property they had to meet this growing need. The sacrifice worked, but just having resources on hand was not enough. Food and other necessities had to be distributed, and this required organization. "And the Lord was adding to their number day by day those who were being saved."[2] This was wonderful, but it also increased the food distribution problem. The church did what it could, but there was a snag. A complaint arose from the Hellenistic Jews—Jews who had adopted the Greek language and some of the Greek culture. Their complaint was that their widows were being overlooked. This implied that the native Jews were receiving preferential treatment. If something were not done to rectify the problem, the concern might grow into a split.

The apostles knew their job was the preaching and teaching of the gospel, and they decided that others should take the task of "serving tables."[3] The decree went out to the congregation: "Select seven men to do this ministerial work." The qualifications are interesting and give us insight into Philip. These men were to have a good reputation, to be full of the Spirit and wisdom.

Seven men made the grade, and Philip was among them. His name appears second in the list. Philip, whose name means "lover of horses,"

---

[1]Acts 2:42. [2]Acts 2:47. [3]Acts 6:2.

was one of the first deacons. Out of thousands, the congregation chose only seven. Philip had the kind of character and reputation to be included in that noble group.

A man by the name of Saul began a scathing persecution of the church that led to the death of one deacon (Stephen) and the forced dispersal of the congregation. "And on that day a great persecution began against the church in Jerusalem, and they were all scattered throughout the regions of Judea and Samaria, except the apostles."[4] Saul, who would later come to Christ in a dramatic conversion on the road to Damascus, mounted a violent campaign against the Jerusalem congregation, "entering house after house, and dragging off men and women"[5] and putting them in prison.

Many of the congregation fanned out from Jerusalem, traveling into the countryside and into the region of Samaria. God works differently than men. While Saul thought he was putting an end to the Christian "cult" (as he viewed it), he actually contributed to its spread. "Therefore, those who had been scattered went about preaching the word" (Acts 8:4). All Saul and his cronies succeeded in doing was throwing fuel on the fire.

Forced from Jerusalem, Philip ended up in the Samarian city of Samaria. There he began preaching Christ to them. He did more than preach: "The crowds with one accord were giving attention to what was said by Philip, as they heard and saw the signs which he was performing. For in the case of many who had unclean spirits, they were coming out of them shouting with a loud voice; and many who had been paralyzed and lame were healed."[6]

Philip was not only a deacon; he was also a preacher and a miracle worker. Thousands responded to the message he delivered, and the Samaritans came to Christ in droves. Here is what is remarkable about this: As a rule, Jews and Samaritans hated each other. They had been at each other's throats for more than seven hundred years. The phrase "shake the dust from your feet" came from an ancient Jewish practice. If a Jew had to cross over Samaritan soil, he would pause before entering

---

[4]Acts 8:1. [5]Acts 8:3. [6]Acts 8:6–7.

his home area and literally shake the dirty Samaritan soil from his sandals so he would not carry the "contamination" with him.

Philip had overcome such prejudices. He did not see Samaritans; he saw people—people for whom Christ died. Later, Philip would be called "the evangelist"[7] and for good reason. From the little the Bible tells us about him, we know he was a godly man who spread the gospel wherever he went. His faith blossomed in his family. He had four daughters who were "prophetesses." They, like their father, spoke the message of God.

In a stroke of holy irony, twenty years later Philip would have house guests. Luke records in Acts: "On the next day we left and came to Caesarea, and entering the house of Philip the evangelist, who was one of the seven, we stayed with him."[8] The "we" in this verse includes the great apostle Paul. Twenty years before, Paul went by the name of Saul and was the man who persecuted the Jerusalem church, sending thousands fleeing, including Philip. Two decades later he was sleeping under Philip's roof and eating Philip's bread.

Philip not only worked miracles in Samaria but also was the object of a miracle himself. It happened while he was ministering in Samaria: "But an angel of the Lord spoke to Philip saying, 'Get up and go south to the road that descends from Jerusalem to Gaza'" (Acts 8:26). Philip did exactly as told.

One of the fascinating things about this man is that he never seemed surprised. He was not surprised by his choice as deacon; not surprised by the positive response in Samaria; not surprised by an angelic message; and not surprised that God moved him from a ministry of many to a ministry of one. This last point is significant. Many people today assume that great ministry means great numbers of people. Sometimes that is true. We should not take away from what God has done in megachurches and megaministries, but we should also remember that God's great concern is for the individual. No matter how large the crowd, God still looks at the one. Jesus even took time out from dying for the world to save and comfort the thief on the cross. For Philip the

---

[7]Acts 21:8. [8]Acts 21:8.

command was to leave a ministry to many to undertake, at least for the moment, a ministry to the one.

The angel told Philip to go to a place many miles south of where he was. A road led down from Jerusalem to the main trade route that ran by the sea. Philip made the trip by foot, cart, or animal. While we are not told how he traveled, we do know that "he got up and went."[9] Once on the road to Gaza, he saw a chariot (probably a covered carriage) with a man in it. "Then the Spirit said to Philip, 'Go up and join this chariot.'"[10]

It is interesting that Philip was sent on his journey by an angel, but was later instructed by the Holy Spirit. Why the difference? There was nothing to keep the Holy Spirit from sending Philip initially. The Holy Spirit often guided people on missions.[11] The key lay in the work of the Holy Spirit, who "will convict the world concerning sin and righteousness and judgment."[12] This is not something an angel can do. The Holy Spirit was in control of this encounter because He was already at work in the Ethiopian eunuch's life.

The Executive from Ethiopia

The case of the Ethiopian eunuch is interesting. We know a few things about him, but this is his only appearance in the Bible. The text states that he was from Ethiopia. This is not the same region as modern Ethiopia. Many scholars think it refers to the Sudan. He is called a "eunuch" (Acts 8:27). This could be literal, meaning that his job required surgical emasculation, but it may be just a reference to his position in the court of the queen of Ethiopia. The term originally referred to guards of royal harems. Castration was required. Later the term referred to the high-ranking servants of kings or queens. This eunuch was the treasurer for the queen of Ethiopia, a lofty and trusted position.

He was also a worshiper of God who had been in Jerusalem to participate in the feasts and religious holidays. If he were a castrated eunuch, then he would be unwelcome in the temple. Mosaic Law prohibited such men from the congregational assembly (Deuteronomy 23:1).

---

[9]Acts 8:27. [10]Acts 8:29. [11]For example, Acts 13:2, 4; 16:6–7. [12]John 16:8.

Whatever his physical state, his spiritual state was one of curiosity and longing. Philip found him reading from Isaiah 53. The fact that the man had a copy of the Scripture is remarkable. Very few individuals could afford a personal scroll of the Bible. Perhaps he had only the writings of Isaiah with him. But because of his position, he may have had the entire Old Testament in scrolls. Perhaps he had purchased the scrolls while in Jerusalem to take home with him.

The rest of the story is a beautifully told account of an encounter between a willing teacher and an eager student. In the end, the Ethiopian executive stopped his chariot, took a short walk with Philip, and received baptism in a nearby body of water. A new name appeared in God's book of life.

This would seem the end of the story, but for Philip there was more.

Spirited Away

The moment the baptism was over, something strange happened. Philip disappeared. He literally disappeared. In a moment, in the blink of an eye, Philip was gone. "When they came up out of the water, the Spirit of the Lord snatched Philip away; and the eunuch no longer saw him."[13]

There's a common phrase in our language: "spirited away." It comes from this passage. Philip was spirited away. The Greek term for "snatched" in this text is *harpazo*. It translates as "catch up," "take by force," "catch away," "pluck," and "pull." The idea is of physical movement caused by an outside force. It's the same word used by Paul to describe the rapture.

The word *rapture* does not appear in the Bible. It is a term that represents a concept taught in the New Testament. Paul wrote, "Then we who are alive and remain will be caught up together with them in the clouds to meet the Lord in the air, and so we shall always be with the Lord."[14] The word he used for "caught up" is the same as in Philip's situation. The Spirit literally, physically snatched the Evangelist from the water and placed him in the city of Azotus. Azotus (Ashdod in the Old Testament) was a coastal city miles to the west. One moment Philip was

---

[13]Acts 8:39. [14]1 Thessalonians 4:17.

in the water with the eunuch; the next he was somewhere in Azotus. The Spirit had moved him from one place to another.

And what did the Evangelist do in Azotus? He evangelized! "But Philip found himself at Azotus, and as he passed through he kept preaching the gospel to all the cities until he came to Caesarea."[15]

Philip traveled in a way very few humans have and certainly in a manner beyond his ability. To the human mind, it is impossible, but that didn't bother Philip. He understood that it was just another one of God's mysterious ways.

Not the First

Apparently, Philip was not the first person to go through this experience. Two Old Testament passages allude to similar events.

The first is chronicled in 1 Kings 18:12. A man named Obadiah (not the prophet, there are a dozen people in the Bible with that name) worked for the evil king Ahab. The great prophet of God, Elijah, troubled Ahab. The king desperately sought him, but Elijah was hard to find. Obadiah, a faithful servant of God who was stuck with a wicked king, was on a mission to find grazing land for the king's stock. Elijah encountered him and instructed the servant to return to Ahab and arrange a meeting. Faithful as Obadiah was, he had concerns.

In sharing his fears, he revealed something about Elijah. Obadiah said, "It will come about when I leave you that the Spirit of the LORD will carry you where I do not know; so when I come and tell Ahab and he cannot find you, he will kill me, although I your servant have feared the LORD from my youth."[16]

Obadiah was afraid that God would transport Elijah to some other place, making him look bad in the eyes of Ahab. No one wanted to look bad in the eyes of the king. Where did he get such an idea? Elijah made a promise that he would not disappear when Ahab arrived. In dealing with Obadiah, Elijah did not correct his notion that the Spirit of God could move him from place to place. Both parties assumed such occurrences to be fact.

---

[15]Acts 8:40. [16]1 Kings 18:12.

Others believed the same thing. After Elijah was taken to heaven by a fiery chariot (itself another mysterious transportation), his successor Elisha was approached by a group of seers who wanted to search for the former prophet. "They said to him, 'Behold now, there are with your servants fifty strong men, please let them go and search for your master; perhaps the Spirit of the LORD has taken him up and cast him on some mountain or into some valley.' And he said, 'You shall not send.'"[17]

They made the same assumption that Obadiah had. God can and has physically moved his prophets from one place to another. Elisha knew that Elijah was gone for good, but the others thought that maybe God had placed him somewhere else.

These were not ignorant or superstitious people. There's a very good chance that they were speaking from eyewitness testimony.

Case 2: Caught Up

Paul wrote a cryptic statement to the church at Corinth. Many interpreters think he was speaking of himself in the third person to avoid boasting. While that is feasible, it's impossible to prove. He wrote: "I know a man in Christ who fourteen years ago—whether in the body I do not know, or out of the body I do not know, God knows—such a man was caught up to the third heaven . . . was caught up into Paradise and heard inexpressible words, which a man is not permitted to speak."[18]

Whether or not this is Paul speaking personally or of some unnamed saint is immaterial to our point. What matters (at least for this chapter) is that the man was "caught up to the third heaven." In Paul's day, the first heaven was where the birds flew (atmosphere); the second was where the stars and planets were (outer space); and the third was where God dwelt (heaven).

The word Paul used for "caught up" is the same as that in Acts 8 for Philip and that in 1 Thessalonians 4 for the rapture. God transported the man to heaven to see whatever it was he saw, and then He commanded him to keep those sights secret. This was a trip no one could initiate on his own.

---

[17]2 Kings 2:16. [18]2 Corinthians 12:2, 4.

A storm breaks across the Sea of Galilee. Several miracles, including one of mysterious transportation, took place on the sea.

Case 3: Rapid Transit

There is one case in the Bible where a group of men made a miraculous trip from one location to another. It began with a storm and ended with an unexplained arrival.

John 6 is a chapter loaded with important events. It begins with Jesus' feeding of the five thousand,[19] segues into a storm on the Sea of Galilee, and then moves into the account of Jesus walking on the water.[20] After feeding the multitudes, Jesus withdrew from the crowd. The miracle had inspired many people to force Jesus into becoming their king. He had not come for that purpose, so He moved away from the multitude. The Gospel of Mark reveals that Jesus sent the disciples away in the boat,[21] something John omits.

The disciples began the hard work of rowing across the large inland lake. They encountered a wind blowing from the west, making

---

[19]John 6:1–14. [20]John 6:15–21. [21]Mark 6:45.

it impossible to finish the journey. They had rowed three or four miles but were losing the battle against the onslaught of weather. Suddenly, the weary men saw someone walking on the dark, churning surface. Naturally, it terrified them, but Jesus comforted them with the words, "It is I, do not be afraid."[22] This calmed them, and they received Him "into the boat."

The story would be impressive if it ended there, but John adds one more line: "And immediately the boat was at the land to which they were going."[23] At its widest point the Sea of Galilee is about eight miles across, meaning that the mysterious transport crossed approximately four miles—certainly a relief for the bone-weary disciples.

Very little is made of this transportation. Just a handful of words document the event. The Gospel writer found it more important to highlight Jesus walking on the water in the storm. That is certainly understandable. Still, crossing four miles of churning water in an instant is certainly worth noting.

Case 4: He Was Here a Minute Ago

Another unusual case of mysterious transportation involves a very ancient man whose name means "dedicated" or "initiated." He is unusual because he never died. History knows only two people who have never died: Enoch and Elijah. God took both alive from this earth without the transition of death.

Enoch appears very early in Genesis. He is the seventh patriarch listed. Mentioned are his father Jared and his son Methuselah (who is remembered as living the longest of any human—969 years![24]). Enoch walked with God for 365 years.[25]

The Bible says very little about this chosen man. Genesis simply says, "Enoch walked with God; and he was not, for God took him."[26] The language is simple. They walked together and God "received" Enoch.

The Book of Hebrews gives us a little more. "By faith Enoch was taken up so that he would not see death; and he was not found because

---

[22]John 6:20. [23]John 6:21. [24]Genesis 5:27. [25]Genesis 5:23. [26]Genesis 5:24.

God took him up; for he obtained the witness that before his being taken up he was pleasing to God."[27]

"Taken" comes from the Greek word meaning "to transfer or change." God transferred Enoch from where he was to another place because of his faith and behavior that so pleased God. Apparently, it was a one-way trip, much to Enoch's benefit.

Case 5: A Slow Rise into Heaven
Acts 1:9–11; Luke 24:50–51

Jesus is remarkable in every way; His teaching is gripping and undeniably authoritative. His command over nature as shown by the miracles He worked is stunning. The sinless life He led inspires and humbles us. Seeing Him on the cross is heartbreaking. Noting the empty tomb is exhilarating. No thinking person can look at Jesus without feeling overwhelmed by the humble grandeur of His life and the difference it has made in the lives of countless millions. Nevertheless, of all that Jesus did, eleven stunned disciples witnessed one of the most amazing events.

It all took place just east of Jerusalem, across the Kidron Valley, on a mile-long ridge of four peaks called the Mount of Olives. It was on this mount that Jesus prayed in the Garden of Gethsemane. Gethsemane means "oil press." Much had happened during the forty days since Jesus stepped alive from the tomb that seemed so permanent to His enemies. He made numerous appearances to individuals or groups, astonishing them each time.

Now a change was about to take place. The work that Jesus started, He would place in the hands of imperfect men. The disciples would become apostles. Guided and empowered by the Holy Spirit, they would become a band of spiritual warriors who would "upset the world."[28]

This passing of the torch took place in a remarkable way. Jesus gathered His disciples on the slope of that verdant hill of olive trees and gave His last direct commands to them. They listened intently, asked a question or two, and then they saw something they never imagined possible. Jesus rose in the air and continued skyward until He was out of their sight.

---

[27]Hebrews 11:5. [28]Acts 17:6.

This was no levitation trick by some magician. Jesus did not merely hover a foot or two above the ground and then settle softly to the earth. He rose, and rose, and rose until the disciples could see Him no longer.

The event is important and like none other in the Bible. Enoch was taken up by God;[29] Elijah was taken in a fiery chariot;[30] but only Jesus ascended bodily in full view of many witnesses. Besides the Luke and Acts passages, several other New Testament books mention the event. For example, Peter wrote, "[Jesus] who is at the right hand of God, having gone into heaven, after angels and authorities and powers had been subjected to Him."[31]

Paul wrote to Timothy: "By common confession, great is the mystery of godliness: / He who was revealed in the flesh, / Was vindicated in the Spirit, / Seen by angels, / Proclaimed among the nations, / Believed on in the world, / Taken up in glory."[32]

The author of Hebrews mentions the great event also: "Therefore, since we have a great high priest who has passed through the heavens, Jesus the Son of God, let us hold fast our confession."[33]

This appearance of the resurrected Savior is also His disappearance.

The Place He Chose

"And He led them out as far as Bethany" (Luke 24:50). Luke gives us the basic area where Jesus physically left this earth. Jesus took them to a specific town, a small town with which He was very familiar. The name *Bethany* means either "house of dates" or "house of misery/affliction." There is some debate as to its exact meaning. Why take them to Bethany?

First, there were some practical reasons. Bethany was close to Jerusalem, just two miles away and nestled on the lower eastern slope of the Mount of Olives. It was also a well-known place. The disciples were familiar with the small town and had been there many times, often staying there when Jesus carried out His ministry in Jerusalem. The streets, the homes, the roads, the wells—all of it was recognizable territory. There they could focus on the event, the meeting with Jesus.

---

[29]Genesis 5:24. [30]2 Kings 2:11. [31]1 Peter 3:22. [32]1 Timothy 3:16. [33]Hebrews 4:14.

There were spiritual reasons too. Bethany was Jesus' "local" head-quarters during His last days of ministry. This was His "staging" area. The small town had special meaning to Jesus. It was from here that His triumphal entry into Jerusalem began. Mary, in a great act of humility and love, anointed the feet of Jesus at Simon the leper's house, fore-shadowing His imminent death. It was also in Bethany where Jesus' close friends—Lazarus, Mary, and Martha—lived. Jesus raised Lazarus from the dead in that town. Bethany was also the last stop for pilgrims on the way to Jerusalem.

The Blessing He Gave

Luke also tells us, "And He lifted up His hands and blessed them. While He was blessing them, He parted from them and was carried up into heaven."[34] This is the only place in the Gospels where Jesus lifts up His hands. His final words were of blessing. How interesting. He was lit-erally taken up mid-blessing. Jesus was not rising into heaven with His face turned toward His destination; He was rising with His gaze resting on His followers. His attention was on them as much as theirs was on Him.

Blessed (eulogia) means "to speak well of someone." Today it is common to hear someone eulogize the deceased at a funeral. Jesus was speaking well of His disciples, but He was not praising them. Instead, He was pronouncing God's blessing on them.

In Numbers 6:23–27 there are words familiar to many church atten-dees. "Speak to Aaron and to his sons, saying, 'Thus you shall bless the sons of Israel. You shall say to them: The LORD bless you, and keep you; the LORD make His face shine on you, and be gracious to you; the LORD lift up His countenance on you, And give you peace.' So they shall invoke My name on the sons of Israel, and I then will bless them." Most likely, Jesus spoke these very words to His disciples, who recognized and found comfort in them.

But that was just the beginning of the blessings. Paul said (count the number of times the apostle used the word "blessed"), "Blessed be the

---

[34]Luke 24:50–51.

God and Father of our Lord Jesus Christ, who has blessed us with every spiritual blessing in the heavenly places in Christ."[35] Note where the blessing took place: In the "heavenly places" Christians are blessed by Christ because of His ascension.

The only other person in the Bible who lifted up his hands while giving a blessing was the first high priest, Aaron. "Then Aaron lifted up his hands toward the people and blessed them, and he stepped down after making the sin offering and the burnt offering and the peace offerings."[36]

There are connections here. Aaron raised his hands and blessed the people after stepping down from making the sin offering. Christ on the cross was our sin offering. Jesus "stepped down" (was resurrected) and could now bless the people before Him.

The disciples got the meaning, and it resulted in joy. "And they, after worshiping Him, returned to Jerusalem with great joy, and were continually in the temple praising God."[37] We might expect sadness. After all, Jesus had left them. But they understood what had happened, and it led to three responses: worship, joy, and praise. Their worship was immediate and intimate, their joy enduring, and their praise public. The more we know Jesus, the more we understand worship, joy, and praise.

The Way He Left

This should have been no surprise to the disciples. Jesus spoke of His ascension several times.

John 6:61–62: "But Jesus, conscious that His disciples grumbled at this, said to them, 'Does this cause you to stumble? What then if you see the Son of Man ascending to where He was before?'"

John 7:33: "Therefore Jesus said, 'For a little while longer I am with you, then I go to Him who sent Me.'"

John 14:28–29: "You heard that I said to you, 'I go away, and I will come to you.' If you loved Me, you would have rejoiced because I go to the Father, for the Father is greater than I. Now I have told you before it happens, so that when it happens, you may believe."

---

[35]Ephesians 1:3. [36]Leviticus 9:22. [37]Luke 24:52–53.

The first person to see Jesus resurrected was Mary Magdalene. So thrilled was she that she seized His feet and clung tenaciously to them. Jesus had to command her to let go. In this command is a statement about His ascension: "Jesus said to her, 'Stop clinging to Me, for I have not yet ascended to the Father; but go to My brethren and say to them, "I ascend to My Father and your Father, and My God and your God"'" (John 20:17).

Another interesting insight into the ascension is this: Jesus was "taken up" (Acts 1:11). All mentions of this event are in the passive. In other words, it was done *to* Jesus, not *by* Jesus. The Father raised Him into the sky, where He disappeared in a cloud. This was something Jesus submitted to joyfully.

One More Thing

The disciples got a friendly nudge from a pair of angels—"men in white" (Acts 1:10). Apparently dumbstruck and paralyzed by what they had just seen, the disciples were jarred from their wide-eyed gazing by the words, "Men of Galilee, why do you stand looking into the sky? This Jesus, who has been taken up from you into heaven, will come in just the same way as you have watched Him go into heaven."[38]

These were exciting, pulse-quickening words. In a way, the angels said, "What goes up must come down," or in His case, "will come back." Jesus said He would return. "If I go and prepare a place for you, I will come again and receive you to Myself, that where I am, there you may be also."[39] The angels were not announcing the fact; they were reminding the disciples of what they already knew. But they did give a gem of knowledge.

Beyond the fact that Jesus will return, the men in white announced that He would return in the "same way." How did Jesus ascend? He ascended bodily, in full view of others, into a cloud, and from the Mount of Olives. That is exactly how Jesus will return.

The ancient prophet who lived half a millennium before Christ said, "In that day His feet will stand on the Mount of Olives, which is in front

---

[38]Acts 1:11. [39]John 14:3.

of Jerusalem on the east; and the Mount of Olives will be split in its middle from east to west by a very large valley, so that half of the mountain will move toward the north and the other half toward the south."[40] Not only do we know that Jesus *will* return, but we know *where* He will return.

It will be an event witnessed by the world: "Behold, He is coming with the clouds, and every eye will see Him, even those who pierced Him; and all the tribes of the earth will mourn over Him. So it is to be. Amen."[41]

The disciples were to stop gazing and start moving. This is understandable, considering that they had just witnessed the most mysterious transportation ever.

Points to Ponder

1. The few mysterious transportations in the Bible are discussed in this chapter. Why do you suppose there are so few? Could there be other such miraculous physical movements not recorded in the Bible?

2. What effect might Philip's sudden disappearance have had on the Ethiopian eunuch? What effect would it have had on you?

3. Obadiah was concerned that the Spirit would move Elijah to another place. How did Obadiah know that the Spirit did things like that?

4. What other significance might there be in the fact that Jesus ascended into heaven with His eyes directed earthward?

5. Angels announced Christ's birth, ministered to Him after His temptation in the wilderness, aided Him after His agonizing prayer in the Garden of Gethsemane, delivered a message at the empty tomb after the resurrection, and stood by the disciples during the ascension. What does that teach us about angels?

---

[40]Zechariah 14:4. [41]Revelation 1:7.

Mysterious Voices, Good and Otherwise

Almost since the beginning of humankind, people have been fascinated with the world of the dead. Harry Houdini spent much time and money searching for a true spiritualist, someone who could contact the dead and allow him to speak to his deceased mother. He found them all to be frauds. Not one to give up, he promised his wife that he would speak to her from beyond the grave within ten years of his death. He arranged a ten-word code known only to them. He died in 1926. Despite claims of many spiritualists who said they had made contact with the departed magician, none could provide the code. Houdini has remained silent.

Today there is a new interest in such things. Ghost hunters tread through eerie buildings and hike through graveyards. They carry with them infrared cameras, recording devices, and magnetometers—all in an effort to prove the existence of ghosts. Talking with spirits has become entertainment. At this writing, several shows run on television, each featuring a person who promises to contact loved ones on "the other side."

Such interest is not new. Ancient peoples often turned to the dead to obtain advice for the living. The variations of belief would fill an encyclopedia. Still most of us look at such things with disbelief, pooh-poohing the idea from the start.

So prevalent was the practice in Old Testament times that God laid down strict rules about consulting with those who practiced such "arts." God repeated the warning several times. "Do not turn to mediums or spiritists; do not seek them out to be defiled by them. I am the LORD your God."[1] Strong words. Consulting these spirits led to defilement! Defilement is pollution of the soul. It is a contamination of what God has made pure and clean.

More strong words are found in Leviticus: "As for the person who turns to mediums and to spiritists, to play the harlot after them, I will also set My face against that person and will cut him off from among his people."[2] Play the harlot? Cut off from among the people? Yes. God isn't kidding. The spiritual danger is too great. In fact, under Mosaic Law, spiritualism was a capital crime. "Now a man or a woman who is a medium or a spiritist shall surely be put to death. They shall be stoned with stones, their bloodguiltiness is upon them."[3]

Why was God's command so severe? There are any reasons, but two rise to the surface. First, it was a pagan practice, and God's people were not to be seduced into following the ungodly habits and beliefs of the people who occupied the land before them. "There shall not be found among you anyone who makes his son or his daughter pass through the fire, one who uses divination, one who practices witchcraft, or one who interprets omens, or a sorcerer, or one who casts a spell, or a medium, or a spiritist, or one who calls up the dead."[4] It's a long list directed at the Canaanite religious system. The children of Israel were to live the message of the one true God, not embrace paganism.

Isaiah made the second reason clear: "When they say to you, 'Consult the mediums and the spiritists who whisper and mutter,' should not a people consult their God? Should they consult the dead on behalf of the living?"[5] To consult the dead is to turn one's back on the living God. It's insulting to Him and to those who have placed their faith in Him.

---

[1]Leviticus 19:31. [2]Leviticus 20:6. [3]Leviticus 20:27. [4]Deuteronomy 18:10–11. [5]Isaiah 8:19.

Still, with all the clear, unambiguous warnings, some people still seek answers from the dead. One such person was a notable, powerful, wealthy man by the name of Saul—King Saul.

The King Who Got More Than He Bargained For
1 Samuel 28:7–19

The first king of Israel was a complicated man, courageous, determined, troubled, and prone to bad choices. One such decision happened on the night before his death.

King Saul spent his life in battle. Once again, he was facing the perennial foe of Israel, the Philistines. Things looked bad. Saul was so seized with fear that his "heart trembled greatly."[6] He sought direction from God, but God remained silent: "The LORD did not answer him, either by dreams or by Urim[7] or by prophets."[8] It's an interesting list. It seemed no avenue of communication with God was working. The lines had been cut. It was at this point where Saul made a horrible mistake.

A Recipe for Disaster

In a sure recipe for disaster, Saul started down a path that would lead to failure and death. It's a formula seen many times in the Bible: A faithful man blessed of God rebels against the God who has done so much for him to pursue a personal path.

During his reign, Saul enjoyed the blessings of God up until he failed to carry out a specific directive concerning the vicious Amalekites. When the great prophet Samuel laid the charge at the monarch's feet, he lied about what he had done (and just as importantly, what he hadn't done).

The Amalekites had mistreated the people of Israel on numerous occasions. Their history went back before the days of Abraham. In the days of Moses, God declared, "Write this in a book as a memorial and

---

[6] 1 Samuel 28:5. [7] The Urim was one of two "stones" used by the priests to determine God's will. They mysteriously appear in Moses' day and remain a mystery throughout history. How they worked has never been determined, nor what happened to them.
[8] 1 Samuel 28:6.

recite it to Joshua, that I will utterly blot out the memory of Amalek from under heaven."[9]

This judgment became the task of Saul many years later: "Now go and strike Amalek and utterly destroy all that he has, and do not spare him."[10]

Saul chose to ignore the order: "But Saul and the people spared Agag and the best of the sheep, the oxen, the fatlings, the lambs, and all that was good, and were not willing to destroy them utterly; but everything despised and worthless, that they utterly destroyed."[11]

This act of wanton disobedience left the warring tribe to trouble David, who would follow Saul as king. They even kidnapped some of King David's family.[12] It also put a barrier between Saul and God. So much so that when Saul sought God's direction, he received only silence.

A new danger arose in the form of the perennial enemies of Israel, the fierce coastal people called the Philistines. Having gathered their armies, they were preparing to do battle. Saul went out to meet the attackers. But after seeing their camp in Shunem, "he was afraid and his heart trembled greatly."[13]

Naturally, he turned to the one who had led him to victory in so many great battles, but God was not answering. "When Saul inquired of the LORD, the LORD did not answer him, either by dreams or by Urim or by prophets." It was the spiritual equivalent of the silent treatment.

Frustration swelled in Saul, and this dissatisfaction led to desperation. He needed to know what lay ahead and how to proceed against the Philistines. Hungry for advice and direction, he did what no believer should ever do: he turned to the occult. "Then Saul said to his servants, 'Seek for me a woman who is a medium, that I may go to her and inquire of her.' And his servants said to him, 'Behold, there is a woman who is a medium at En-dor.'" (1 Samuel 28:7).

If God wouldn't speak to him, then Saul would find someone who would. It was a lousy decision. A better course would have been to fix the problem he had with God. Confession and repentance certainly

---

[9]Exodus 17:14. [10]1 Samuel 15:3. [11]1 Samuel 15:9. [12]1 Samuel 30:1–31.
[13]1 Samuel 28:5.

would have reopened the door of communication, but Saul chose a different and disastrous course. Rather than repair the problem, he compounded it with a foolish and desperate act.

It boggles the mind to know that with all the clear, unambiguous warnings he received, the notable, powerful, wealthy man Saul would do what he did.

What made matters worse was the depth of hypocrisy Saul sank to when he consulted the medium at En-dor. Saul himself had banished all such practitioners from the land. Those who continued the practice took their lives in their hands. The king sent his aides out to find a medium. We have no idea how long that took, but they came back with a report of a woman in the town of En-dor not far from where Saul and his troops had pitched camp. Still, the night journey must have been difficult as he made his way through the uneven valley. In one of the supreme acts of hypocrisy, Saul did the very thing he (as well as God) had forbidden others to do.

A thousand years later, the apostle Paul made it clear that God does not take such disobedience lightly: "Do not be deceived, God is not mocked; for whatever a man sows, this he will also reap."[14] Saul was about to reap a nightmare.

In Search of Stupidity

Saul was a desperate man, and desperate men often resort to actions that would seem foolish in the light of less stressful times. This, however, is not an acceptable excuse. Indeed, such times often reveal the true heart of a person. Saul's behavior unveiled the inner man.

His actions showed that he had given up on God. God's silence was not the disease; it was a symptom. Saul's best course of action would have been to fix the spiritual problem first. That was the greatest enemy. More dangerous than facing thousands of sword-wielding, helmeted Philistines is flaunting sin in the face of God. From Saul's point of view, the prayer, the dreams, the Urim didn't work, and the prophets were not

---

[14]Galatians 6:7.

receiving a word from God. So he thought he was free to seek someone who would speak to him. He was wrong.

Turning to the medium was a direct, personal affront to God. Saul knew exactly what he was doing. Turning to the spiritualist was not only foolish on Saul's part; it endangered the woman's life. This she clearly recognized. She asked, "Why are you then laying a snare for my life to bring about my death?"[15] She feared for her life.

What is ironic and amazing was Saul's attempt to comfort her: "Saul vowed to her by the LORD, saying, 'As the LORD lives, no punishment shall come upon you for this thing.'"[16] He took a vow before the Lord— the same Lord he knew had refused to answer his prayers.

The Horror of Getting What You Ask For

The mysterious medium did as she was told, perhaps intimidated by Saul and his two servants. We know nothing of her ancient technique. She did whatever incantations, meditations, or procedures were common to her profession. Perhaps she, as many ancient practitioners did, peered into a bowl of water, using it like a modern crystal ball.

Then something happened. The medium got exactly what she asked for. The result terrified her, probably because it had never happened before. Then, as now, those who offer to speak for the dead are cheats who use trickery to fool their clients. That was what Harry Houdini learned. It has always been so. There is no reason to believe this woman was any different. Her stark terror indicates that the unexpected had happened. The "ghost" she called for answered her by appearing.

The woman saw Samuel and somehow recognized him. Samuel was closely associated with King Saul; she discerned the truth of the matter. Her client was king of Israel.

"The king said to her, 'Do not be afraid; but what do you see?' And the woman said to Saul, 'I see a divine being coming up out of the earth.'" (1 Samuel 28:13). It is interesting that he would tell her not to be afraid when it was fear that brought him to her door.

---

[15]1 Samuel 28:9. [16]1 Samuel 28:10.

The phrase translated "divine being" comes from the Hebrew word *elohim*. Normally the word refers to God, but on a few occasions it refers to angels, pagan gods, and even men. Her point was that she was seeing something that was not strictly human. She also described what she saw as an old man wrapped in a robe.[17] This would be the form most easily recognized by Saul.

At this point, something changed. At first, only the medium saw Samuel. Saul had to ask for a description, but suddenly Saul could speak directly to Samuel and hear the prophet's words—and they were not friendly words.

"Why have you disturbed me by bringing me up?" the prophet wanted to know. He considered it a disruption that he should be called from his resting place back to a place he left in death. This leads to a question: Just where was Samuel?

The Old Testament taught that the soul of the deceased went to a place called Sheol. The word means "pit," "grave," or "place for the departed soul." Context dictates if it is the place of the soul or the physical grave. In Luke 16, Jesus told the story of the rich man and Lazarus. Both men died, and both ended up in Sheol, but their conditions were very different. The evil rich man was in physical torment, experiencing pain, thirst, and more. He was also aware of his surroundings and could see Lazarus in "Abraham's bosom," a place of comfort and peace (see Luke 16:19–31).

After Christ's work on the cross and His resurrection, things changed dramatically. Today when a believer dies, his or her soul is immediately in heaven with the Father. Paul made that clear when he wrote, "We are of good courage, I say, and prefer rather to be absent from the body and to be at home with the Lord."[18] The unsaved dead wait in Sheol for the great white throne judgment.[19] Hell is a future punishment, and it follows the great white throne judgment.

Samuel would have been on the "good" side of Sheol, what Jesus called Abraham's bosom[20] and Paradise.[21] The prophet was not pleased

---

[17]1 Samuel 28:14. [18]2 Corinthians 5:8. [19]Revelation 20:11–15. [20]Luke 16:22. [21]Luke 23:43.

to have been disturbed. Even Saul's pathetic appeal failed to move the dead prophet. In essence, Saul said, "I'm afraid; God won't answer my prayers; and the prophets are useless. I'm turning to you for advice. Tell me what to do."

That didn't fly. Samuel said, "Why then do you ask me, since the LORD has departed from you and has become your adversary?" Samuel had a point. How could Saul believe that the faithful prophet of God would do what God Himself would not? The prophet had more to say, and none of it was what Saul wanted to hear. Samuel described grim facts for the next day: Saul would be defeated; his kingdom overthrown and given to David; his army crushed; and he and his sons would die (or as Samuel put it, "Tomorrow you and your sons will be with me"[22]).

The phrase "with me" is puzzling. Samuel had been faithful to the end and was receiving the earned rewards, but Saul had damaged his fellowship with God. Does this mean that the prophet was merely saying, "Tomorrow you will be with me in death"? Or, could he also have meant that Saul, in spite of his recent foolish behavior, would still inherit eternal life?

Most likely, it was the latter. God is not fickle. He knows we fail and will fail in the future. We may pay for those failures in the present life, but God's love and justice are balanced. Saul had done many good things, but he was far from perfect. God, who is perfect, is free to reward Saul in the next life if He chooses to do so.

In the Old Testament Book of 1 Chronicles is a summary of Saul's spiritual crimes: "So Saul died for his trespass which he committed against the LORD, because of the word of the LORD which he did not keep; and also because he asked counsel of a medium, making inquiry of it, and did not inquire of the LORD. Therefore He killed him and turned the kingdom to David the son of Jesse."[23]

The passage makes four charges. First, Saul trespassed against God, going where he should not have gone. Second, the king had refused to keep God's command. Third, he sought counsel of a medium. Fourth, he did not inquire of the Lord.

---

[22]1 Samuel 28:19. [23]1 Chronicles 10:13–14.

It's the last one that causes confusion. From Saul's testimony, he prayed, consulted the Urim, sought revelatory dreams, and inquired of the prophets. Is this not seeking the Lord? Yes, in action. But consulting the Lord requires more than words and religious practices. It requires that a vital and active relationship with God be in place. That is where Saul failed. Rather than remove the obstacle of sin, he let the obstacle remain in place. This cut him off from the God he needed so desperately.

Had he repaired the relationship, things might have concluded differently.

What Really Happened

Did a medium really call up the ghost of the dead prophet Samuel? Did she exercise a mystical skill and draw Samuel's soul from its home in Sheol? It is very doubtful.

The work was not an achievement of the medium but of God. Only God has the ability to raise the dead physically or any other way. This was God's way of answering Saul's prayer. He sought direction; he hungered for a glimpse of the future battle. He got it not through the Urim or living prophets or dreams, but through a manifestation of the dead Samuel. It was poetic justice.

Of Preachers and Mules
Numbers 22:1–25:10

Fear is a powerful thing. Not only does it cause the heart to trip in the chest, but it can cloud otherwise reasonable thinking. It was because of fear and faulty assumptions that one of the Bible's strangest stories came to be.

In many ways, it is an international story. The children of Israel had wandered in the wilderness for many years, enduring hardship from without and spiritual weakness from within. Moses' long journey was ending. God would transfer leadership to Joshua in the days ahead, but that remained in the distance. For now, the people had settled east of the Jordon River, opposite the walled city of Jericho. The mere sight of them was enough to weaken the knees of most kings. The king of Moab was no different. Having heard that the people had crushed King Og and his

*As in Balaam's day, travel
by donkey remains common
in the Middle East.*

Amorites, King Balak was shaken to the core. He felt he needed help—
and needed it soon. To his mind, his land was going to be the next to fall
before the Israelites.

Here's the irony. God had commanded the Israelites not to attack
Balak's land.[24] They were distant kinsmen and therefore protected. All of
Balak's fears were unfounded and needless, yet there they were, eating at
him, depriving him of sleep. From his point of view, he was in trouble
and needed supernatural help.

There was a man who had a reputation for such things. People said
that those whom he blessed received a great blessing and those he cursed
were doomed. The solution seemed simple to the pagan mind of Balak:
bring the renowned prophet to the land and pay him to curse the
Israelites. The problem was one of geography; the prophet lived in
Pethor on the Euphrates River. It was a distance of hundreds of miles.

---

[24]Deuteronomy 2:9.

The Euphrates ran through Mesopotamia *(Mesopotamia* means "between the rivers") and was on the eastern edge of the Fertile Crescent. Archeological finds there have shown the existence of a large fraternity of pagan prophets and seers. The man whom Balak was interested in lived in that region. There was nothing to do but to send representatives and buy the man's services.

Balak sent messengers to Balaam with a message: "Behold, a people came out of Egypt; behold, they cover the surface of the land, and they are living opposite me. Now, therefore, please come, curse this people for me since they are too mighty for me; perhaps I may be able to defeat them and drive them out of the land. For I know that he whom you bless is blessed, and he whom you curse is cursed."[25]

The message had it all: praise, pressing need, and the implication of payment. Balaam[26] was an interesting mix of true prophet and pagan seer. He received the messengers and gave them a place to stay for the night while he consulted with God.

What was a pagan mystic doing consulting God? All pagan nations of the day believed in multiple gods. They were polytheistic. It seemed logical to them, as it surely did to Balaam, that Israel had a few gods of their own, just like the rest of the nation. The idea of one God was foreign to all people but the Israelites. The representatives had arrived "with the fees for divination in their hand." The word translated "divination" comes from the Hebrew *qesem* and refers to the price paid to a mystic to interpret dreams, practice witchcraft, or interpret omens. Generally, it refers to pagan practices.

Balaam sought God's advice and received an answer. God "came to Balaam" with a question: "Who are these men with you?" One of the details that is often overlooked in this passage is that while Balaam prepared to seek the God of Israel, God had already found him and initiated the conversation. Balaam explained the situation to the One-Who-Needs-No-Explanation.

---

[25]Numbers 22:5–6. [26]Balaam's name is debated. Some think it means "glutton" while others suggest "consumer of nations" or "not of this people." The latter makes sense.

God was ready with the direction Balaam sought: "Do not go with them; you shall not curse the people, for they are blessed."[27] The statement was clear and unambiguous. Balaam got the picture and sent the messengers packing. But there is something in the way he did it that opens the door and lets us peer into his heart. God not only told the mystic he could not curse the people, but He also gave a reason: They were blessed. That meant God had chosen them. Balaam left that bit of information out, saying only, "Go back to your land, for the LORD has refused to let me go with you." He didn't share the reason, just the bottom line.

Why would he do this? Balaam was working both sides of the fence. By not telling the messengers the whole story, he left open a door for a return trip, which was exactly what happened.

King Balak was not one to take *no* for an answer, so he sent more emissaries. He sent more than servants; he sent people of power and money, stepping the negotiations up to a new level. His message carried his concern: "Thus says Balak the son of Zippor, 'Let nothing, I beg you, hinder you from coming to me; for I will indeed honor you richly, and I will do whatever you say to me. Please come then, curse this people for me.'"[28]

"Please?" "Beg you?" "Honor richly?" "Do whatever you say to me?" Odd words for a king to say, yet here was the offer carried by the rich and famous of the day. The blank-check offer must have been very inviting. Still Balaam refused to go unless he received permission from God.

Balaam gave a good response: "Though Balak were to give me his house full of silver and gold, I could not do anything, either small or great, contrary to the command of the LORD my God."[29] Despite those noble words, Balaam provided a place for his visitors to stay the night and sought the Lord's guidance again.

God's reply has puzzled many people. On the surface, it seems as if He had changed His mind. "If the men have come to call you, rise up and go with them; but only the word which I speak to you shall you do." The emphasis is on *do,* not *say.* Certainly, God meant that Balaam was not to

---

[27]Numbers 22:12. [28]Numbers 22:16–17. [29]Numbers 22:18.

curse Israel, but He meant more. Balaam was to be obedient to God's direction, not just in word, but also in behavior.

Why would God change His mind? Actually, He didn't. Balaam was under the same restrictions as before, but God was allowing the trip to take place. Balaam cheated on the message the last time by not mentioning all that God had actually said. This time he was to deliver the message personally. Balaam wasted no time rising in the morning and saddling his donkey for the trip west.

The next verse is jarring and has puzzled scholars and Bible students for centuries. "But God was angry because he was going, and the angel of the LORD took his stand in the way as an adversary against him. Now he was riding on his donkey and his two servants were with him."[30]

Wait a minute! Didn't God give him permission to go? Yes, He did. So what happened? The Wycliff Bible Commentary makes an interesting suggestion. It translates the verse, "God's anger was kindled as he was going." In other words, something happened on the trip. Perhaps Balaam's desire was getting the better of his head. God didn't change His mind between verses; Balaam changed his commitment, and God knew it.

How could Balaam do something that is so obviously flawed? Balaam was a product of pagan culture. This culture taught that gods dwelt in geographical areas. Those who worshiped Baal, for example, had different Baals for different cities. It is possible that Balaam thought that since he had left the city where God spoke to him but had not arrived where the children of Israel were, he was out of God's reach and influence. If so, then it was a bad assumption.

When Farm Animals Speak

The angel of the Lord took his stand in front of Balaam, who was riding a donkey. The angel of the Lord is a mystery himself. At times, it is clear that the angel is a manifestation of God (what theologians call a theophany); at other times he appears to be a messenger of God. Each

---

[30]Numbers 22:22.

time he appears, something dramatic or significant takes place. In this case, the angel of God was God.

The most intriguing part of this story is the manner in which the angel worked. At first, only the donkey (technically, a she-donkey) was able to see the powerful being who stood directly in the animal's path. The angel held a sword. The donkey, frightened by what it saw, veered off the path and into a field. This brought about a beating from Balaam, who was angered at the animal.

The angel appeared before the donkey again, but this time the creature was on a narrow, wall-lined path that crossed a vineyard. To avoid the angel, the donkey moved as far to one side as possible. Unfortunately for Balaam, the animal crushed his foot against the wall. The animal endured a second beating.

A third incident occurred, this time on a narrow path that did not allow room for the donkey to pass. Unable to turn around, unable to veer off, the donkey did the best it could. It stopped, and then lay down. Balaam used the stick again, for the third time.

Next, the impossible happened. God enabled the donkey to speak. Many interpreters object to this, citing the fact that a donkey doesn't have the anatomical apparatus necessary to vocalize. Everything about the creature is wrong for oral communication. Those who object for these reasons are right. God did not design donkeys to carry on conversations. Nor are their brains capable of abstract thought or logic.

Nevertheless, by the power of God,[31] this donkey not only spoke but also argued its case in a manner worthy of a debate team.

Donkey: "What have I done to you, that you have struck me these three times?"

Balaam (hopping on one foot): "Because you have made a mockery of me! If there had been a sword in my hand, I would have killed you by now."

Donkey: "Am I not your donkey on which you have ridden all your life to this day? Have I ever been accustomed to do so to you?"

Balaam: "No."[32]

---

[31]Numbers 22:28. [32]Numbers 22:28–30.

The donkey out-thought Balaam! It was a good thing too. The angel stood ready to do the prophet in, but the donkey's sudden changes of direction prolonged Balaam's life. This is an interesting detail. The angel had no problem moving from place to place. It certainly wasn't required that Balaam come to him. The angel could have taken a few more steps and let the sword fly, but he didn't. This is one of the clues that there is more going on in the account than what appears on the surface. As we will see, the donkey represented more than a domesticated farm animal.

There are only two accounts in the pages of the Bible where an animal speaks. The first mention is in Genesis 3 where the mysterious serpent appears. The serpent is described as "more crafty than any beast of the field which the LORD God had made."[33] In the next phrase, this enigmatic creature begins a dialogue with Eve that includes lies and misrepresentation.[34]

The situation of Balaam's donkey is different. The animal had never before spoken, and apparently, aside from those three questions, it never spoke again.

The dialogue with the angel shows the danger that Balaam was in without his realizing it. The angel of the Lord was ready to spare the donkey but to kill Balaam. Balaam should have been thankful that his beast was as insightful as it was.

The angel also made a provocative remark that shows that he was none other than God. First, he told Balaam of his crime: "Behold, I have come out as an adversary, because your way was contrary to me."[35] *Contrary*—in this context—appears only here in the Bible. It means "to be reckless" or "to perverse." Its basic meaning is to toss or rush headlong, that is, to proceed along a path with no thought to the consequences. Balaam had started down a path that was dangerous. Although his words were those of obedience and submission to God, he had a hidden agenda. Balaam was learning that God "knows the thoughts of man, that they are a mere breath."[36]

Second, the angel permitted Balaam to continue the trip but reiterated what God had said to the seer earlier: "Go with the men, but you

---

[33]Genesis 3:1. [34]See chapter 3, "Mysterious People." [35]Numbers 22:32. [36]Psalm 94:11.

shall speak only the word which I tell you."[37] This shows again that the angel of the Lord, at least in this case, was a manifestation of God.

Talked About for Centuries

This event is so remarkable that it became an object lesson mentioned several times throughout the ages.

The butler-turned-builder, Nehemiah, used Balaam as an example of disobedience and God's intervention: "Because [the Moabites] did not meet the sons of Israel with bread and water, but hired Balaam against them to curse them. However, our God turned the curse into a blessing."[38]

The prophet Micah did the same: "My people, remember now what Balak king of Moab counseled and what Balaam son of Beor answered him, and from Shittim to Gilgal, so that you might know the righteous acts of the LORD."[39]

The apostle Peter gives us insight into Balaam's hidden agenda. Peter, in writing about false teachers in the church, said, "Forsaking the right way, they have gone astray, having followed the way of Balaam, the son of Beor, who loved the wages of unrighteousness; but he received a rebuke for his own transgression, for a mute donkey, speaking with a voice of a man, restrained the madness of the prophet."[40] Balaam "loved the wages of transgression." In other words, he was money driven and loved prestige. That took precedence in his life.

The New Testament doesn't overlook the devious man's actions. The little Book of Jude is a letter condemning false teachers who were misleading the church. Jude drove his point home by comparing these teachers to the hated Balaam: "Woe to them! For they have gone the way of Cain, and for pay they have rushed headlong into the error of Balaam, and perished in the rebellion of Korah."[41]

Jude even uses the phrase "rushed headlong" to reflect the Hebrew word that was translated as "contrary" or "perverse."

Balaam is even mentioned in the Book of Revelation, and not in a good light. Writing to the church at Pergamum, John records Jesus' words as, "But I have a few things against you, because you have there

---

[37]Numbers 22:35. [38]Nehemiah 13:2. [39]Micah 6:5. [40]2 Peter 2:15–16. [41]Jude 11.

some who hold the teaching of Balaam, who kept teaching Balak to put a stumbling block before the sons of Israel, to eat things sacrificed to idols and to commit acts of immorality."[42]

The world will remember Balaam and his treachery forever.

More than Just a Donkey

Why make the donkey speak at all? In this long account of Balaam and his sin, the animal plays a pivotal role. Why did God bother with the creature? As is often the case in the mysterious passages of the Bible, there is more than first meets the eye.

Gather a group in someone's home, play an old record from the 1940s, and ask, "What do you hear?" Several answers are sure to be voiced. After listening carefully to the scratchy phonograph sounds, someone will say, "I hear jazz." Another will add, "It's a clarinet piece." Seldom will anyone say, "I hear a lot of background noise and scratches." We tend to tune things out to focus on the obvious. Often in the Bible the obvious floats on the page like a large ship on the pulsing ocean, but there is always more just below the surface.

Most people will say that the story of Balaam is about a talking donkey, but it goes beyond that. The donkey, although it truly did speak by a miracle of God, is also a metaphor. A metaphor is a device of language used to imply a comparison. If some unhappy voter calls a politician a "snake in the grass," he is saying the politician exhibits traits associated with snakes: sneaky, dangerous, and unpleasant (to most people). *Metaphor* comes from a Greek word that means "to transfer between."

Who or what does the donkey represent? To answer that question, we must first summarize what we know about the animal and its behavior.

First, the donkey was an unclean animal under Mosaic Law. The law prohibited the eating of its meat. It was a useful and respected animal, a beast of burden, and was often used to carry a rider. Jesus rode on a donkey during His triumphal entry into Jerusalem.[43] Kings rode on donkeys if they wanted to show that they were coming to an area or city in peace.

---

[42]Revelation 2:14. [43]Matthew 21:1–11; Mark 11:1–11; Luke 19:28–38; John 12:12–19.

The donkey also showed more insight than Balaam and was able to see the angel of the Lord when the "seer" could not. The donkey showed more concern for Balaam's welfare than Balaam was showing for the Israelites, whom he was retained to curse. The donkey endured harsh treatment for doing what was right. His work was unappreciated, and Balaam was clueless about the danger he was in.

These facts open a range of possibilities for the metaphor. Does the donkey represent Israel? The Gentile nations? Balaam? God? It's hard to be dogmatic, but the possibility that seems most likely and most meaningful is that the animal represented Christ. The following chart makes the comparison.

The Typology of Balaam's Donkey	
Donkey	Christ
Bore the weight of a sinful man	Bore the weight of a sinful world
Endured the anger of the one it was saving	Endured the anger of His people
Tried to take a safer path	Tried to lead to a better way
Endured three beatings	Endured three "trials"[44]
Endured pain for the person it was protecting	Endured pain and death for the world
Balaam was worthy of death, and the donkey was worthy of life	Christ was worthy of life and we of death
Beast of burden	Suffering Messiah who "bore" our sins and punishment
Undeserving of beating	Undeserving of death
Balaam's complaint was "you make a mockery of me."	The Jewish religious leaders resented Jesus because He made a mockery of the bloated system of laws.

[44]Technically, Jesus passes through seven stages of rejection and trial. Three represent Christ's rejection by the religious establishment: (1) before Annas the former high priest and still religious heavyweight (John 18:12–14); (2) before Caiaphas the high priest and son-in-law of Annas (Matthew 26:57–68); and (3) before the Sanhedrin, the religious ruling body (Matthew 27:1–2). He then endured one appearance before Herod (Luke 23:6–12) and two appearances before Pontius Pilate (John 18:39–19:6). These were Jesus' civil trials. One last "trial" occurred when Pilate displayed Jesus and Barabbas to the crowd and let them judge whom they found more important and valuable. They chose Barabbas. Therefore, Jesus experienced a set of religious trials, a set of civil trials, and a public trial.

The Ubiquitous Number Three

The number three appears hundreds of times in the Bible, and it carries the idea of holiness. Oddly, the number three keeps popping up in this account. There are three travelers: Balaam and two servants. The angel of the Lord appears three times, causing the she-donkey to turn from the path three times. Balaam beats the beast three times. Not to be outdone, the donkey asks three questions. Later Balaam will bless the children of Israel three times. This is not coincidence.

The Rest of the Story

When Balaam arrived at the border of Moab, the angry King Balak met him and made his dissatisfaction quite clear. Balaam could only say, "I'm here now."

King Balak took the pagan prophet to the "high places of Baal" to show him the camp of Israel. Even from that elevated height, he could see only a portion of the people.[45] Then the bizarre rituals began. Balaam called for seven altars, seven bulls, and seven rams. Each altar was the site of a pair of sacrifices, one bull and one ram. This is not the prescribed sacrifices God gave to the Israelites, but something Balaam took upon himself. Very likely, he was auguring—a divination practice meant to determine the future or learn the will of the gods by examining the entrails of a sacrificed animal. To Balaam's credit, each time he carried out this bizarre act, he went off to seek the Lord's will. Each time God "put a word in his mouth" and then told him what to say.

Three times Balaam listened to the Lord and blessed Israel, refusing to curse them even at the king's command. He then took King Balak aside to advise him what would happen to his people in the future.[46]

Balak was furious. Nothing more could the king do. Balaam refused to curse the people of God. Balaam had enough fear of the Lord to refrain from that act. However, he advised the king about a different approach. If cursing the people was out, it might be possible to cause them to curse themselves.

---

[45]Numbers 22:41. [46]Numbers 24:14.

"Behold, these caused the sons of Israel, through the counsel of Balaam, to trespass against the LORD in the matter of Peor, so the plague was among the congregation of the LORD."[47] It was devious advice that played on the carnal nature of all humans. The pagan practice of Baal worship included fertility rites—rites that involved public sexual immorality. A Canaanite (in this case Moabite) priest and priestess would engage in public sex. This soon led to an orgy of immorality. Some in the camp of Israel thought it was a good practice. It wasn't. A plague swept through the people, taking twenty-four thousand lives,[48] and all because of Balaam's last-minute advice.

The story of Balaam is long and complicated. He was a man of some spiritual insight who received direct visitations from the Lord, yet he flirted with disaster by stretching God's patience to the limit. While he refused to curse the people, he gave advice that led to the death of a great many and contributed to corruption of thousands. While those Israelites who participated in the sin bear responsibility for their actions, it is clear that the Bible lays much of the blame at the feet of the Mesopotamian mystic who could not leave well enough alone.

When God Speaks

One thing is certain: God makes His will known. He has communicated with humankind in many ways and on many levels. That is His prerogative. He has spoken from a burning bush, from over the ark of the covenant, and, as we have seen, through the mouth of a dead prophet and even a donkey.

The writer of Hebrews said it best: "God, after He spoke long ago to the fathers in the prophets in many portions and in many ways, in these last days has spoken to us in His Son, whom He appointed heir of all things, through whom also He made the world."[49]

Many portions, many ways—all meant to guide us into righteousness. However, of all the means of communication used by God, the most significant is His Son, Jesus Christ.

---

[47]Numbers 31:16. [48]Numbers 25:9. [49]Hebrews 1:1–2.

Points to Ponder

1. Some interpreters have suggested that what Saul saw was not the prophet Samuel but a demon. Does that idea fit the text?

2. The medium at En-dor did what the law prohibited, but the Bible makes no mention of punishment. Why do you suppose this is true?

3. The story of Balaam is a strange one with lots of twists and turns. Why do you think God became so upset with Balaam?

4. It is possible that the donkey represents, in some ways, Christ and His work. Does it seem odd that a donkey could be used as such a reference?

5. Why did God speak to Balaam in the first place? Since no person can curse another, let alone an entire nation, why did God care what Balaam said?

Mysterious Symbols

The Bible is a unique book for many reasons. No other writing can claim the level of sophistication and complexity as the Bible. While the Bible is intricate, it is also simple enough to touch uncountable lives every day.

In many ways, the Bible is an engineered book. As an engineer might design a bridge to accommodate cars and foot traffic safely over a wide canyon, so God has designed His Word to meet the needs of humanity.

This is no easy task. The fact that we have a Bible resting on our desk or coffee table is testimony to its miraculous nature. The Protestant Bible consists of sixty-six books written by about forty authors over a fifteen-hundred-year span. The writing took place on three continents and was penned by those with the best education as well as those with very little schooling.

How can a book endure so long and touch so many lives? How can a volume composed of many smaller books be substantial enough to challenge the finest minds while simple enough for a child to understand? Engineering, planning, and forethought are the things that make it possible.

The kind of engineering necessary to make a written word that was pertinent two thousand years ago still life-changing today requires more skill than any purely human effort could provide.

The Bible is inspired. Paul told Timothy, "All Scripture is inspired by God and profitable for teaching, for reproof, for correction, for training

CHAPTER ELEVEN

in righteousness; so that the man of God may be adequate, equipped for every good work."[1] The word *inspired* comes from *theopneustos,* meaning "God-breathed." It pictures God exhaling His Word to the human author. The Bible originated with God, is designed by God, is inspired by God, and is protected by God.

Like a wedding cake, the Bible has many layers. The most obvious layer is historical. We read about David and learn that he was king of Israel and did many good things, but was also a willing victim of sin like the rest of us. The Scriptures record his sin with Bathsheba as an actual event, and we should understand it as such. However, there is another layer, a layer that shows the spiritual side of the issue.

Other layers exist. These lay out truth in subtle ways, often pivoting on a change in a word, or a detail in the background. With a little extra work, a whole new panorama of understanding comes into view. Much of this detail is in types and symbols. In many ways, the Bible is lyrics set to the music of symbolism. Everyday things—common, everyday things—take on new meaning in the pages of Scripture. Here are some examples.

Common Things Made Uncommon

Fish

Except to the sports fisherman and ichthyologist, fish are dull. They swim in rivers, lakes, and oceans. They are beautiful to see, and some are tasty to eat. In Jesus' day, fish was a dietary staple. Four of the twelve disciples were fishermen, and they came from a line of people who made their living taking fish from the Sea of Galilee.

The Jews did not divide fish by name as we do, nor did they distinguish between freshwater and saltwater varieties. They did, however, differentiate between clean (and therefore edible) and unclean (to be avoided) fish. Fish with fins and scales were acceptable, and all others were declared unfit.

Still, there are some interesting distinctions in the Bible. Jesus worked five miracles related to fish. In each case, the details reveal a great truth.

---

[1] 2 Timothy 3:16–17.

An Arab vineyard worker examining grapes on the vines in his field. One of the many symbols Jesus used to describe Himself was the grape vine. "I am the vine," He said, "and you are the branches."

Twice, Jesus fed the multitudes by multiplying a small amount into enough to feed thousands. Both events are recorded in the Gospel of Matthew. In the first case (Matthew 14:15–21), Jesus stood before a large crowd that had followed Him into a desolate region. The disciples numbered the crowd at five thousand men. This means that, counting women and children, the group could have been greater than fifteen thousand. The congregation needed to eat and Jesus was determined to feed them, but all that was available to Him were five loaves of bread and two fish. That was plenty for the Savior. Jesus multiplied the paltry amount so much that twelve baskets full of leftovers remained.

The word used here for *fish* was the typical Greek term *ichthus,* and it appears in the New Testament about twenty times. By itself, there is nothing special in the term. It is the expected word.

Strangely, however, John in his account of the miracle[2] uses a different word—*opsarion.* The meaning of the word is hard to nail down, and only John uses it in the Bible. It appears to refer to a smaller fish, but even that is uncertain.

We need to know one other fact about this event: This was the Jewish version. That is, the crowd was predominately Jewish, and the

---

[2]This is the only one of Jesus' miracles recorded in all four Gospels. See John 6:5–14.

miracle occurred in Galilee at a region near Bethsaida whose name means "house of fish."

Jesus worked a similar miracle but with a primarily Gentile crowd of four thousand men (Matthew 15:32–38). As before, the number of people present may have been three or four times larger. Again, Jesus had little with which to work. When asked how many loaves of bread were available, the disciples said, "Seven, with a few small fish" (v. 34). The word for *fish* here is *ichthudion*. It is the diminutive of fish. It is as if Jesus used trout in the first feeding and sardines in the second.

There was a third feeding that often goes overlooked. It occurred during the third appearance of Jesus after the resurrection. John 21:1–13 tells the story of seven disciples who decided to go fishing. This occurred during the forty-day span after the resurrection in which Jesus made multiple appearances.

The disciples, including the experienced fishermen Peter and John, had labored all night, throwing and dragging the net, and had nothing to show for it. On shore, there was a man who watched for a while, then asked the question every angler hates to hear when the fish aren't biting. "Children, you do not have any fish, do you?" (John 21:5). Except the word is not *fish*. Translations such as the King James Version use the word "meat" instead of *fish*. The New King James Bible updated this to "food." Jesus used the word *prosphagion*, which refers to meat of some kind but can, as in this context, mean *fish*. That, by itself, is not extraordinary, but what follows is. The English translations render two different words as *fish*. What's more, Jesus used one term while the disciples consistently used another. Charted, it looks like this:

Association/Point of View	Term	Number
Jesus (v. 5)	*prosphagion*	Singular
Disciples (v. 6)	*ichthus*	Plural
Disciples (v. 8)	*ichthus*	Plural
Jesus (v. 9)	*opsarian*	Singular
Jesus speaking (v. 10)	*opsarian*	Plural
Peter (v. 11)	*ichthus*	Plural
Jesus (v. 13)	*opsarian*	Singular

The pattern is peculiar. Why would John, under the inspiration of the Holy Spirit, use different words for *fish*? Was it coincidence or writer's prerogative? It goes beyond happenstance. The pattern is drawn too finely and the structure is too obvious to be without meaning.

The event contains two miracles. First, the disciples who had no luck fishing that night followed Jesus' instruction to fish from the "right-hand side of the boat."[3] The request made no sense, but the weary disciples recognized the command. It was not the first time they had heard it. Many months before, Jesus said to do the same thing and the result was a huge catch, so much so that the boat nearly sank under the weight of the fish.[4] The disciples did as told and again, their net bulged with an enormous amount of fish.

So excited was Peter that he could not be bothered with fishing any-more (it was his idea to go in the first place). He "jumped ship" and swam to shore. The remaining six disciples struggled to bring in the catch.

When they arrived on shore, they found that Jesus already had breakfast ready: a single fish *(opsarian)* and a single loaf of bread. Not much food for eight men, seven of whom had been working all night.

Jesus did tell Peter, "Bring some of the fish which you have now caught."[5] But there is no mention of that fish being prepared and cooked. The text reads, "Jesus came and took the bread and gave it to them, and the fish likewise."[6] *Fish* is in the singular. He shared one fish among eight men, and one loaf of bread. And if *opsarian* means "small fish," then this is even more remarkable.

This brings us back to why John recorded Jesus using a different word for *fish* than expected. The other place where John used that term is in his account of the feeding of the five thousand.[7] If we were reading the Gospel of John in the original language, we would first come across the feeding of the multitudes with five loaves and two fish *(opsarian)*, then later reach this account and see that John used the same word. Our thoughts would snap back to that event and realize that Jesus was multi-plying the fish and bread for the disciples and making a statement at the same time.

---

[3]John 21:6. [4]Luke 5:4–7. [5]John 21:10. [6]John 21:13. [7]John 6:9, 11.

What is that statement? No matter how faulty the disciples' skill, Jesus can do something great and unexpected. They would become a force that forever changed the world. The net they cast would bring in believers of all kinds, Jews and Gentiles.

More Fishy Symbolism

Fish are a common metaphor in the Bible. Generally, they represent either humanity as a whole or some large segment of it.

Jesus told a parable about the end of the world. He said, "Again, the kingdom of heaven is like a dragnet cast into the sea, and gathering fish of every kind; and when it was filled, they drew it up on the beach; and they sat down and gathered the good fish into containers, but the bad they threw away. So it will be at the end of the age; the angels will come forth and take out the wicked from among the righteous, and will throw them into the furnace of fire; in that place there will be weeping and gnashing of teeth."[8]

Jesus compared the kingdom of heaven to a net that has captured all the fish in the sea. The fishermen (angels) separate the good (clean) from the bad (unclean). In this case, the good are those who are Christ's followers, and the bad are those who reject Him. Jesus used the image of fish to represent all of humankind. The event on the Sea of Galilee would remind the disciples of this teaching too.

Fish can indicate nations under judgment. God said through the prophet Ezekiel that Egypt would be taken up like fish.[9] Habakkuk described the powerful, conquering Chaldeans as people who bring their enemies "up with a hook, drag them away with their net, and gather them together in their fishing net."[10]

The Sign of the Fish

It is common to see cars on the road with a plastic fish emblem glued to the bumper or trunk. The symbol has become a universal sign for Christianity. It is an ancient symbol that dates to the first century. Many symbols could have been used by the early church to signify a connection

---

[8]John 13:47–50. [9]Ezekiel 29:4–5. [10]Habakkuk 1:15.

with Christ: bread, an oil lamp, a shepherd, even a lamb. Jesus used these metaphors to describe His work and person. Never did He describe Himself with the image of a fish. Perhaps the symbol came about because of those miracles associated with fish.[11] *Ichythus,* the Greek word for *fish,* became an acrostic to the early Christians: Jesus *(i)* Christ *(ch)* God's *(th)* Son *(y)*, Savior *(s)*. For two thousand years, the fish has represented Christ, but it goes beyond the acrostic. Fish, for many, was one of the basic elements of life. Bread and fish were part of the daily diet of many. What could be more fitting for the giver of life, the sustainer of our souls?

Mountains of Meaning

There are few things more impressive than a mountain rising out of the plain. Dusted with snow and crowned with clouds, it looks unconquerable, immovable, and eternal. They are a beauty to behold, and they carry a measure of the mystic.

The Bible mentions mountains frequently, often showing a symbolic meaning. There are twenty-six specific mountains mentioned in Scripture, but certain ones take on special meaning because of the events that occurred on their slopes or peaks.

Ancient people associated deities with mountains, often setting up shrines and other places of worship. While God revealed Himself on certain mountains, the mountain itself was never the holy object. God was the Holy One, and the mountain was the stage of His revelation. Early in His ministry, Jesus met a woman at a well in Samaria. There He revealed Himself as the Christ and revealed the woman's need for forgiveness and salvation. She was a Samaritan, a half-Hebrew race hated by the Jews. They believed that worship was to take place on Mount Gerizim, a nearby peak that was the focal point of worship for the Samaritans. Gerizim was, to the Samaritans, a place of blessing.[12] The Samaritans used it as a substitute place of worship to compete with the temple in Jerusalem.

---

[11]The miracles involving fish are two miraculous catches (Luke 5:6–9; John 21:6–11), two feedings of the multitudes (Matthew 14:17–21; 15:34), the coin in the fish's mouth (Matthew 17:27), and the feeding of the disciples on the shore (John 21:9).
[12]Deuteronomy 11:29; 27:12–13.

Jesus corrected the misunderstanding, showing that God was beyond the mountains: "Woman, believe Me, an hour is coming when neither in this mountain nor in Jerusalem will you worship the Father."[13] It is a mistake to think that the infinite God can be narrowed to a specific peak on this planet.

A survey of the Bible shows that mountains have been important places in God's plan.

Ararat. The first mention of mountains in the Bible occurs in the account of Noah's flood. "The water prevailed more and more upon the earth, so that all the high mountains everywhere under the heavens were covered. The water prevailed fifteen cubits[14] higher, and the mountains were covered."[15] The next mention is when Noah's ark ran aground on the mountains of Ararat. It's important to note the plural use of "mountain." As is often the case in the Bible, a single name can apply to a ridge or set of peaks.

The meaning of *Ararat* is lost. Most likely, it's a cognate (a word in two or more languages that come from the same root word) of an Assyrian word, *urartu.* The mountain that bears the name *Ararat* today is in Turkey and rises nearly seventeen thousand feet. Unless the ark itself is found on the mountain, we have no way of knowing if present-day Ararat is the same as the mountain Noah stepped foot on after leaving the ark.

It was on Ararat that humanity got a fresh start. Noah's first act after releasing the animals was to make a sacrifice to God. It was a place of new beginning and worship. From there humanity spread to fill the earth.

Ararat symbolizes a new beginning and the end of judgment.

Moriah. Genesis 22 contains the account of Abraham and Isaac (see chapter 5, "Mysterious Requests"). God asked of Abraham something He had never asked before nor would ever ask of any other man: to sacrifice his son on an altar. Abraham had to make a three-day journey to a mountain that God would show him. That mountain was Moriah. As Abraham was ready to do the deed that would forever break his heart, God interceded and provided a nonhuman sacrifice—a ram entangled in

---

[13]John 4:21. [14]Approximately twenty-two and one-half feet. [15]Genesis 7:19–20.

a thicket. The act was symbolic of God's sacrifice of His only Son. Jesus was the substitution sacrifice—a sacrifice demanded by God, then provided by Him. The symbolism is impossible to miss.

The name *Moriah* means "chosen of Jehovah"—and chosen it was. It was on this same mountain, generations later, that the temple was built. There priests sacrificed for the sins of the people. This lasted until A.D. 70, when the Romans destroyed the temple. The greatest sacrifice for sin, and the only one that is enduring through the ages, was Christ upon the cross. It was on Mount Moriah that Jesus gave Himself for us; where God sacrificed His Son, something portrayed by Abraham and Isaac—except God spared Isaac; Jesus died.

Moriah symbolizes God's love and sacrifice. As Ararat was a place of a new beginning, Moriah was a place of new life.

Horeb. Moses knew something about mountains, especially the mountain chain called Horeb. *Horeb* means "wilderness" or "desert." It was in these mountains in the Sinai Peninsula that the great man received his commission from God in the form of a voice from a burning bush,[16] brought water from a rock,[17] and met with God.[18] Mount Sinai is one of the mountains of Horeb. It was where Moses received the Ten Commandments. There is some dispute about the location of the actual mountain. The meaning of *Sinai* is uncertain, but it may be a derivation of a word describing a Mesopotamian moon god called Sin.

Mount Sinai was also the place where the prophet Elijah fled after the evil Jezebel threatened his life. While Elijah was hiding in a cave, God spoke to the prophet and manifested Himself as wind, earthquake, fire (as He did with Moses), and then a gentle wind. God was not in the noise and destruction, but in the breeze.

Mount Sinai is symbolic of the Law of Moses and the bondage to that law. Paul uses it that way in his book to the Galatians: "Now this Hagar is Mount Sinai in Arabia and corresponds to the present Jerusalem, for she is in slavery with her children."[19] Sinai remains a reminder of God's giving of the law.

---

[16]Exodus 3:1–2. [17]Exodus 17:6. [18]Exodus 32:1–35. [19]Galatians 4:25.

Carmel. Mount Carmel is a 1,650-foot peak overlooking the Mediterranean Sea. In 1 Kings 18 is the historical account of how the great prophet Elijah stood toe-to-toe with the prophets of Baal in a test of gods. Each side prepared an altar and offering but put no fire to it. The challenge was to have the real God answer with fire from heaven. The prophets of Baal failed, but God answered unmistakably and quickly. Fire came down and consumed the offering, the altar, and much more. Elijah put to death 450 prophets of the pagan god Baal and 400 prophets of Asherah on the slopes of that mountain.

An Arab shepherd tends his herd in the Judean hills. Jesus often used everyday objects and things as symbols of Himself. Jesus is the "Lamb of God who takes away the sin of the world."

The name *Carmel* means "garden" or "orchard," but it has been the site of bloodshed and judgment. Mount Carmel is representative of judgment.

Hermon. Matthew 17 recounts one of the most unusual events in the Bible, usually referred to as the transfiguration. Jesus and three of His disciples traveled to this mountain. There, on the slope of one of the three peaks that make up the ridge, Jesus physically changed before the eyes of Peter, James, and John. Stranger still, two people who did not make the ascent up the steep slope joined the group: Elijah and Moses. Moses had died 1,400 years before, and Elijah had "translated" to heaven 850 years before. Now they stood in conversation with Jesus. It was shocking to Peter, James, and John, who wanted to build three booths in commemoration. Rounding out the number to a perfect seven was God who spoke audibly from heaven, "This is My beloved Son, with whom I am well-pleased; listen to Him."[20]

Mount Hermon represents the eternal life in Christ. It was a place where the living met with the dead.

Olives. One of the best-known mounds is the Mount of Olives, a rise just east of Jerusalem. There Jesus wept over Jerusalem, prayed, preached His final message, agonized in the Garden of Gethsemane, and submitted to betrayal by one of His own disciples. Jesus spent many hours on that mount, some of them grueling hours.

The Mount of Olives is symbolic of the suffering of Jesus and the price He paid for our forgiveness. There is great irony in this. The olive tree was a symbol of peace and prosperity. The olive market was crucial to the economy of Israel and represented all that was good. For Jesus, the Mount of Olives was the opposite of all the good that the trees around Him symbolized. Christ completes the metaphor. Our peace with God comes through a great price paid by Jesus. *Gethsemane* means "oil press." There in the garden by that name, Jesus "being in agony He was praying very fervently; and His sweat became like drops of blood, falling down upon the ground."[21]

Peace has a price.

Christ, More Than Symbolic

The Bible uses symbols to make great truths memorable, but by far the most meaningful and enduring symbols are those associated with Christ Jesus. An entire book might be too small a forum to discuss the scores of references to Jesus in the Old and New Testament. Some stand out, however, as the following chart shows.

---

[20]Matthew 17:5. [21]Luke 22:44.

Alpha and Omega	Revelation 22:13

A term used by Jesus of Himself. "I am the Alpha and the Omega, the first and the last, the beginning and the end." Alpha is the first letter of the Greek alphabet, and Omega is the last. If English were the language of choice for the New Testament, then Jesus would have said, "I am the A and the Z." The symbol shows Christ as existing from the eternal past and into the eternal future. There was never a time when Christ was not.

Interestingly, the same phrase is applied to God the Father twice (Revelation 1:8; 21:6). The phrase occurs only in the Book of Revelation.

Bread, Manna	John 6:31–35

"Jesus said to them, 'I am the bread of life; he who comes to Me will not hunger, and he who believes in Me will never thirst'" (John 5:35).

Earlier, Jesus had said, "The bread of God is he who comes down from heaven and gives life to the world." This was a clear reference to manna, the mysterious food sent by God to feed the wandering children of Israel. It was a miraculous provision that sustained life. Jesus referred to Himself as that bread of heaven—the giver and sustainer of life. Manna was a food created by God for a specific purpose, so Jesus was the Savior with a specific plan. He was and continues to be the source of eternal life.

Firstfruits of a Harvest	1 Corinthians 15:20

The apostle Paul gives a lengthy and powerful lesson on the resurrection in 1 Corinthians 15. In making his case, he describes Jesus as "the first fruits of those who are asleep." In a predominately agricultural society, this was a powerful description. Farmers harvested some crops more than once in a season. By using the symbol of the firstfruits, Paul is saying that Jesus is the first of the resurrected (never to die again) and that another harvest would soon be coming. The "second fruits" are all the believers whom God will physically resurrect to live in their bodies forever.

Lamb	John 1:29; Revelation 5:6

Jesus as the Lamb of God is an unbroken image that began deep in the Old Testament. John the Baptist, who announced in his powerful, boisterous style "Behold, the Lamb of God who takes away the sin of the world," first mentions it in the New Testament.

What was a descriptive phrase for John the Baptist became a graphic image for John the apostle. "And I saw between the throne (with the four living creatures) and the elders a Lamb standing, as if slain, having seven horns and seven eyes, which are the seven Spirits of God, sent out into all the earth."

He saw a slain lamb. The words are not graphic, but the image is startling. Priests, by cutting the throats of animals, killed sacrificial lambs. What John saw is a vision manifestation of Jesus with His throat cut. Of course, Jesus died on the cross not by the knife, but the image is symbolic of a Savior who became the sacrificial Lamb killed for the sins of the world.

| Light | John 1:9 |

This same John describes Jesus as Light. "There was the true Light which, coming into the world, enlightens every man." Light was a mysterious and magical thing to ancient people. Despite the advance in physics, light remains mysterious, defying exact definition and description. One thing known then and now is that light is the only means of dispelling darkness. We are unable to sweep darkness from a room. That's because darkness does not "exist." It is merely a word used to describe the effect of missing light. Only light can remove darkness. Jesus is the light that pushes back the obsidian blackness of life. Light is an appropriate description of the Savior.

| The Word | John 1:1; 1 John 1:1 |

"In the beginning was the Word, and the Word was with God, and the Word was God." With those words, the apostle John begins his unique Gospel of the life of Christ. While the other Gospels begin with a historical background, John chose a different approach. Instead of referring to Jesus by name, he begins his account before time, showing that Jesus was before creation and was indeed the agent of creation.

He chose to use a very common term: *logos*. Logos refers to the spoken word. While used by Greeks and Jews in their philosophies, John defines the term differently and uniquely. To him, the Logos was Jesus who was with God from time eternally past and was indeed God.

In his first letter, John starts in similar fashion, but enhances the phrase to read "Word of Life." He wanted to make clear that Jesus is the source of eternal life—before, then, and forever.

| Serpent | John 3:14–15; Numbers 21:4–9 |

One of the most unexpected symbols of Christ is the serpent. Generally the serpent is associated with Satan, sin, or judgment, yet Jesus Himself used the serpent as a representation of His work and sacrifice—not just any serpent, but one that became a symbol of healing 1,400 years before. Numbers 21 is the account of another rebellion of the Israelites who had become "impatient" and grumbled about the journey in the wilderness, the food, and the water. They went so far as to call the provision of God "this miserable food." Judgment came quickly in the form of "fiery serpents." The people called them "fiery" because of their appearance, or perhaps because of their burning venom. Whatever the reason, the people were soon pleading for relief. God answered their request, but not in the expected fashion. Instead of removing the snakes, God instructed them to construct and raise a bronze serpent on a pole: "Everyone who is bitten, when he looks at it, he will live" (Numbers 21:8).

Their salvation rested in their willingness to look to God's solution—the bronze serpent. It was the only answer; no other cure was available.

A millennium and a half later, Jesus called the event to mind when He said, "As Moses lifted up the serpent in the wilderness, even so must the Son of

Man be lifted up; so that whoever believes will in Him have eternal life" (John 3:14–15).

The image Jesus portrayed was that of Himself on the cross. He was saying it in a way that every Jew of the day would have understood—that He was the solution to the sin problem. As the people were required to look to the bronze snake on the pole, so the world must look to Jesus on the cross to have the cure for their sin affliction.

Stone	1 Peter 2:4

Peter the apostle penned a letter to the persecuted church, encouraging and advising them during a difficult and frightening time. He also reminded them of whom they served and for whom they suffered. In that reminder, he referred to Jesus as "a living stone." Of course, in the natural world, stones are inanimate, lifeless things, but in the world of faith, Jesus is a living stone. Part of the irony of this passage is that Peter used the stone metaphor for Jesus and His followers. Peter's name comes from *petra,* which means "a rock."

Earlier in the book, he referred to Jesus as a "living hope" (1:3), then as the "living and enduring word of God (1:23)," and next as a "living stone."

Stones were important in the ancient world. The construction of a home began with the careful selection of a cornerstone to serve as the beginning of the foundation. The builder joined the first two walls over that stone. From that point, the rest of the house took shape.

Someone not looking for such a stone could easily trip and fall. Such a person might not see it as the beginning of something, seeing instead just a painful nuisance. That was Peter's point. Those who recognize Jesus see Him as the one whom we build our lives upon. Others simply trip over Him as the religious leaders of His day did. Jesus used this image Himself (Matthew 21:42).

Temple	John 2:19–21

Upon entering the temple courts, Jesus saw the money changers and merchants making themselves rich off those who had come to worship. Not willing to tolerate such sinful behavior, He overturned tables and drove off the perpetrators. When challenged to state by what authority He did this and what sign He could offer that indicated He had a right to do it, "Jesus answered, 'Destroy this temple, and in three days I will raise it up'" (John 2:19).

The religious leader thought He was speaking of the massive temple complex. "It took forty-six years to build this temple, and will You raise it up in three days?" (John 2:20). Jesus was not speaking of stone and wood. He was speaking of flesh and blood. The sign they wanted would come when He rose from the dead after spending three days in the tomb.

Jesus replaced the temple. It is through Him that worship is possible and productive. No building can achieve what the living Savior can.

Other	
Jesus used many other images and metaphors to help His followers understand Him and His mission. A short list must include the following:	
Vine	John 15:1–11
Door	John 10:7
Shepherd	John 10:14
Light	John 8:12
The Way	John 14:6

Why does the Bible contain all these images and metaphors? Why is there so much symbolism in the Scriptures? Symbols often communicate a truth in a way that a lecture cannot. The brain processes images by the thousands and is able to remember images better than any other stimulus. By using images familiar to the common man, Jesus gave educated and uneducated alike insight into His nature, purpose, and work.

Pictures of the Church

Jesus only founded one institution. He did not start schools, governments, or businesses. He did create an organization called the church. The church is at the center of much of the New Testament. Jesus "loved the church and gave Himself up for her."[22] As might be expected, something so important also has many symbols in the Bible:

Body	1 Corinthians 12:27; Ephesians 3:6; 4:4; Colossians 1:18
Branches	John 15:1–11
Bride	Revelation 19:7
Building and field	1 Corinthians 3:9
Lampstands	Revelation 1:20
Lights	Matthew 5:14; John 12:36; Ephesians 5:8; Philippians 2:15; 1 Thessalonians 5:5
Pearl	Matthew 13:45–46
Chosen race and priests	1 Peter 2:9
Salt	Matthew 5:13
Sheep, lambs	John 10:11; 21:15–17
Stones	1 Peter 2:5
Temple	Ephesians 2:19–22

God has chosen to reveal Himself in many ways. His work and will are complex and difficult to take in quickly. But He has, by the use of symbols, emblems, and metaphor, made the truth simple and accessible to everyone. Great mysteries made understandable in simple terms—that is something to be thankful for.

Points to Ponder

1. This chapter touched on just a few of the symbols in the Bible. Other than fish, mountains, Jesus, and the church, what other symbols come to mind?

2. If you were describing Christ in today's terms, what contemporary metaphors might you use?

3. How much weight and value should we apply to the symbolic nature of Scripture?

4. In our society, are the symbolism in the Bible easier or more difficult to understand?

5. Why do you suppose the Bible uses so many symbols?

---

[22]Ephesians 5:25.

Mysterious
Numbers

Design is the direct result of intelligence. When traveling around San Francisco, one eventually will come upon the beautiful Golden Gate Bridge. Only the most cynical person could look at the steel beams, concrete surface, support cables, and guard rails and assume that it had all fallen together by chance. In the structure, intent and design are evident. Clearly, there was an engineer.

When astronomers searched the deepest parts of space looking for intelligent life, they did it by listening for signals that could not have originated naturally. Their guiding principle was "nonrandomness." That is, if a radio telescope picked up a signal that followed an identifiable pattern and repeated itself, it would be evidence of intelligence.

When we come to the Bible, we quickly see its design. Of course, it uses language (Hebrew, Aramaic, and Greek), which is proof that it is the result of intelligent work; that much is obvious and beyond debate. Nevertheless, there's more just beneath the surface, an indication that this book called the Bible is more than the sole product of men.

The sheer task of getting forty different authors, most of whom had never met, to write a cohesive work that not only isn't contradictory but also enhances the work of the other authors is beyond imagination. Then to see subtle imprints of numbers and patterns from beginning to end makes the whole thing even more amazing. We might expect some pattern, since humans think in those terms, but the very nature of biblical patterns is unmistakable and impressive. God's fingerprints are everywhere.

CHAPTER TWELVE

Almost everyone who has studied the Bible has encountered numbers that repeat with regularity. These numbers do more than quantify; they qualify—that is, they do more than count; they teach. One of the mysterious ways God communicates is through the numbers that appear in the Bible.

This is not numerology; let's be clear on that. By definition, numerology is an occult practice that studies the supposed effects of numbers (or combination of numbers) on individuals and history. Some people use numbers to predict the future. Such practices have no place in the Christian life.

One

Although not as prevalent as others, the number one is still important. It is the number of unity and has its greatest expression in the Shema. The Shema comes from Deuteronomy 6:4: "Hear, O Israel! The LORD is our God, the LORD is one!" We call it the "Shema" because the first word of the verse is "Hear," which translates the Hebrew *shama*. The purpose of the verse is to remind us that there is only one God. As Moses said, "To you it was shown that you might know that the LORD, He is God; there is no other besides Him."[1]

Jesus taught His unity with the Father when He said, "I and the Father are one."[2] As the time of His betrayal drew near, while He was in the upper room with the disciples, Jesus prayed. In His prayer He said, "The glory which You have given Me I have given to them, that they may be one, just as We are one."[3]

Jesus' prayer was for unity among the disciples, and that concern continues today. Unity is a major theme of the New Testament (something many churches need to learn). Paul instructed the church in Ephesus about the important matter, saying that the people should be "diligent to preserve the unity of the Spirit in the bond of peace."[4] He then illustrated the point with the "oneness" of God. "There is one body and one Spirit, just as also you were called in one hope of your calling;

---

[1]Deuteronomy 4:35. [2]John 10:30. [3]John 17:22. [4]Ephesians 4:3.

one Lord, one faith, one baptism, one God and Father of all who is over all and through all and in all."[5]

One is the number of unity.

Two

Two is a powerful number and has deep significance. It signifies mutual support and often stands for work done on behalf of God.

The first mention of the number two is in Genesis and reveals that "God made the two great lights, the greater light to govern the day, and the lesser light to govern the night."[6] The sun and the moon are partners in the sky, providing light and marking the passage of time.

God's creation included two humans, Adam and Eve, the world's first couple.

Noah was ordered to take two "of every living thing of all flesh, you shall bring two of every kind into the ark, to keep them alive with you; they shall be male and female."[7] Noah also took seven "clean animals," animals that could be used for food and sacrifices.[8]

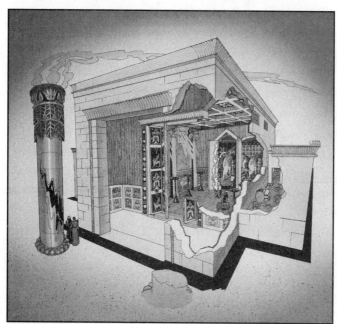

Cut-away view of Solomon's temple at Jerusalem, showing the porch, the holy place, and the holy of holies— where giant protecting cherubim and the sacred ark of the covenant were placed.

[5]Ephesians 4:4–6. [6]Genesis 1:16. [7]Genesis 6:19. [8]Genesis 7:2.

Before God destroyed the cities of Sodom and Gomorrah, two angels went in to rescue Abraham's nephew Lot and his family.[9] The pair succeeded in their mission and demonstrated their amazing power.

The gold-cased box called the ark of the covenant had a pair of sculpted gold cherubim on its lid (the mercy seat).[10] When the ark came to rest in the temple's Holy of Holies, it rested under the outstretched wings of two fifteen-foot-tall cherubim statues. Interestingly, the Bible usually shows cherubim in fours. Once in the temple, the number of cherubim on the ark and the two standing cherubim statutes make the expected four.

When the Ten Commandments were given, they were "written by the finger of God" on two tablets of stone.[11] These two tablets were carried in the ark of the covenant under the lid with the two cherubim on two poles carried by two pairs of priests.

The "twos" carry on. Under Mosaic Law, at least two witnesses were necessary to convict a person of a crime. Their testimony had to agree.[12] During Jesus' trial, His accusers had difficulty finding two such witnesses who could agree, even though they committed themselves to lie. They just couldn't keep their stories straight.[13]

Under Moses' leadership, twelve spies went into the land of Canaan to make what contemporary military leaders would call a threat assessment.[14] When they returned, the survey party gave a lopsided assessment. Ten gave a woeful report that frightened the people. Only two, Caleb and Joshua, had the courage to encourage advancement. The bad report led the people to rebel against God, threatening to kill their leaders by stoning. Their rebellion nearly cost the people their lives. Only the quick intercession of two men, Moses and Aaron, spared the people.

The number two is repeated many times, and not just in the Old Testament. After the Magi had spoken to Herod about the birth of Christ and then were warned by God in a dream "not to return to Herod,"[15] the Magi left by a different route. This enraged the off-balanced king. He gave the orders, and his men killed "all the male children who were in

---

[9]Genesis 19:1. [10]Exodus 25:22. [11]Exodus 31:18. [12]Deuteronomy 17:6. [13]Matthew 26:60. [14]Numbers 13–14. [15]Matthew 2:12.

Bethlehem and all its vicinity, from two years old and under, according to the time which he had determined from the magi."[16]

When Jesus began calling His disciples, He chose two sets of two; that is, He picked two sets of brothers—Peter and Andrew,[17] and James and John.[18]

Jesus often interacted with people who came to Him in pairs, including two demon-possessed men,[19] two blind men who followed Him,[20] and two blind men sitting on the roadside.[21] When John the Baptist had questions for Jesus, he sent two of his disciples to meet with the Lord.[22]

Jesus had a huge impact on the Samaritans. What started with a conversation between Him and the woman at the well led to an entire city encountering the Messiah. "So when the Samaritans came to Jesus, they were asking Him to stay with them; and He stayed there two days."[23] Jesus' witness among them lasted two days.

The list goes on. Jesus multiplied five loaves and two fish to feed thousands.[24] He sent out seventy of His disciples on a mission trip. When He did, He sent them in pairs.[25]

A man came to Jesus with a question. He wanted to know which of the commandants was the greatest of all. Jesus did not confine His answer to the man's expectation. Instead, He gave two commandments as being the greatest: "And He said to him, 'You shall love the LORD your God with all your heart, and with all your soul, and with all your mind.' This is the great and foremost commandment. The second is like it, 'You shall love your neighbor as yourself.' On these two commandments depend the whole Law and the Prophets."[26]

Jesus taught that where two agreed on earth, the Father in heaven would do it for them.[27] He followed that with the reminder that "where two or three have gathered together in My name, I am there in their midst."[28]

We can add to all of that the fact that when Jesus died on the cross (between two thieves), the veil—a heavy curtain that separated the Holy

---

[16]Matthew 2:16. [17]Matthew 4:18. [18]Matthew 4:21. [19]Matthew 8:28. [20]Matthew 9:27. [21]Matthew 20:30. [22]Luke 7:19. [23]John 4:40. [24]Matthew 14:17. [25]Luke 10:1. [26]Matthew 22:36–40. [27]Matthew 18:19. [28]Matthew 18:20.

of Holies from the rest of the temple—was "torn in two from top to bottom."[29] After Jesus' resurrection, two angels were "seen sitting, one at the head and one at the feet, where the body of Jesus had been lying."[30]

Three

The number three is one of the best known and most used numbers in the Bible. It is the number of completeness, although that one word doesn't carry enough meaning to cover adequately all the varied uses of the number. No single word could do justice to it.

There are three parts of creation: the heavens, the earth, and "under the earth." Paul wrote, "At the name of Jesus every knee will bow, of those who are in heaven and on earth and under the earth."[31] All of humanity can be traced back to Noah's three sons, Shem, Ham and Japeth. Israel celebrated three yearly feasts: the Feast of Unleavened Bread (Passover), the Feast of Harvest (Firstfruits), and the Feast of Tabernacles.

Jonah was in the belly of the great fish for three days, and he became an example of Christ's time in the tomb.[32] Jesus' ministry lasted three years. Jesus was on the cross between two thieves, making three people who died that day.

At the heart of Jerusalem was the temple that King Herod had enhanced over a period of four decades. The temple was a permanent reflection of the mobile tabernacle. Each had three major parts: the outer court, the inner court, and the Holy of Holies.

There are more "threes."

Jesus holds three offices: prophet,[33] priest[34] and king.[35] His work in each of these areas brings about our salvation. Salvation itself is threefold and includes justification (being declared righteous), sanctification (being set apart for service) and glorification (eternal life).

On the Mount of Transfiguration, Jesus' appearance changed before the wide eyes of three disciples, who formed the "inner circle" of followers. Peter, James, and John witnessed Jesus' physical change and

---

[29]Mark 15:38. [30]John 20:12. [31]Philippians 2:10. [32]Jonah 1:17; Matthew 12:39–41. [33]Matthew 13:57. [34]Hebrews 5:1–10. [35]Luke 1:31–33.

overheard His conversation with Elijah and Moses. These two great men from the past miraculously appeared next to Jesus, forming yet another set of three.

The Trinity is the supreme use of three. As one author said, "Human reason, however, cannot fathom the Trinity, nor can logic explain it, and, although the word itself is not found in the Scriptures, the doctrine is plainly taught in the Scriptures."[36]

He is not alone in this opinion. "The doctrine of the Trinity is a deep mystery that cannot be fathomed by the finite mind. That it is taught in the Scripture, however, there can be no reasonable doubt. It is a doctrine to be believed, even though it cannot be thoroughly understood."[37]

For the purposes of this chapter, it is only important to note that the Trinity, as the word implies, defines the three Persons who make up the single triune God. The number three is at the very nature of God.

Four

Four is the "earth" number. While that may sound like something from a New Age book, it is not. Four describes the earth or its surface in some way. For example, the first mention of four is in the Book of Genesis. Speaking of Eden, the text states, "Now a river flowed out of Eden to water the garden; and from there it divided and became four rivers."[38] In the Book of Isaiah, God speaks of "the four corners of the earth."[39] God designed our planet to have four seasons: summer, fall, winter, and spring.

The number is symbolic in the Book of Daniel, where it describes the number of coming kingdoms.[40] Jesus told a parable of a farmer who went out to sow his field. Farmers in those days planted the seed by throwing seeds in an arch in front of them. Since this was not an exact process, seed would fall on good soil as well as bad. In Matthew 13, Jesus describes four types of soils that represent the hearts of those who hear His message.

---

[36]Paul P. Enns, *The Moody Handbook of Theology* (Chicago, Ill.: Moody Press, 1989, 1997). [37]William Evans, *The Great Doctrines of the Bible* (Chicago, Ill.: Moody Press, 1974, 1998), 26. [38]Genesis 2:10. [39]Isaiah 11:12. [40]Daniel 7.

On a darker note, Revelation 6 describes the "four horsemen of the apocalypse." Each horse represents a judgment to take place during the tribulation—conquest, famine, war, and death—all related to events on earth.

Four Gospels record Christ's ministry, and each shows the Lord's work in a slightly different light. Taken together, we get the complete picture. Matthew emphasizes Christ the King, while Mark shows the servant aspects of Jesus' work. Luke emphasizes the humanity of the Savior, while John shows His deity. Together they make a complete package, a portrayal rich in detail and facts. We must read all four Gospels to see the many aspects of Jesus' ministry.

Five

Five is a number that is associated with worship. The number is repeated many times in the construction of Solomon's temple. For example, the wing length of the standing cherubim statues in the Holy of Holies was five cubits for each wing.[41] There were ten lampstands, five on one side of the building and five on the other (see 1 Kings 7:49).

Leviticus 1–5 dictates the five offerings made by the priests, again showing that the number five is closely associated with worship and grace.

Jesus described the kingdom of God as being like ten virgins waiting to join the groom's procession from the bride's home to his own, where the wedding feast waited. There was a delay, and when the groom (Jesus) arrived, only the five wise virgins were ready to greet him with working lamps. They joined the procession while the others were left behind (see Matthew 25:1–12).

Six

Of all the numbers in the Bible, six gets the most attention. In Revelation, there is mention of the mark of the Beast.[42] The infamous number 666 has clouded the actual meaning of the basic numeral. Six is the number of man. It is not an evil number. Indeed, in many ways it is

---

[41]2 Chronicles 3:11. [42]Revelation 13:18.

a holy number. While the mark of the Beast mentioned in Revelation is a hideous thing, it is the diabolic Beast that is evil, not the number six.

God created the universe and all it contains in six days and pronounced it good. "God saw all that He had made, and behold, it was very good. And there was evening and there was morning, the sixth day."[43]

The biblical workweek was six days long to match the number of days that God spent creating the universe. This pattern was so important that God gave it as part of the Ten Commandments. "For in six days the LORD made the heavens and the earth, the sea and all that is in them, and rested on the seventh day; therefore the LORD blessed the sabbath day and made it holy."[44]

God designed humans to have a day of rest. Many have pushed that design to its limits and found it less productive than they thought. Rest is part of God's plan for man.

The Bible also describes six cities of refuge. When the children of Israel took possession of the Promised Land, the country was divided among the tribes. Six cities—three on each side of the Jordan River—were designated as cities of refuge. In ancient Israel, if one man killed another, a blood avenger would pursue the killer and take his life, avenging the death. This avenger (the *goel*) was the nearest male relative, and it was his job to exact justice. But if the killing was not premeditated, then the pursued man could flee to one of the six cities of refuge and be safe as long as he remained there.[45] In many ways the six cities of refuge are symbolic of Christ, who is the one to whom we flee for protection from death.

Seven

Every Bible student knows this number well. It is the crown prince of numbers. The number of explicit usages of seven, as well as those hidden a layer or two deeper in the text, is enormous. Seven is the "God number," the number of perfection.

---

[43]Genesis 1:31. [44]Exodus 20:11. [45]Numbers 35:6.

It appears very early in the Bible when Genesis records that God rested from His creative work on the seventh day. That day became the basis for the Sabbath, a day God commanded us to keep holy.[46]

When Peter asked Jesus how often he should forgive his brother, and then suggested seven times, the Lord multiplied the number. "Jesus said to him, 'I do not say to you, up to seven times, but up to seventy times seven.'"[47] This was Jesus' way of telling Peter to stop counting and start forgiving.

Jesus made seven comments from the cross: (1) "My God, My God, why have You forsaken Me?"[48] (2) "Father, forgive them; for they do not know what they are doing."[49] (3) "Truly I say to you, today you shall be with Me in Paradise."[50] (4) "Father, into Your hands I commit My spirit."[51] (5) "Woman, behold, your son!"[52] (6) "I am thirsty."[53] (7) "It is finished!"[54]

The apostle John was the recipient of a long and detailed revelation from God. What he saw and experienced is described in the Book of Revelation. During that symbolic vision, he was commanded to write to seven churches. He also saw seven lampstands, seven stars in Christ's hands, seven angels pronouncing judgment, and a book with seven seals.

The always interesting Chuck Missler, building on the works of Ivan Panin, shows that the number seven appears in other fashions.[55] The first eleven verses of Matthew contain a heptadic (sevenfold, grouped by seven) structure that goes well beyond surprising. Those verses contain the genealogy of Jesus. Missler notes that in the original language:

- The number of words in the passage is divisible by seven.
- The number of letters is divisible by seven.
- The number of vowels is a multiple of seven.
- The number of consonants is a multiple of seven.
- The number of words beginning with a vowel is divisible by seven.

---

[46]Exodus 20:8. [47]Matthew 18:22. [48]Matthew 27:46. [49]Luke 23:34. [50]Luke 23:43. [51]Luke 23:46. [52]John 19:26. [53]John 19:28. [54]John 19:30. [55]Chuck Missler, *Hidden Treasures* (Coeur d'Alene, Idaho: Koinonia House, 2000), 27–28.

- The number of words beginning with a consonant is divisible by seven.
- The number of words that occur in more than one form is divisible by seven.
- Likewise, the number of words that appear in only one form is divisible by seven.
- The number of nouns is divisible by seven.
- In the text, only seven words are not nouns.
- The number of names is divisible by seven.
- The number of male names is a multiple of seven.
- The number of generations listed (twenty-one) is divisible by seven.

From this list, Missler has calculated that the odds of such a structured list occurring by chance are well over one in forty million. To see the great difficulty in constructing such a list, one only has to try to do it himself. Of course, another aspect to this is that the list must also be true and historically accurate.

We could spend a lifetime examining the obvious and subtle appearances of the number seven in the Scriptures.

Eight

Eight is also a significant number. It represents a new start. Eight people survived the great flood: Noah and his wife, his three sons and their wives. Peter noted, "When the patience of God kept waiting in the days of Noah, during the construction of the ark, in which a few, that is, eight persons, were brought safely through the water."[56]

Nine

Nine is a number of spiritual empowerment. In the Book of Galatians, Paul lists nine segments of the fruit of the Spirit: "But the fruit of the Spirit is love, joy, peace, patience, kindness, goodness, faithfulness, gentleness, self-control; against such things there is no law."[57] What

[56]1 Peter 3:20. [57]Galatians 5:22–23.

makes this passage so interesting is the play on numbers. There are nine descriptions of the fruit, but the word *fruit* is in the singular. In other words, there is only one fruit of the Spirit (remember, one represents unity), but there are nine evidences of that fruit. As a single orange has many segments, so the single fruit of the Spirit has nine segments.

In a similar vein, there are eighteen (9 x 2) gifts of the Spirit, given by Him to equip the believer for the work and the Christian life. There are three lists of spiritual gifts in the New Testament.[58]

Abraham was the father of a nation. Where there is a father, there must also be a mother. The Bible tells the remarkable story of Sarah, Abraham's wife, who gave birth to her only son, Isaac, when she was ninety years old. That is amazing, even back in a time when age spans were significantly longer than today (Abraham lived to be 175 years old[59]).

The number nine carries the idea of empowerment from God.

Ten

This number is associated with human government and kingdoms. Daniel and Revelation speak of ten nations. When the nation of Israel split into two kingdoms, the Northern Kingdom was composed of ten tribes.

Twelve

Twelve is a highly symbolic number and refers to God's appointment and plan. There were twelve tribes of Israel. These tribes could trace their lineage back to Abraham. Twelve became the number of Israel. Jesus twice fed the multitudes by multiplying a small amount of fish and bread. He did this for a primarily Jewish group, then later for a predominantly Gentile group. After the first miraculous feeding, the disciples picked up the remaining bread and filled twelve baskets.[60] They gathered seven baskets[61] after the Gentile feeding, representing the seven nations driven out by Joshua.[62]

---

[58]1 Corinthians 12:7–10, 28–30; Romans 12:6–8; Ephesians 4:11. [59]Genesis 25:7.
[60]Luke 9:17. [61]Matthew 15:37. [62]Deuteronomy 7:1.

Jesus called twelve men to be His core disciples. After Judas's betrayal, that number dropped to eleven, but God had a man selected to replace the traitor. His name was Saul, later known as Paul. The disciples jumped the gun in Acts 1 when they cast lots and chose Matthias to replace Judas. We hear nothing more of Matthias after this.

When the apostle John had his revelation, he saw twenty-four elders (perhaps representing Israel's twelve tribes and the twelve apostles). In that revelation, John also saw New Jerusalem, a city with twelve gates (three gates on each of the four walls).[63]

Thirty

Thirty is associated with sadness and mourning. The people mourned Aaron and Moses for thirty days after their deaths.[64]

Forty

Forty is a number that appears many times in the Bible and is associated with judgment or testing. A short list shows:

- It rained forty days and nights in Noah's flood (Genesis 7:4).
- The life of Moses divides into three forty-year segments: forty years in Egypt, forty in Midian, forty leading the children of Israel.
- When Moses sent spies into the Promised Land, they surveyed the situation for forty days (Numbers 13:25).
- Moses spent forty days and forty nights on Mount Sinai (Exodus 24:18).
- Israel wandered in the wilderness for forty years (Numbers 14:33).
- The Philistine giant Goliath mocked the army of Israel for forty days (1 Samuel 17:16).
- The rebellious prophet Jonah preached in the city of Nineveh for forty days (Jonah 3:4).

---

[63]Revelation 21:12. [64]Numbers 20:29; Deuteronomy 34:8.

- Jesus fasted for forty days and nights during His temptation in the wilderness (Matthew 4:2).
- Jesus made twelve appearances over forty days following His resurrection.

Two Other Numbers

The number fifty also appears many times in the pages of the Bible. It is associated with celebration. Pentecost, called in the Old Testament the Feast of Weeks, came fifty days after Passover. It was on that day, fifty days after Jesus died, that the Holy Spirit came upon the disciples who preached the message of Christ. More than three thousand people received salvation.

Under God's economic system, every fiftieth year the economy was to reset. All debts were released, Jewish slaves were freed, and land that had been sold reverted back to the original owners.[65] It was the completion of seven seven-year cycles (7 x 7 = 49). The fiftieth year began the cycle all over again.

Seventy is the number associated with human leadership. Under God's command, Moses appointed seventy elders to help him rule the people.[66] Jesus appointed seventy disciples and "sent them in pairs ahead of Him to every city and place where He Himself was going to come."[67]

The Sanhedrin was the civil and religious ruling body that sat in judgment of Jesus and the apostles. The word *Sanhedrin* does not appear in the English translation of the Bible (the words *council* or *courts* are generally used), but rabbinical writings tell us of their function. They ruled on matters of law and high cases. They were composed of seventy men from the religiously conservative Pharisees, the more liberal Sadducees, and others.

So What?

God's revelation of Himself is detailed and multilayered. Most of what we know comes to us through the inspired text of the Bible. Even

---

[65]Leviticus 25:8–17. [66]Numbers 11:16. [67]Luke 10:1.

a casual reading shows that it is a book like none other. The number patterns in the Bible show us the depth of inspiration. In some ways, numbers and patterns are the fingerprints of God. They show a layer of meaning beyond the surface text, and that takes us deeper and further in our understanding.

The Bible is one of God's ways of reaching those whom He loves. The deeper we dig, the more of God we will know.

Points to Ponder

1. Why do you suppose God would inspire His Bible in such a way that numbers carry more meaning than their numerical value?

2. There is always a danger of taking things too far. Some people have attempted to predict Christ's return based on certain numbers that appear in the Bible. Why is this wrong?

3. After seeing the numerical structure of the Bible, what can we learn about God and His ways?

4. How might you use this information about numbers to help people see the inspiration of the Bible?

5. Sometimes numbers are just numbers. How can we tell the difference between those times when numbers represent something and those when they don't?

Mysterious
Science

For many people, the Bible is little more than a collection of ancient writings penned by superstitious men more than two thousand years ago. Some have suggested that the influence of the Bible has little place in the technoscientific twenty-first century. This is the age of enlightenment and scientific pursuits. We live in a world in which astronauts visit space with such regularity that it no longer garners more that a five-second comment on the TV news. What could people of two millennia ago have to offer a world connected by copper wire, fiber optics, and satellite transmissions? And the Old Testament is older still; certainly that must be outdated.

All of this would be true if the Bible were a mere book, if it were a collection of the musings of old men in an old time. In such a case, the Bible would have little effect on our modern world. The Bible would be nothing but a collection of the dusty, moldering past. But the Bible is an inspired book, divine in origin and engineered to speak to humankind. While it is true that our society has changed greatly and that engineering, science, and technology have changed much, it has yet to change the heart of man or to remove sin. While our sky is dotted with jetliners unimagined by men like Abraham and Moses, the heart of humanity remains unchanged. It still has a longing and a vital need for a loving God. It was true in the days of Moses, and it is true today. The Bible is not out of date. It never will be. It remains the unchanging boulder on the shifting shore of history.

CHAPTER THIRTEEN

There is a myth that the Bible is primitive, that its human authors believed in a flat earth and had no hint of how the world worked. Such a belief could not be more wrong. Indeed, the Bible shows the opposite. In fact, it hints at scientific discoveries centuries before contemporary men and women of science realized them.

The Sky Above

Ancient people were sky watchers. The sun, moon, and stars were part of their daily life. Many myths sprouted around the celestial objects. Today we turn telescopes skyward to learn what is out there. The ancient people had no such tools, but the Bible records some facts that would remain hidden from most people for centuries.

Rounding Out Earth and the Moon

One of the most prevalent and enduring myths is that the people of the biblical era believed the world was flat. While that may be true of some cultures, it is not true of the Scriptures.

Approximately 2,700 years ago, the prophet Isaiah proclaimed God's word and attempted to lead His people from idolatry back to faith. He recorded God's words: "It is He who sits above the circle of the earth, and its inhabitants are like grasshoppers, who stretches out the heavens like a curtain and spreads them out like a tent to dwell in."[1]

What a revealing verse. God sits "above the circle of the earth." *Circle* translates the Hebrew *chug* and appears only three times in the Bible. Each time it shows God as superior to space and time.[2] The word means "vault," "circle," or "horizon."

Isaiah's point is that God as Creator sits (is enthroned) beyond the curve of the horizon, beyond the sphere of the earth.

Solomon wrote his proverbs one thousand years before Christ. The Bible preserved his wisdom through the ages. In Proverbs 8:27, using the literary device that personalizes a nonliving thing, he puts words in Wisdom's mouth. Wisdom says, "When He established the heavens, I was there, when He inscribed a circle on the face of the deep." Again,

---

[1]Isaiah 40:22. [2]Job 22:14; Proverbs 8:27.

the word *circle* refers to the earth. King Solomon believed the earth was a sphere.

The oldest writings in the Bible are in the Book of Job. Conservative scholars put Job in the time of the patriarchs, meaning that he lived about 1,800 to 2,000 years before Christ. Not only does the book show a spherical planet but much more. First, he shows a round earth. "Clouds are a hiding place for Him, so that He cannot see; and He walks on the vault of heaven."[3] *Vault* is the same term as above, meaning a circle.

The Book of Job shows that the Bible anticipated what science would discover many centuries later. For example, Job showed that some other celestial creature did not support the earth. While some cultures taught that the earth rested on the back of a turtle, or an elephant, or rode in a chariot, or sat upon the shoulders of Atlas, Job said, "He stretches out the north over empty space and hangs the earth on nothing."[4] Our society is accustomed to seeing pictures of the earth taken from space, but 3,500 years ago, no one had seen anything like that. To have something solid "resting" on nothing was a foreign concept and too far in the future for most to imagine. Yet the Book of Job records the reality of the situation long before there was a way to determine the truth.

The Book of Job goes even further, anticipating something that would be unknown to most people for thousands of years when it said, "If even the moon has no brightness and the stars are not pure in His sight."[5] The implication of the verb translated "has no brightness" is that the moon reflects light rather than shining on its own. That's common knowledge now, but it was not in Job's day. While other cultures believed that the light of the moon came from the moon itself, the inspired Book of Job shows the truth of the matter.

Twinkle, Twinkle

Those people who are fortunate enough to live away from city lights can stare through a cloudless sky and see flecks of light called stars. They captivate the attention as much today as they did in ages past. Still, our eyes are limited in what they can see. No matter how long we look or

---

[3]Job 22:14. [4]Job 26:7. [5]Job 25:5.

how long we stare, we can see only a fraction of the stars that fill the stretches of space.

Some people have attempted to count the visible stars and have arrived at various numbers. Kepler, Ptolemy, Brahe—all names familiar to astronomers—have counted the stars in the night sky, each reaching their limit at approximately one thousand. In 1609, the Italian Galileo Galilei turned his primitive telescope skyward. Able to see twenty times more than anyone had ever seen before, he discovered mountains on the moon, some of Jupiter's moons, and the uncountable stars of the Milky Way. That was a revolutionary moment as the world learned that there were more stars than ever thought before. However, the Bible was ahead of the great Galileo. Jeremiah recorded God reiterating a promise made long before: "As the host of heaven cannot be counted and the sand of the sea cannot be measured, so I will multiply the descendants of David My servant and the Levites who minister to Me."[6]

The "host of heaven" refers to stars in the sky. God made it known that there were, at least from a human perspective, more stars than could be counted. The Milky Way, that band of stars that stretches across the night sky, has about one trillion stars. Counting one or two stars per second, it would take a person thousands of years to number the Milky Way—and the Milky Way is just one galaxy in the universe. God was not exaggerating.

Two thousand years ago, the apostle Paul made a subtle statement that presages another scientific discovery: "There is one glory of the sun, and another glory of the moon, and another glory of the stars; for star differs from star in glory."[7] Variations in the stars? Today we know there are many types of stars, such as red giants and white dwarfs, but we know this because of the invention of the telescope, spectroscope, and more. No such instruments existed in Paul's day. At best, someone with good eyesight might see that some stars are brighter than others, but little more. Yet, Paul was inspired to mention the different "glory" of stars. *Glory* comes from the Greek *doxa* and means "brightness," "shining,"

---

[6]Jeremiah 33:22. [7]1 Corinthians 15:41.

or "radiance." Paul was saying that the stars are not all the same but have unique qualities—not bad for an ancient rabbi.

A Touch of Physics

One of the most remarkable scientific foreshadowing passages comes again from the Book of Job. Light is something we take for granted. Flip a switch, and the light comes on. Turn it off, and it goes away. The sun rises above the horizon and bathes the landscape in golden light. Light, however, is still a puzzle, not fully understood by physicists. Depending on the testing method, light behaves as a particle or it can behave like an electromagnetic wave.

Biblical people knew that daylight came from the sun and that a lamp with a wick in oil could be made to burn for light at night. Such basic information was as obvious then as it is now. What is remarkable is the higher concept that light travels.

Every student learns in elementary school that light travels from one place to another at about 186,000 miles per second. Common knowledge has not always been common. The concept of light traveling through space is a high notion for ancient thinkers. Yet, God revealed that very fact in His challenge to Job: "Where is the way to the dwelling of light? And darkness, where is its place, that you may take it to its territory and that you may discern the paths to its home?"[8]

God uses the word *way (derek)*. It is used more than seven hundred times in the Bible and means "way," "manner," "journey," "distance," "path," "street," and similar words. Darkness is also mentioned as having a "home," but God's point is that Job knew much less than he thought he knew. Only God has a full understanding of these elements. Job may not have understood the process of light, but God certainly did—He created it.

Job holds another startling revelation that was beyond the understanding of men of his era. "Where is the way that the light is divided, or the east wind scattered on the earth?"[9] Divided light? The Hebrew word for "divided" *(chalaq)* means to "apportion," "distribute," or

---

[8]Job 38:19–20. [9]Job 38:24.

"disperse." How can light be divided? Anyone who has seen a beam of sunlight pass through a prism knows the answer. Isaac Newton correctly explained the phenomenon in 1666. Sunlight is a composite of several colors of light. The red, orange, yellow, green, blue, indigo, and violet combine to make the "white" light we see.

A prism can divide light, breaking it down into its component wave lengths. The rainbow we see during rainy weather is the result of sunlight passing through airborne water droplets that act like millions of tiny prisms.

How is it that the Bible describes the ability to divide light when science did not explain the process until the seventeenth century?

Our Home Planet

Until American astronauts stepped foot on the moon, humankind had never traveled far from earth. Even then, the distance crossed was a mere 240,000 miles, small when compared to the vast distances of outer space. While robot craft have traveled through the solar system and landed on Mars, humankind has been rooted to earth.

This planet we call home is a complex system with intricate dynamics that make life possible. This system has been the source of curiosity and investigation through the ages. Still, most of what we know has come about in the last few hundred years.

Heavy Air

Job again gives us insight into science in the Bible. "When He imparted weight to the wind and meted out the waters by measure."[10] What an unusual phrase: "Imparted weight to wind." We seldom think of air as having weight, but it does. At sea level, air exerts a pressure of about fourteen pounds per square inch. Since God designed us to live in such an environment, we take no notice of it.

If the Bible were a purely human invention, then how would the writer of Job know that air had weight? A barometer is a device used to measure atmospheric pressure (the pressure exerted by the weight of air).

[10]Job 28:25.

Galileo's successor Evangelista Torricelli invented the first device to measure atmospheric pressure in 1643. Yet the Bible clearly states that air has weight.

Moving Air

King Solomon, a man with special wisdom from God, wrote the Book of Ecclesiastes. A contemplative book, it forces the reader to think and evaluate life. In its pages is a fascinating passage: "Blowing toward the south, then turning toward the north, the wind continues swirling along; and on its circular courses the wind returns."[11]

By definition, wind is air in motion. Everyone experiences wind. It is a useful force and is necessary for life. However, it can become destructive. What Solomon described is the normal, large-scale movement of air. He was doing more than saying, "The wind blows." He described the direction and course changes that match what we now know about air movement and predating the science of meteorology.

Water Cycle

Life requires a constant source of water. That water is in constant movement. Evaporation from lakes and oceans and transpiration from plants fill the atmosphere with water vapor that returns to the ground in the form of precipitation. Much of the rain and snow flows to the seas through rivers and steams, and the cycle repeats. Every day, seventy cubic miles of precipitation waters the planet; twenty-four cubic miles of water flow to the seas through rivers; and that water returns to the atmosphere as vapor. Our atmosphere holds 2,900 cubic miles of water.

The water cycle is well known. It's part of every child's education. Still, our knowledge of the cycle is recent, yet King Solomon wrote, "All the rivers flow into the sea, yet the sea is not full. To the place where the rivers flow, there they flow again."[12] Three thousand years ago, Solomon knew what science would not demonstrate for centuries. And he wasn't the only biblical personality who understood the process.

---

[11]Ecclesiastes 1:6. [12]Ecclesiastes 1:7.

The Jordan River just north of the Sea of Galilee. Like all bodies of water, the river contributes to the water cycle.

The prophet Isaiah noted, "For as the rain and the snow come down from heaven, and do not return there without watering the earth and making it bear and sprout, and furnishing seed to the sower and bread to the eater."[13] The key phrase is "do not return there without watering the earth." The passage describes perfectly the endless cycle of water. Rain was certainly something Isaiah and other ancient people understood, but evaporation and transpiration (water from plants released into the atmosphere) would have been a stretch. Still, the Bible shows the process clearly.

Atomic Bible

The author of Hebrews hinted at something that was unknown for many centuries: Everything that exists is composed of small blocks of

---

[13]Isaiah 55:10.

matter called atoms. "By faith we understand that the worlds were pre-pared by the word of God, so that what is seen was not made out of things which are visible."[14] What an intriguing verse. It wasn't until 1803 that the modern theory of atomic structure got its start under John Dalton, a British physicist and chemist. The writer of Hebrews alluded to the concept a little less than 1,800 years before Dalton and those who corrected and furthered his work.

Visible things made from the invisible. While the author doesn't launch into a discussion of atomic theory, he does make it known that God constructed the physical world from things that people cannot see. That certainly describes our understanding of matter. Atoms are so small that one hundred million of them strung in a line would barely make a centimeter.

Again, the Bible anticipates what science would discover only cen-turies later.

Biology Basics

People may appear different, have divergent interests and tastes, but all of us have something in common—blood. The sticky fluid that flows through our arteries and veins is essential for life. The average person carries one to two gallons of blood in his body, depending on age and size. Roughly 8 percent of a person's weight is blood.

Blood carries oxygen from our lungs, delivering it to the entire body. It also transports waste products away from our tissue. Without blood, we would die in minutes.

Blood is an important issue in the Bible. The ancient Jews were pro-hibited from eating blood. In one such prohibition, God said, "For the life of the flesh is in the blood, and I have given it to you on the altar to make atonement for your souls; for it is the blood by reason of the life that makes atonement."[15]

Long before the medical science of hematology, the Bible was teach-ing that life was resident in the blood—no blood, no life.

---

[14]Hebrews 11:3. [15]Leviticus 17:11.

The idea that some diseases are communicable was known in Bible times. Today it seems obvious, but in a world that had no concept of viruses and bacteria, the concept was not so clear. One such communicable disease was problematic for Middle Easterners and others—leprosy.

Biblical leprosy referred to a number of skin disorders, including leprosy proper. It was required that lepers avoid contact with other people. While this might seem cruel, it was crucial to a world with limited medical skill and medications.

"As for the leper who has the infection, his clothes shall be torn, and the hair of his head shall be uncovered, and he shall cover his mustache and cry, 'Unclean! Unclean!' He shall remain unclean all the days during which he has the infection; he is unclean. He shall live alone; his dwelling shall be outside the camp."[16]

This makes the number of times Jesus touched a leper all the more poignant. Technically, He was breaking the Mosaic Law, but since the person was "cleansed" each time, no violation was committed on Christ's part.

Again, the Bible anticipated later scientific discovery. In this case, that some diseases could be contagious.

The Book that Saw the Future

The Bible is not a book of science. In many cases, it describes the world in terms of appearance rather than scientific fact. As we do today, biblical people spoke of the rising and setting sun, not the rotation of the earth on its axis. Still, the Bible shows itself to be accurate on everything it touches, including science.

A book written by mere humans could not have anticipated the advances that science would bring one day, but the Bible does just that. It is one more piece of evidence that the Scriptures are inspired and true in all things.

If the Bible is trustworthy in the things that were secondary to its primary purpose of revealing God to man, then it must be all the more trustworthy when it speaks to spiritual matters.

---

[16]Leviticus 13:45–46.

Points to Ponder

1. Many people speak of a conflict between science and the Bible. Is there really such a conflict?

2. The Bible speaks very little about how things work in the universe, but when it does speak, it does so accurately. Why doesn't the Bible speak on scientific issues more?

3. Does the information in this chapter show that the Bible is inspired, or is it possible that ancient people just knew more than previously supposed?

4. When the human authors penned the Bible, do you think they understood everything they were writing?

5. Someone once called science the sixty-seventh book of the Bible. Can that be true?

Mysterious
Relatives

The Bible holds as much nail-biting action and edge-of-your-seat thrills as any major motion picture. What one of us has not heard of the exploits of David, his great wars, his grand poetry? What one of us has not read of the miracles of Peter and Paul as they took the message of Christ to the world?

Yes, we know well the champions of the Bible. We are well acquainted with David, Solomon, Elijah, John the Baptist, Peter, Paul the apostle, and so many more. What we may not know, however, are the interesting characters who become heroes in unexpected, sometimes mysterious ways. At first glance, some seem insignificant, but they rose to do mighty things, like the boy David killing Goliath. Some were drawn into outrageous schemes that were doomed to failure but succeeded because of the grace of God.

Notable people are not always noble. Hitler is as famous (perhaps *infamous* is a better word) as Albert Schweitzer, but they were very different people working from very different motives. Each changed the world, bringing either hope or fear. History is a mix of the good with the bad, the noble with the ignoble, heroes and fiends. Some are surprised to find that such people make up the lineage of Jesus. We find their genealogies in Matthew 1:1–17 and Luke 3:23–38.

The greatest hero of all time is Jesus Christ. However, not everyone would have readily agreed. In Jewish culture, genealogy was highly important. In order for the world to recognize Jesus as "the King of the

Jews," He had to have the family tree to prove it. For this reason, both Matthew and Luke record the lineage of Jesus in their Gospels.

These lines, however, have a few kinks. They don't match up exactly. Many people have pointed to this as a flaw in Scripture, an inconsistency. Such accusations are far from the truth. Matthew records the Jewish heritage of Joseph, the "foster" father of Jesus. Luke, however, records the heritage of Mary, the biological mother of Jesus, and there is good reason for this.

In Matthew's record, we see some interesting names. Most people skip over these names. They don't seem like exciting reading. Names represent people and people have experiences. Some of those experiences are graphic and even shocking. A deeper study of these names reveals some very unlikely heroes.

Of the unexpected champions in Jesus' family tree, the women are perhaps the most overlooked and underrated. Four women are in the list: Tamar, Rahab, Ruth, and Bathsheba. These were unusual women with difficult life stories. They teach us that God is able to make anyone—regardless of race, age, or gender—into a hero.

Tamar (Genesis 38:6–30)

Tamar's is a sad story. As an ancient woman living in a male-dominated society, she had very few rights. In order to survive and prosper, she had to marry. Her livelihood depended solely upon her husband's well-being. If he were to die, her children, primarily any sons she might have, would be responsible for her care. Tamar, however, at the death of her husband, became a childless widow. There was more at stake than just physical comfort. A husband who died before his wife bore children had no heir to carry on his name. This was a tragedy in Jewish thinking.

Jewish law, however, had an answer. For a situation like this, it was required of the brother-in-law to go in to the widow and conceive a child with her so she would have a means of survival in her elder years and, just as importantly, continue the family line. The practice predated Moses but became a part of the law that governed the Jewish people.

Called Levirate[1] marriage, the command occurs in Deuteronomy: "When brothers live together and one of them dies and has no son, the wife of the deceased shall not be married outside the family to a strange man. Her husband's brother shall go in to her and take her to himself as wife and perform the duty of a husband's brother to her."[2] This practice was still binding in Jesus' day and was used by the Sadducees as a theological test for Jesus.[3]

Tamar was a Canaanite woman. Judah chose her to be the wife of his son Er. Judah had also taken a Canaanite wife, a decision that would cause him much trouble. The error wasn't in marrying outside his race, but outside his faith. Canaanites were notorious pagans and would be, through the ages, a constant source of spiritual pollution to the Israelites.

Er, whose name means "watchful," was no prize himself: "But Er, Judah's firstborn, was evil in the sight of the LORD, so the LORD took his life."[4] No details are given. What the man did is unknown, but it was enough to compel God to take his life. This divine capital punishment left Tamar a widow in need of a husband. Judah assigned his next son, Onan ("strong"), to take Tamar as his wife and have a son by her.[5]

Onan was a greedy man. He knew that any son of Tamar's would inherit Er's property—and not him. That was because the child would legally be Er's son, not Onan's. Despite being the biological father, he would not have the rights or privileges fathers normally had. He refused to follow through with his duty. God saw this and was not pleased. "But what he did was displeasing in the sight of the LORD; so He took his life also."[6]

Now Judah, father of three sons, had only one surviving son, Shelah ("prayer"). Two had died suddenly, each struck dead by God. This tragedy was hard for any man to endure, yet there was still the problem of Tamar. What should Judah do? Fearing he might lose his last son as he had the previous two, Judah backed away from his obligation. Using Shelah's age as an excuse, he insisted that his last son was too young to

---

[1]*Levirate* comes from the Latin *levir*, which means "a husband's brother."
[2]Deuteronomy 25:5. [3]Matthew 22:25. [4]Genesis 38:7. [5]Genesis 38:8–10. [6]Genesis 38:10.

fulfill the duty of the brother-in-law. Instead, he instructed Tamar to come live with him, and he would provide for her needs until Shelah grew up.[7]

At first, this appears reasonable. Judah seemed genuinely concerned for Tamar's well-being, and he may have been. However, fear controlled him. Although his sons had died because of their own evil, not because of Tamar, Judah could not make that distinction. His two older sons, who had been with Tamar, had died. He would not run the same risk with his only surviving boy. Ultimately, the offer was a ruse. Judah did not intend to fulfill his duty.

After the death of Judah's wife and after the time for grieving had passed, Tamar set her plan into motion. Understanding that it was still her right to bear a child through her husband's family, she knew that her only option was to seduce Judah. As terrible as it sounds to our Western minds, it was acceptable, even expected, in Tamar's culture. Judah was depriving her of her right to have a child of her own and cutting off the lineage of his dead son. Tamar, a woman of strength, intelligence, and diligence, was unwilling to let Judah get away with his transgressions.

When she heard that Judah had left to shear his sheep in a distant pasture, she quickly took off the clothes that identified her as a widow and put on the dress of a religious prostitute. This involved wrapping a veil around her face. Religious prostitutes *(kedeshot)* were common in the land. Baal worship often included prostitution. Tamar, disguised beyond recognition, waited for Judah "in the gateway of Enaim."[8]

Judah arrived in town after working with the sheep and found the disguised Tamar waiting for him in the gate of the city. Ancient walled cities usually had several gates. They were popular places to meet and conduct business. In pagan cities, it was also the ancient equivalent of the red-light district. Thinking she was a prostitute, he chose to avail himself of her "services." She agreed, but asked for collateral until he could return with proper payment. Judah gave her his seal, cord, and staff.[9] The seal was a device that left an impression in wax or clay. It was the

---

[7]Genesis 38:11. [8]Genesis 38:14; also known as Enam (Joshua 15:34). [9]Genesis 38:18.

The Dung Gate was the entry to Jerusalem from the area of the Tyropoeon Valley. It was a gate similar to this that Tamar began her seduction of Judah.

equivalent of a signature. The seal hung from a cord around Jacob's neck. The staff refers to a shepherd's staff and may have had some markings that identified it as belonging to him.

The deal was set; the deed was done.

After the rendezvous, Judah sent one of his servants back with a young goat to make payment, but she was missing. The servant searched diligently, and asked others where the "temple prostitute" was. The reply was surprising, "There has been no temple prostitute here."[10] There was nothing Judah could do.

Three months later, it became apparent that Tamar was pregnant. To be pregnant out of wedlock was an offense punishable by death. Furthermore, since she was in the house of Judah, he would suffer great humiliation. He was unwilling to endure that shame. Tamar was to die by burning.[11]

---

[10]Genesis 38:21. [11]Genesis 38:24.

Tamar was ahead of the game, knowing that this day would come. She approached Judah and played her trump card—the seal, cord, and staff. "I am with child by the man to whom these things belong."[12] Seeing the property he left with the prostitute, Judah realized what had happened. The pieces of the puzzle dropped into place. "She is more righteous than I, inasmuch as I did not give her to my son Shelah."[13]

Six months later, Tamar gave birth to twins.

To most of us, what Tamar did was deceitful and motivated by selfish desires. Nonetheless, it was still an act of faith. Because of her faithfulness to God, she was willing to seduce her own father-in-law to keep the line of Judah intact. Because of that, she is in the lineage of Jesus.

We would not normally think of a woman who willfully engages in a semi-incestuous relationship as respectable, but in this rare and unique situation, Tamar did the difficult thing to achieve a greater good.

God is not limited by the actions or motivations of His people.

Rahab (Joshua 2:1–24)

Centuries after Tamar and her seduction of Judah, another woman would make history and earn a place in the lineage of Jesus. She was a woman with a tarnished past, a pagan upbringing, an immoral lifestyle, and the ability to recognize truth.

In the wilderness outside of Jericho, Joshua was beginning his conquest of Canaan, the Promised Land. Moses had died, and the mantle of leadership now rested heavily on his shoulders. The Israelites moved closer to the land that had been promised to them by God. Victory had been theirs in the past, and God promised more victory in the future. Now a fortified city lay before them.

The setting was the walled city of Jericho—an ancient city situated a few miles north of the Dead Sea and nestled in the Jordan valley. Across the river, the Israelites were massing for their next campaign. Word had come from God: Joshua was to lead the people in a miraculous attack against the city—an attack that would see its mighty walls crumble to the ground.

---

[12]Genesis 38:25. [13]Genesis 38:26.

Joshua sent two spies to infiltrate the city and find its weaknesses. The spies entered the house of Rahab, a known prostitute. Why a prostitute? A prostitute's home was one of the few places a stranger could go without arousing suspicion. The neighbors had certainly seen men passing through her doors before.

Rahab's home became, for a short time, a base of operations. She let the Israelites stay because she recognized something about their people. Based on the battle accounts and the tales of miracles that preceded the people, Rahab concluded, "I know that the Lord has given you the land, and that the terror of you has fallen on us, and that all the inhabitants of the land have melted away before you."[14] Rahab had been paying attention.

Someone, however, had seen the spies. Word was delivered to the king of Jericho, "Behold, men from the sons of Israel have come here tonight to search out the land."[15] The situation escalated quickly when the king's men arrived, banging on Rahab's door and demanding, "Bring out the men who have come to you."[16]

Rahab faced a big decision. Would she give up the spies to save her own life? Or would she risk her life, and the life of her family, to save them? She made the hard decision, and the decision she made says a great deal about her belief in the power of God.

Putting her faith in the God of Israel instead of the pagan gods she had known all her life, she chose to help the Hebrew spies escape. This was a monumental decision. Everything in her life, everything she had known, was the opposite of what she was choosing to embrace. First, she hid the spies on the roof of her house under stalks of flax. Most houses of that era had flat roofs that served as decks. It was the place where people dried stalks of flax.

She sent word to the king, "Yes, the men came to me, but I did not know where they were from. It came about when it was time to shut the gate at dark, that the men went out; I do not know where the men went. Pursue them quickly, for you will overtake them."[17]

---

[14]Joshua 2:9–11. [15]Joshua 2:2. [16]Joshua 2:3. [17]Joshua 2:4–5.

It was a lie, but a lie that bought the spies more time, a lie that saved their lives. It was time well used. She made a request of the Israelites, a plea for her safety and for her family's, which included a father, mother, brothers, sisters, and "all who belong to them."[18]

The spies agreed: "Our life for yours if you do not tell this business of ours; and it shall come about when the LORD gives us the land that we will deal kindly and faithfully with you."[19] Then they made their escape through her window, which was on the city wall.

True to their word, the spies returned to Rahab shortly thereafter and helped her family escape the destruction that would soon fall upon Jericho. They even allowed Rahab's family to camp with them and to live among their people. Because of her faithfulness to God, she eventually married and had a family. Centuries later, one of Rahab's relatives would be Jesus.

Not only does her name appear in the genealogy of Jesus, but she is also one of the heroes of the faith mentioned in the "hall of faith" in the New Testament Book of Hebrews: "By faith Rahab the harlot did not perish along with those who were disobedient, after she had welcomed the spies in peace" (Hebrews 11:31).

One might think that a prostitute was too far removed to be of use by God in a noble cause, but Rahab was just such a person. Her faith caused her to recognize that God was with the children of Israel, and that knowledge enabled her to trust Him for her deliverance when the walls of Jericho came crashing down.

Ruth (Ruth 1:1–4:22)

The small Book of Ruth could parallel countless fairy tales. Everything Ruth had, she lost. Not only did her husband die, but her brother-in-law and father-in-law were both dead as well. She had no child to support her, nor did her mother-in-law, Naomi. The only option for them was to leave the land of Moab and return to Judah, where they could rely on the kindness of relatives.

---

[18]Joshua 2:12–13. [19]Joshua 2:14.

Naomi, however, thought it might be better for Ruth to stay in Moab. After all, she had some family and friends there. She would stand a better chance of survival if she stayed in the country of her birth where she could remarry. Ruth, however, was unwilling to leave her mother-in-law, Naomi: "Do not urge me to leave you or turn back from following you; for where you go, I will go, and where you lodge, I will lodge. Your people shall be my people, and your God, my God. Where you die, I will die, and there I will be buried. Thus may the LORD do to me, and worse, if anything but death parts you and me."[20]

This is perhaps one of the most poignant passages in all of Scripture. It tugs at the heart strings. Seldom has the world seen such unselfish faithfulness. Ruth was saying that she didn't care if she died, so long as she was with Naomi. Ruth understood the importance of family and the power of love. She also understood that no matter how bad off she was, Naomi was in a much worse position.

Naomi was an elderly widow with sons who preceded her in death. She had no means of support. She was far too old to work for herself, and too old to remarry. She had all but resigned herself to a lonely death.

Ruth had a different idea. If Ruth could go to Naomi's country of Judah with her, and maybe even remarry, then she could support Naomi. It was the older woman's only chance for survival.

When they arrived in Judah, Ruth immediately set out to find food for them. She went after the reapers in the barley fields and gathered what they left behind. It wasn't much, but it was enough to get them by.

Over time, she came to the field belonging to Boaz. Boaz was a close relative of Naomi's. When he saw Ruth, her plight moved him with compassion. He instructed his servants to take care of her by leaving more food behind for her to gather.

Naomi, after she had heard all Ruth told her, began to formulate a plan. Ruth was to go to Boaz as he was sleeping and "uncover his feet."[21] There is speculation about what that phrase means. Some have suggested that some immorality was at play, but the character of Boaz and Ruth

---

[20]Ruth 1:16–17. [21]Ruth 3:7.

rules that out. What Ruth did was aboveboard and proper. Boaz was sleeping near the grain to guard it. Ruth lay at his feet, a position of humility, and then uncovered the man's feet. This awakened him, and she made a straightforward request that he fulfill his role as kinsman redeemer.

Boaz went to great lengths to make the request a reality. God was working in the details. In the end, the two married, all because of Ruth's faithful and bold act. Because of it, Ruth was in the lineage of Jesus. She was an ancestor of the Messiah. God didn't care where she was from. Her faith pleased Him, and He blessed her in return. Like Tamar, Ruth was an outsider. God brought her in.

Bathsheba (2 Samuel 11:1–5)

Perhaps of all the women listed in the genealogy of Jesus, none is more surprising than Bathsheba.

In the midst of a war, while his generals and soldiers were off in battle, King David chose to stay home. The Bible says that David rose from his bed in the evening and took a stroll on the flat roof of his palace. It was most likely late. Peering through the spring night, he saw a beautiful woman bathing nearby. He demanded that his servants find out who she was, and he quickly learned that it was Bathsheba, wife of Uriah, a leader in David's army.

At this point, David should have had the wisdom to walk away, but he lingered over Bathsheba's beauty. This proved more dangerous to his well-being than all the wars he had previously fought. Unwilling to deny himself his desire, he commanded that she be brought to him. When she arrived, he took her to his bed. She conceived, and the one-night affair becomes a lifelong problem.[22]

David was concerned about the people learning of his adultery and disobedience to God. In order to cover his transgressions, he called for Uriah to return home and urged him to "go down to [his] house." David's hope was for Uriah to believe that it was he—Bathsheba's own husband—who had conceived with her.[23]

---

[22]2 Samuel 11:3–5. [23]2 Samuel 11:8.

What David did not count on was Uriah's deep sense of pride and brotherhood with the men who were at war. He stoically denied himself any comfort of home and family while his friends and brothers were still in battle. Unable to convince him, David resorted to another plan—a deadly plan.

Uriah's resolve was stronger than David's desperation. No amount of cajoling could get the military man to avail himself of wife and home. Even drunk, he was more righteous than David. Time was running short. In a month or so, people would realize what had happened. David was beloved by the people, a truly great king. Above all else, he was righteous and obedient to God—most of the time. If the news of his adulterous affair became known, the ramifications would be impossible to control.

David sent Uriah back to the war with a message for Joab, the commander-in-chief of Israel's army. Uriah was to go to the front line of the fiercest battle. Then the army was to withdraw suddenly from him, leaving the faithful man exposed to the enemy. With Uriah dead, David could legally marry Bathsheba. Then the child could be his, and no one would have to know about his secret sin.

Again, it seemed like the perfect plan. Uriah died in battle, the result of David's scheme. David sacrificed a man's life to protect his own image. Time passed. Bathsheba became the king's wife and gave birth. David certainly thought he was in the clear. He wasn't. In 2 Samuel 12, God sent the prophet Nathan with a message. The communication was that God knew what David had done, and would deal harshly with him. Because he had killed Uriah, God would take the child who was born to Bathsheba. That very night, the child became ill. Seven days later, he died.

Psalm 51 is the record of David's heartfelt repentance. While the repentance restored his relationship with God, it could not undo the damage he had done.

A new child was born to the couple—a child loved by God. His name was Solomon.

Bathsheba's story does not end there. Years later, David fell ill and was bedridden. His death was near. The balance of power for the kingdom was swaying. David's most powerful son, Absalom, had died.

Adonijah, David's son from another wife, was claiming the throne. He gathered Joab, along with other prominent members of the kingdom, and amassed an army. It looked as if there was no way to challenge Adonijah. He would take control of the kingdom—or so it appeared.

Nathan, the same prophet who rebuked David for his sin with Bathsheba, came and told Bathsheba of all that was happening in the kingdom and instructed her to inform David.

Bathsheba did tell David and pleaded with him to name Solomon as king. David did, and Solomon went on to become one of the greatest kings the world has ever known.

What can we learn from this? That God hates sin and is a God of justice. He will punish sin; He will never condone it. However, God is a merciful God who loves sinners in spite of their sin. As easily as God can punish, He can bless the sinner for what righteousness they may have, as He did here.

Romans 8:28 says, "And we know that God causes all things to work together for good to those who love God, to those who are called according to His purpose." Again we see that God is unlimited by our actions or our failings. Bathsheba was more victim than conspirator, but her image still suffered. Nonetheless, she was in the line of David.

Four women were in the lineage of Jesus, each one with an unpleasant history. The inclusion of Tamar the seductress, Rahab the harlot, Ruth the outsider, and Bathsheba the adulteress reminds us that our past need not dictate our future. No matter what we have done, God is willing to listen to a confession.

But it wasn't just the women in Jesus' lineage who had challenges and failings.

Uzziah, Manasseh, and Jehoiachin

There is an abundance of kings found in Jesus' family tree. This should not surprise us, since we know Him to be the King of kings. The type of kings, however, may surprise some.

Consider Uzziah. He was just sixteen when he ascended to the throne, but that did not stop him from doing great things. Second Chronicles 26:4 says, "He did right in the sight of the LORD."

He made war against the pagan nations and broke down altars to false Gods. He was enthusiastic for the Lord, taking great pains to follow His every command. He even built temples and altars to worship God. But it was this zeal that eventually brought his downfall.[24]

Toward the end of his fifty-two-year reign, Uzziah entered the temple of God to burn incense. At first, this doesn't sound like such a horrible act, but there's more to it than first appears. What he did was strictly forbidden. Only the priests were to burn incense to God. The Bible puts it this way: "But when he became strong, his heart was so proud that he acted corruptly, and he was unfaithful to the LORD his God, for he entered the temple of the LORD to burn incense on the altar of incense."[25]

"Then Azariah the priest entered after him and with him eighty priests of the LORD, valiant men. They opposed Uzziah the king and said to him, 'It is not for you, Uzziah, to burn incense to the Lord, but for the priests, the sons of Aaron who are consecrated to burn incense. Get out of the sanctuary, for you have been unfaithful and will have no honor from the LORD God.'"[26]

Uzziah's heart had become proud and arrogant. Instead of humbling himself, as he should, he became enraged with the priests, and God became enraged with him.

As he lashed out at the priests, a leprous spot appeared on Uzziah's forehead. Realizing what was happening, the priests quickly hurried him out of the house of God and into a separate house where he could remain isolated as required by law. He died a leper, leaving the kingdom to his son Jotham.[27]

Uzziah was a man of great character and great pride. He was a man who loved God but who came to love himself more. He was a man who believed in the holiness of God, and in his own holiness. An arrogant heart will not be a heart used by God. Uzziah shows us that even the best of us can stumble. Even righteous, upright Christians can fall prey to temptation. Uzziah was in the line of Jesus Christ, a reminder that Jesus is the Lord of imperfect people.

---

[24]2 Chronicles 26:6. [25]2 Chronicles 26:16. [26]2 Chronicles 26:17–18. [27]2 Chronicles 26:19–23.

Enter Manasseh. He and Uzziah were polar opposites. Early in his reign, Manasseh did virtually everything wrong. Although he reigned for eleven years with his father Hezekiah, a great king and a man of God, the young king learned nothing from his father and cared nothing for what he was taught. Immediately Manasseh set out to rebuild all the pagan places of worship that his father had torn down. He reinstated Baal worship as well as the worship of Asherah.

That's not all. Manassah's evil campaign continued as he turned to astrology, divination, and sorcery. As if that weren't enough, he turned to child sacrifice. He "made his sons pass through the fire in the valley of Ben-hinnom."[28] Babies were sacrificed to worship the pagan gods. Manasseh had descended as low as a man could go.

Instead of immediately destroying Manasseh and his people, God was patient and provided a means of escape. We see in 2 Chronicles 33:10 that "the Lord spoke to Manasseh and his people, but they paid no attention." They were without excuse for their sins. God acted.

God's punishment was severe. Using Assyria as His divine instrument of destruction, He struck the country of Judah down. Assyria captured Manasseh and bound him with chains and hooks as if he were a wild animal, and led him off to Babylon, where he remained captive.[29]

It is in the midst of this captivity that we see the true difference between Uzziah and Manasseh. In the darkness of imprisonment, something changed in Manasseh. In a Grinch-like epiphany, Manasseh remembered the words and acts of his father Hezekiah. He remembered God—the true God of Israel—whom he had worshiped as a child before he turned to idols.

Confronted with his own sin, Manasseh cried out to God in distress. He humbled himself and prayed for mercy. God heard the cry of his repentant, humble heart. God granted him freedom from Babylon and allowed him to return to Judah, where he continued his reign.[30]

Wisely, Manasseh used the remainder of his time as king to undo some of the evil he had brought upon the land. He undertook great construction

---

[28]2 Chronicles 33:6. [29]2 Chronicles 33:11. [30]2 Chronicles 33:12–13.

projects, building walls and making the armies stronger. Even greater than that, he removed all the foreign gods that he had brought into the land. He built an altar to God and made sacrifices and peace offerings.[31]

The name of a man so evil, so vile as to sacrifice his own children is listed in the lineage of Jesus. An idol worshiper and a sorcerer? It boggles the mind. This account shows us that no one is beyond the saving grace of God. If Manasseh could turn back to God, after all he had done, how much wider is the door of repentance open for us? There is no one who is so far removed from faith that God cannot reach him. Manasseh became a hero.

Perhaps the strangest wrinkle in Christ's genealogy fabric is a king by the name of Jehoiachin (sometimes called Jeconiah). The record about him is thin, aside from the fact that he did evil in the sight of the Lord.[32]

We also know that he was young when he took the throne, only about eight years old. Like many kings before him, Jehoiachin proved himself foolish by doing evil in the sight of the Lord.

The great prophet Jeremiah made a telling statement: "Write this man down childless."[33] These are harsh words for anyone, but especially for a king. The phrase meant that none of his physical descendants would have a legal claim to the throne of David. The fact that he was in the line of Jesus should compromise Jesus' claim to the throne and to the title, "King of the Jews."

However, God does not overlook such details. He is able to make good from bad and success from failure. Jehoiachin was a descendant of Joseph, but Joseph was not the physical father of Jesus. He provided a father's role, but there was no genetic connection to Joseph's family line. There was, however, a legal connection. The ancestors of Joseph were the "legal" ancestors of Jesus, but Jesus' bloodline descended through Mary. This gave Jesus a legal right to the throne of David while keeping him above the sins of his forefathers. Therefore, God was able to pronounce judgment on the wicked acts of Jehoiachin without jeopardizing His Son's future rule.

---

[31] 2 Chronicles 33:15–25. [32] 2 Chronicles 36:9. [33] Jeremiah 22:30.

Amon and Josiah

Two interesting names in the genealogy of Jesus are father and son—one good, one bad. Amon, the king of Judah, took the throne when he was twenty-two years old. The Bible describes him as an evil man, addicted to gross idolatry.[34] He was so evil that his own people plotted his death. They killed him two years into his reign.[35]

Why is a man so evil that his own people killed him listed in the names of the ancestors of Jesus? Perhaps it's for the simple reason of the royal bloodline. His real contribution was providing a nobler son. The Bible records no acts of generosity or selfless giving from Amon. He was a man who "multiplied guilt."[36]

If Amon made any contribution to the world, it was through the acts of his son, Josiah. Josiah was a great king, though he was only eight years old when Amon was killed. The Bible says, "The people of the land made Josiah his son king in his place."[37] It's an odd thing to kill a boy's father, then make the boy king, but it points up the fact that the people did not rebel out of greed, but out of necessity. Josiah was young, but his age did not prevent him from doing many significant things. He, like his great-grandfather Hezekiah, was one of the greatest kings in Judah's history.

As far as God is concerned, age is irrelevant. He can use whomever He wishes whenever He wishes. Though we would not normally think of an eight-year-old king as one to be renowned and revered, God brought Josiah up throughout his thirty-one years of rule to be a man of God, a purposeful leader of a powerful nation.[38] His list of accomplishments is recorded in 2 Chronicles 34:1–35:27.

The Bible has always been fair, true, and accurate. It records the failings of men as well as their successes. The Bible does not create plastic heroes; it shows them as humans who, like King David, may live a righteous life for many years, only to fail at the end.

---

[34]2 Chronicles 33:22. [35]2 Chronicles 33:24. [36]2 Chronicles 33:23. [37]2 Chronicles 33:25. [38]2 Chronicles 34:1–7.

In the lineage of Jesus are some unlikely heroes. Each one served a purpose and provided a lesson for us. No matter what we have done in the past, God can help us to forge a new future.

Points to Ponder

1. Having seen the successes and failings of some of the people in Jesus' family tree, what can we learn about God's choice of leaders?

2. Each of the four women listed in Jesus' lineage had what would appear to be problems that would make them outcasts. What does that say about God's ability to work in difficult situations?

3. Three of the four women discussed in this chapter were involved in some unusual sexual situation. Is that important or significant?

4. Israel's history was marked by a roller coaster of good and bad kings. Both types ended up in Jesus' lineage. Is there an underlying moral to that fact?

5. The genealogies of Jesus show His legal and biological right to be king. Are there other reasons why the genealogies are included in the Gospels?

Mysterious
Connection

The greatest discovery in history occurred on a cool spring morning just outside Jerusalem. The discovery was made not by an explorer or a scientist but by a heartbroken woman. The previous hours had been more grueling than any person should have endured.

Mary Magdalene had worked her way through the deserted streets of Jerusalem just before sunrise. She was on a mission, a pilgrimage to the tomb of Jesus. His trials, beatings, and horrid execution were still fresh in her mind. It is doubtful that she had slept much since the Friday when she saw Jesus breathe His last breath.

We can't know what thoughts were on the surface of her mind; nor can we know what fear churned in her heart. We do know that she was the first of many to discover that the tomb of Christ was empty.

The resurrection of Christ is the heart and soul of Christianity. All doctrine, all churches, all baptisms, everything associated with Christ is wrapped up in the truth that Christ died on the cross but was raised to life. If that is not true, then the church is a sham. The apostle Paul drove that point home in his letter to the Corinthians. In chapter 15, the apostle shows how futile faith would be with a dead Savior. He said, "If Christ has not been raised, then our preaching is vain, your faith also is vain."[1] He went on to say that he would be a "false witness" and that we would all remain in our sin. As if that image isn't chilling enough,

---

[1] 1 Corinthians 15:14.

Paul added the fact that the dead have perished—forever. Without the resurrection, "we are of all men most to be pitied."[2]

But Christ did rise from the grave, and He was seen by many people.

The resurrection is the bright spot of the Gospels. It shows victory over death and verifies Christ's claims and message. So bright is the event that many fascinating things often get overlooked. When staring into a bright light, the human eye cannot distinguish nearby objects. Any object in front of the light becomes silhouetted. So it is with the resurrection. The mind immediately runs to the risen Savior as it should, but there are other details to be noticed too. And what amazing details they are.

For example, there is more to the tomb than most people know. It is more than a cave in a hill; it is symbolic of something amazing and meaningful.

Four Views

Anchoring the New Testament are four books that cover the same material. The Gospels ("good news") each tell the story of Christ's life, message, miracles, death, and resurrection. Each emphasize a different aspect of Jesus' ministry. Some Gospels record events not found in the others. This is not only to be expected, but it brings greater meaning to the accounts.

As expected, each of the Gospels records the resurrection, but they do so differently, emphasizing particulars not found in the others. This has caused some confusion. It is difficult to get a uniform, chronological picture, but that is to be expected. More went on in those first few hours than most people realize. The event itself is so unusual that it would be impossible to avoid some confusion.

Does this mean that the Gospels are in error? Not at all. Like a diamond that shines more brightly because a skilled jeweler has cut facets into the gem, so the resurrection takes on a deeper, more colorful meaning because of the inspired facets of the writers.

Some people have maintained that the four accounts contradict one another. On the contrary, they complement one another. Taken together,

---

[2] 1 Corinthians 15:19.

they give a picture that is far richer and more meaningful. It is when we take all four Gospels together that we find one of the most mysterious and little known symbols in the New Testament. The tomb itself was more than it appeared to be.

Burial Practices

Unlike most of today's cultures, the Jews of Jesus' day did not embalm the dead. Consequently, they buried as quickly as possible, generally the same day. Family and friends prepared the body of the deceased by washing it, anointing the corpse with spices, and then wrapping it in linen. The linen was in the form of long strips, wound mummy-like around the body from foot to under the arms. Spices and perfume were laid between the layers of linen. Another piece of linen was wrapped under the jaw and over the top of the head to keep the mouth from gaping. A face "napkin" covered the face. The hands and feet were also tied with linen strips.

Friends would then carry the body on a wooden bier to the burial place. Jesus encountered such a scene when He came across a widow burying her only son.[3]

Depending on the wealth of the family, they buried the body in the ground or entombed it in a sepulcher. Cremation was rare, done only under extreme conditions, such as advanced decomposition. Many Jews buried their dead in family tombs. These were natural caves or cavities cut out of rock. The latter was extremely expensive.

After Jesus died on the cross, Joseph of Arimathea and Nicodemus took His body down and prepared it for burial.[4] As was the custom, the two men wrapped Jesus and covered Him with a mixture of myrrh and aloes weighing about one hundred pounds.

Several people have suggested various tombs for the one used that day, but it is impossible to be certain. We do know that the place where Jesus was buried was a new tomb, recently cut out of the rock.

Once in the sepulcher, they placed His body on a wood bench or rock ledge. All of this happened hastily since the Sabbath was about to

---

[3]Luke 7:12–15. [4]Matthew 27:57–60; John 19:38–42.

begin. Once inside, the two men would have left the tomb and released the large stone that sealed the opening. The stone was like a large disk they rolled into place. Such stones kept animals out.

Jesus' death was uncommon. Although the Romans had crucified many people, Jesus presented a different kind of problem for the religious leaders and Pontius Pilate, the local Roman leader. The concern revolved around two problems.

First was the number of people who followed Jesus. At times in His ministry, they came out in the tens of thousands. While many people had fallen away, the number—as far as His enemies knew—was still significant.

The second concern came from Jesus Himself. On many occasions, He had said He would rise from the dead. Such an act would prove disastrous to the religious leaders' cause. Once He was in the grave, they wanted to keep Him there. They held no belief that Jesus could deliver on His promise, but they feared the disciples would steal the body and lie about it. It is amazing how untrusting untrustworthy people are.

Their fear came out in their conversation with Pilate. Oddly, the only other person whom the Pharisees hated more than Jesus was Pilate, yet they were willing to set aside the years of animosity to further the conspiracy. "Sir, we remember that when He was still alive that deceiver said, 'After three days I am to rise again.' Therefore, give orders for the grave to be made secure until the third day, otherwise His disciples may come and steal Him away and say to the people, 'He has risen from the dead,' and the last deception will be worse than the first."[5]

Pilate agreed, saying, "You have a guard; go, make it as secure as you know how."[6] They needed no further encouragement. "And they went and made the grave secure, and along with the guard they set a seal on the stone."[7] There is no description of the seal, but it was most likely a dab of clay into which the impression of Pilate's personal seal was imprinted. They attached the seal to a cord that stretched across the stone door. To break the seal could be punishable by death.

---

[5]Matthew 27:63–64. [6]Matthew 27:65. [7]Matthew 27:66.

There it was. They had done the deed. They orchestrated Jesus' arrest, tried Him repeatedly, beat Him, rejected Him, and nailed Him to a cross. Hours later, He died, was removed from the cross by friends, was hastily prepared for burial, and was laid in a borrowed tomb. The door was shut, sealed, and guards were set in place. The disciples went into hiding.

On Sunday morning, the world changed forever.

Mystery 1

Mary Magdalene had invested her life in Jesus. She along with several other women supported the itinerate ministry of the Savior.[8] As the sun pushed back the ebony night, she made her way to the grave, but she found something she could not understand.

The grave was open. The seal had been broken. Jesus was gone. And there was more mystery waiting. John 20 gives the account of how Mary, shocked to see an empty tomb, raced to the disciples and told Peter and John the news. Peter and John ran to the site, John outracing Peter. John stopped short of entering the tomb. Instead, he stopped, stooped, and looked in. From the outer edge of the opening, he was able to peer in and see the linen wrappings that had once held Jesus.

Peter was not so timid. He may have been the second to arrive, but he was the first inside. He also saw the linens and the "face-cloth which had been on His head," not lying "with the linen wrappings, but rolled up in a place by itself."[9] This is the first oddity and indicates several things.

First, taking the time to roll up the face-cloth shows the leisure of time. There was no rush. A police detective would find it unusual. If someone had stolen the body of Jesus, they would have cast the cloth to the side, not meticulously folded it and set it in a place by itself. We can't help but wonder who folded the napkin. Perhaps an angel was helping the Savior, or perhaps Jesus set the face-cloth to the side Himself.

When John could restrain himself no longer, he joined Peter in the tomb. He studied the linens more intently. The text uses several words

---

[8]Luke 8:2–3. [9]John 20:7.

for "look." First, John *looked* in the tomb. The term comes from the Greek for "to perceive, to see" (from *blepo)*. It's the basic word for "see." Next Peter charged into the tomb and "saw" the linens, but the word here (from *theoreo*) means "to gaze intently and with interest." Peter was looking for clues, trying to make sense of what he was seeing. This indicates a greater puzzle. Something about the linens caught and held the disciple's attention. What was he seeing?

John saw the same thing when he entered the tomb. He "saw" (from *eidon*) the linens, but the word carries the idea of seeing with understanding—not just gazing, not just puzzling, but seeing with insight. This is why the passage states that John "saw and believed" (John 20:8). What he saw was convincing.

The text implies that there was something unusual about the linens themselves. As John stared down at the spot where Jesus had been laid the previous Friday, he saw not a pile of linen wrappings but a chrysalis, a cocoon, as if Jesus had passed right through the material. The wrappings that had covered Jesus from the feet to under the arms may have retrained its form, held in place by the aloe and myrrh mixture pasted between the strands. John knew that no person could wiggle out of such bindings without destroying the linens. He also knew that no grave robber would steal the body and leave the death clothes behind. Even if it were possible, it would take too much time.

Peter and John left the empty tomb, taking with them the unforgettable sight they had just witnessed. The text tells us, "For as yet they did not understand the Scripture, that He must rise again from the dead."[10] That doubt would be removed later.

Mystery 2

Mary Magdalene returned to the tomb. Her heart was still broken, her fear still piercing. Peter and John left the tomb as they found it, their thoughts their own. Something had changed. Through tear-filled eyes, Mary noticed visitors. The empty tomb was no longer empty. In fact, it was becoming crowded. "But Mary was standing outside the tomb

---

[10]John 20:9.

weeping; and so, as she wept, she stooped and looked into the tomb; and she saw two angels in white sitting, one at the head and one at the feet, where the body of Jesus had been lying."[11]

The Bible is a book of details. So much gets overlooked when we don't ask, "Why is this here? Why would the Bible have this detail?" This is certainly true of this passage. The details seem to flash before our eyes. Why tell us the number of angels? Why record that they were sitting? Is this just general background or pertinent detail? It is more than coincidence.

Two angels sat where the body of Jesus had been. Between them lay the empty cocoonlike chrysalis, face napkin, linen straps used to tie Jesus' hands, and the one used to hold His jaw shut. The symbolism is magnificent, but not apparent.

The most obvious fact is that there were two angels. *Angel* is the generic word for "messenger." It doesn't tell us the type of angels Mary saw, only that they were angels. The word carries the idea of an envoy sent on a mission. So it was with these two. They had a message to give: spoken and unspoken.

The spoken message came in the form of a question: "Woman, why are you weeping?"[12] At first, it seems an odd, even silly, question. The answer should be obvious. Mary Magdalene had come to grieve over her executed Savior, and now His corpse was gone. The question may seem silly, but it has an implied statement: "There is no need to weep." Mary's tears, while understandable, were rooted in a misunderstanding. She assumed that the final indignity had occurred—Jesus' body had been stolen. To her, this was one more cruelty meant to crush those who loved Jesus, and there was nothing to be done about it.

A moment later, Jesus corrected that misconception in a glorious way. Turning, Mary saw a man she did not recognize.[13] He asked the same question: "Woman, why are you weeping? Whom are you seeking?"[14] Within moments, Mary came to understand the truth of the matter: Jesus

---

[11]John 20:11–12. [12]John 20:13. [13]For a discussion of the unrecognizable Jesus, see the author's book *Uncovering the Bible's Greatest Mysteries* (Nashville, Tenn.: Broadman & Holman, 2002). [14]John 20:15.

had delivered on His promise to rise from the dead. At this point all attention shifts away from the two angels in the tomb to Jesus. That is understandable, but we miss something remarkable if we let our attention shift too quickly.

The unspoken message is thrilling. Picture the scene again: Two angels sitting at the head and the foot of where the lifeless body of Jesus had been for three days. Nowhere else in Scripture are angels said to be sitting. Only at the tomb do we find sitting angels. As we will see, there were four such angels.

We need to ask a question: Of all the places in the world to sit, why sit on the bier that once supported the lifeless body of Jesus? It's a symbolic act meant to call to mind two other messengers in a similar situation.

Fourteen hundred years before, God had given specific information to Moses to build a special chest called the ark of the covenant. God not only called for its construction but also gave verbal blueprints for its design.

The word *ark* simply means "box." Not to be confused with Noah's ark, which translates a different Hebrew word, *ark* in the ark of the covenant comes from the word *aron* and means "a chest or coffin." The boat Noah built comes from the Hebrew *tebah* and is used to describe the basket in which Moses was laid as a child.[15]

The ark of the covenant was a wooden box, covered inside and out with gold. It was measured in cubits, an imprecise unit that was equivalent to the distance between a man's elbow and his fingertip. A cubit could measure from sixteen to twenty-two inches. Most scholars consider a cubit to be eighteen inches. Using that number, the ark would measure 3.75 feet by 2.25 feet by 2.25 feet. It was about the size of a large travel trunk.

Using God's dimensions and descriptions, two men, Bezalel and Oholiab, undertook its construction. God had chosen and gifted them for the work.[16] Exodus 25:10–21 gives the details of the ark's construction. There were only two building materials used: gold and wood. The wood

---

[15]Exodus 2:3. [16]Exodus 35:4–35.

was acacia, a dark, hard-grained wood that repelled insects. It was the perfect wood for an object designed to last centuries.[17]

Over this base of hardwood, the workmen laid gold. Gold covered everything, inside and out. Once finished, the wood was impossible to see. The Bible doesn't state how thick the gold was. It could have been a thin layer, like gold leaf, but it may have been more substantial. Even the poles used to carry the ark were covered in gold, as were the rings through which the poles passed. Ironically, as beautiful as the ark was, very few people ever saw it. When moved, it was always covered.[18]

The lid of the ark was special on several counts. Referred to as the mercy seat *(kapporeth)*, it was placed over the open top of the box, sealing the contents inside.[19] It was constructed with a continuous layer of gold, out of which were formed two cherubim whose faces were forever turned toward the mercy seat and whose wings extended above them and forward until they met over the middle of the ark. On the Day of Atonement *(Yom Kippur)* the high priest would enter the Most Holy Place of the temple. It was the only time of the year when such entrance was permitted. Before he could enter the hallowed room, the priest had to make a sacrifice for his own sin. Sacrificing a bull, he would enter the Holy of Holies and sprinkle the blood on the mercy seat. When he went into the room, he wore a white linen robe.

The parallels between the tomb and the ark of the covenant are amazing. What Mary saw is a symbolic reflection of what the high priest would see once a year—or used to see. In Jesus' day, the Holy of Holies was empty, the ark having mysteriously disappeared sometime around King Solomon's reign. In the first century, the high priest made the same offerings but sprinkled the blood of the bull on the spot where the ark *used* to be.

If we could see through the eyes of Mary, we would see two angels in white sitting on a stone bier[20] (possibly wood) in the same positions as the cherubim on the ark of the covenant. Between them lay the spot where the sacrifice for the world had rested, in essence, the sprinkling of His

---

[17]This wood is sometime called *shittim*. [18]Numbers 4:5–6. [19]Exodus 25:17.
[20]There is something poetic in the knowledge that at Jesus' birth He was laid in a manager, a stone feeding trough, and that in death He was laid upon a stone bier.

Tombs in one of the numerous Etruscan cemeteries north of Rome. After His cruci-fixion, Jesus was laid in a tomb crowded with angels.

blood. All that remained were the linens, which correspond to the linen robe the high priest used to wear. Instead of sprinkling the blood of a bull for the remission of sin, Jesus our High Priest "sprinkles" His own blood.

Inside the ark of the covenant were several key items: the tablets of stone upon which God had written the Ten Commandments, a golden jar of manna, and the rod of Aaron. Each of these symbolizes some aspect of Christ. As the ark carried the tablets of the law, so Jesus came not to "abolish the Law or the Prophets" but to "fulfill" them.[21] The ark carried a jar of the miraculous food called manna that was literally bread from heaven. Jesus used this as an example of Himself: "I am the living bread that came down out of heaven; if anyone eats of this bread, he will live forever; and the bread also which I will give for the life of the

---

[21]Matthew 5:17.

world is My flesh."[22] Aaron's rod budded miraculously to prove that he and his descendents were God's choice for the priestly work. The author of the Book of Hebrews shows Christ as the High Priest.[23]

The author of Hebrews makes another interesting remark: "But when Christ appeared as a high priest of the good things to come, He entered through the greater and more perfect tabernacle, not made with hands, that is to say, not of this creation; and not through the blood of goats and calves, but through His own blood, He entered the holy place once for all, having obtained eternal redemption."[24]

What Mary saw would force the mind of any Jew to the image of the ark of the covenant. The two angels, the stone mercy seat, the linen—all of it a silent, symbolic statement about what Christ achieved for humanity. Forgiveness came because of that work. "And according to the Law, one may almost say, all things are cleansed with blood, and without shedding of blood there is no forgiveness."[25]

But it doesn't end there.

The Crowded Tomb

When we take all the Gospel accounts together, the big picture appears. The Gospel of Mark records: "Entering the tomb, they saw a young man sitting at the right, wearing a white robe; and they were amazed."[26] *They* refers to a group of women that included "Mary Magdalene, and Mary the mother of James, and Salome."[27]

Mark's words are intriguing. First, he says that the women entered the tomb and saw a "young man sitting at the right." What rich detail. Most commentators assume this is the same angel seen sitting on the stone outside the tomb, but the text shows that the young man was already seated inside. This is a different person from the one who sat on the stone.

Two other details catch our attention. Mark doesn't call the person an angel. His description matches that of other angels, but Mark specifically

---

[22]John 6:51. [23]Hebrews 9:11. Hebrews 9 is a great study of the symbolism of the temple and how it relates to Jesus. [24]Hebrews 9:11–12. [25]Hebrews 9:22. [26]Mark 16:5. [27]Mark 16:1.

called him a young man.[28] Why? Most likely, he was an angel. He wore the same white robe that angels wore. Those who sat on the bier wore white.[29]

Add to that the specific detail that he was sitting. Why not standing? Why not pacing? Why seated when the women entered? In ancient cultures, sitting represented the stop of work, that an assigned task was completed. But what was the young man's assignment?

If the bier upon which the two angels sat does indeed represent the ark of covenant, then the symbol is strengthened with the introduction of a man who would represent the high priest. He sat because no other sacrifice is possible beyond what Christ has already done. Christ's work on the cross "offered one sacrifice for sins for all time."[30]

Mark uses the term *young man* in lieu of the expected "angel" to strengthen the image that the tomb is a representation of the temple. The young man delivered a simple but profound message: "Do not be amazed; you are looking for Jesus the Nazarene, who has been crucified. He has risen, He is not here; behold, here is the place where they laid Him."[31]

So far, we have seen three angels, but the tomb had other otherworldly visitors. The Gospel of Luke mentions two more angels. Some interpreters have suggested that these were the ones who sat upon the bier, but the passages make more sense if these were a pair of additional angels.

"While they were perplexed about this, behold, two men suddenly stood near them in dazzling clothing."[32] Like Mark, Luke avoids the typical word *angel* and uses the Greek term for man *(aner)*. Unlike Mark, he doesn't indicate any age. Their clothing was "dazzling."[33] The word is used of lightning and means "to flash forth." So awesome was the sight that "the women were terrified and bowed their faces to the ground."[34]

Why two angels? Inside the Holy of Holies, overshadowing the ark of the covenant, were a pair of cherubim statues, fifteen feet tall, each with a fifteen-foot wingspan.[35] These statues were made of olive wood and

---

[28]*Neaniskos.* [29]John 20:12. [30]Hebrews 10:12. [31]Mark 16:6. [32]Luke 24:4. [33]*Astrapto.* [34]Luke 24:5. [35]1 Kings 6:23–28.

covered in gold. Gold would reflect any light that fell upon it, making the statues shine and flash. The two dazzling angels in the tomb round out the picture.

The tomb of Christ stood in the shadow of the temple, but because of His work on the cross, the temple falls under the shadow of the tomb. Christ did what no high priest could achieve; He became the sacrifice that no animal sacrifice could achieve. Consequently, the need for ritual sacrifice was finished. No longer is there a need for an annual sacrifice for sin. Jesus took our sin upon Him as He died and became the perfect sacrifice.

This symbolism began the moment Jesus died on the cross. "And behold, the veil of the temple was torn in two from top to bottom; and the earth shook and the rocks were split."[36] The veil was a thick curtain that separated the Holy of Holies from the rest of the temple. Only the high priest ever went behind the curtain. The tearing of the veil was a graphic statement that the final sacrifice had been made. For centuries, only one priest could go into the room where it was believed that God dwelt. With the ripping of the veil, the hidden was clearly seen. It was by design that the tomb was open and the women were encouraged to enter.

Who invited them in? The sixth angel in the Gospel accounts. Matthew gives the details: "And behold, a severe earthquake had occurred, for an angel of the Lord descended from heaven and came and rolled away the stone and sat upon it. And his appearance was like lightning, and his clothing as white as snow."[37]

This description is similar to the two angels who suddenly appeared inside the tomb, but different from the other three "sitting" angels. This being sat on the stone as if to show contempt for its ability to keep him out or the Savior in. Incidentally, the stone was not rolled away to let Jesus out, but to let others in.

If we chart the pertinent information, we see an interesting pattern.

---

[36]Matthew 27:51. [37]Matthew 28:2–3.

Gospel	Term	Number	Location	Position	Seen by
Matthew 12:1–7	An angel (*angelos* x2)	One	Outside	Seated on stone outside	Women
Mark 16:1–8	Young man (*neaniskos*)	One	Inside	Seated "on right" inside	Women
Luke 23:55–24:10	Men (*aner*)	Two	Inside	Standing (suddenly) inside	Women
John 20:1–18	Angels (*angelos*)	Two	See inside	Seated at head and foot of bier	Mary Magdalene

A schematic of the accounts is on the next page.

The Temple that Made the Difference

Outside the walls of Jerusalem, three days after Passover, Jesus exited a common tomb. It was common in the sense that it belonged to a man and his family. No tomb could hold Jesus. The resurrection is a fact of history that changes everything. The empty tomb attests to the fact that Jesus is the one who was dead but is alive forevermore.[38]

In many ways, that empty tomb became a temple. Whereas the activities and practices of the temple could not provide an enduring cure for sin, Jesus could. The tomb is the temple that makes all the difference.

Points to Ponder

1. In chapter 12, "Mysterious Numbers," it was argued that numbers in the Bible carry symbolic meaning. Is there any significance to the fact that there were six angels seen at the tomb?

2. The temple was a magnificent structure of massive cut stones, beautifully adorned with wood and gold. The tomb was simple and rough. Is there any significance in this?

---

[38]Revelation 1:18.

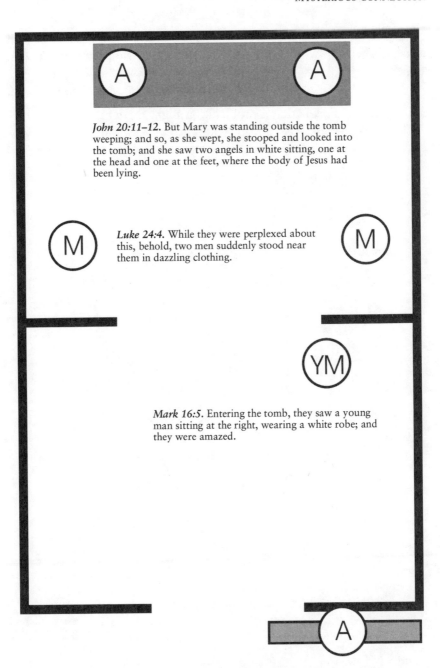

John 20:11–12. But Mary was standing outside the tomb weeping; and so, as she wept, she stooped and looked into the tomb; and she saw two angels in white sitting, one at the head and one at the feet, where the body of Jesus had been lying.

Luke 24:4. While they were perplexed about this, behold, two men suddenly stood near them in dazzling clothing.

Mark 16:5. Entering the tomb, they saw a young man sitting at the right, wearing a white robe; and they were amazed.

Matthew 28:2. And behold, a severe earthquake had occurred, for an angel of the Lord descended from heaven and came and rolled away the stone and sat upon it.

3. When Peter and John arrived at the tomb, there is no mention of angels. When the women arrived, they and they alone saw the angels. Why?

4. It is very difficult to correlate all the events at the tomb into an unbroken time line. Is that a problem, or might there be a reason for it?

5. Are there other symbols in and around the tomb not covered in this chapter?

Why I'm a Skeptic

"To you it was shown that you might know that the LORD, He is God; there is no other besides Him."[1]

"The secret things belong to the LORD our God, but the things revealed belong to us and to our sons forever, that we may observe all the words of this law."[2]

If you've read the chapters that precede this one, the title of this chapter may surprise you. After discussing everything from mysterious punishments to the symbolic lesson of Christ's tomb, my sudden admission to being a skeptic seems out of place. But it is true.

I grew up in a very trusting world and was by nature unquestioning of others . . . until I reached my teen years. Then it seemed no one trusted anyone, including me. Over the years of my life I have learned to have confidence in many things, I have also learned that there is as much falsehood in the world as there is truth; as much evil as good; as much deception as honesty.

That knowledge has not come easily to me. Some of the lessons came by painful processes, others through observation, and some by grace. Now, as I approach my fiftieth birthday, I believe I've reached a biblical, godly balance between belief and doubt.

I have come to believe that all the Bible teaches is true. This is not blind faith. The Bible has proven itself correct in everything I've examined.

---

[1]Deuteronomy 4:35. [2]Deuteronomy 29:29.

This conclusion is borne out daily. The more I learn, the more convinced I am that every word in the Bible is there for a reason.

I've also learned that the greatest meaning is in the smallest details. While our duties in this world push us to "get the big picture" and then move on, I've learned there is depth in the details.

I watch very little news that comes across commercial television. My patience with sound bites has run out. Too often, the commercials run longer than the news reports. A quick glossing of facts is frustrating. Others feel the same. The same can be said of Bible study. A quick glance at a passage may be interesting, but it is seldom enlightening.

God is in the details. I've said that before in this book, but I can't help repeating it. God is truly in the details. Jesus Himself said, "For truly I say to you, until heaven and earth pass away, not the smallest letter or stroke shall pass from the Law until all is accomplished."[3]

He was referring to the small marks on Hebrew letters. Those tiny marks make a difference. The tiny things in the Bible are the big things in life. This much I have come to believe without reservation. Still, I'm a skeptic, and I think you should be too.

The older I've grown, the more skeptical I've become. I no longer believe that when a telemarketer calls my home at 8:00 in the evening, he has my best interest at heart. I don't believe everything said by a preacher on television simply because he's introduced by the title Reverend or Doctor. I don't believe everything I read in the papers, and even less of what I see on television.

I'm a skeptic, and I take a measure of pride in it.

The Meaning of Skeptic

A definition is in order. The word *skeptic* has fallen on hard times, and it is used by those who would be better described by other words. The *American Heritage Dictionary* describes skepticism as "a doubting or questioning attitude or state of mind." I define the term a little differently. I believe biblical skepticism is harvesting the jewels of truth from the cut glass of opinion. That is hard work, but it is worth the effort.

---

[3]Matthew 5:18.

The church remains strong as long as its members keep the Bible and its teaching central.

Perhaps it is important for me to explain what I don't mean. There are those who believe the United States did not land men on the moon. They preach that the whole thing is a conspiracy. Others believe the world is flat and even have their own organization called the Flat Earth Society. That is not what I mean by skepticism. I have something more reasonable in mind.

Skepticism—biblical skepticism—appears many times in the Bible. The bold and colorful John the Baptist was a skeptic. His skepticism was recorded for us by Matthew: "But when he saw many of the Pharisees and Sadducees coming for baptism, he said to them, 'You brood of vipers, who warned you to flee from the wrath to come? Therefore bear fruit in keeping with repentance; and do not suppose that you can say to yourselves, "We have Abraham for our father"; for I say to you that from these stones God is able to raise up children to Abraham.'"[4]

Yes, John the Baptist was a skeptic, and he was in good company. Jesus said something very similar: "You brood of vipers, how can you, being evil, speak what is good? For the mouth speaks out of that which fills the heart."[5]

In New Testament times, there was a group known as the Bereans. They knew the joy of positive skepticism. Acts 17:10–12 tells us of their character: "The brethren immediately sent Paul and Silas away by night to Berea, and when they arrived, they went into the synagogue of the Jews. Now these were more noble-minded than those in Thessalonica, for they received the word with great eagerness, examining the Scriptures daily to see whether these things were so. Therefore many of them believed, along with a number of prominent Greek women and men."

Once again, the apostle Paul had been run out of town, this time from a city called Thessalonica. He and Silas entered the town of Berea, which was forty-five miles or so from Thessalonica. There they began their work again, but this time they were welcomed. Instead of enemies, they found a group of Jews who received them gladly and examined the Scriptures to see if Paul was on the level. In short, they were skeptics— the best kind of skeptics.

Their goal was not to prove others wrong. They simply wanted to discover what was right and true. Consequently, they learned more, discovered more, and were forever changed in the process.

Skepticism and God's Mysterious Ways

It is one thing to know that God works in mysterious ways. It is quite another to examine those ways for yourself. This book contains some examples of the unexpected ways in which God has worked. We've seen harsh punishment and great grace. All of these are little more than curiosities if we do not realize the greater meaning behind it all.

---

[4]Matthew 3:7–9. [5]Matthew 12:34.

A few of the topics I've approached are controversial. My hope and prayer in all of it is that you the reader will open the Word of God—as the Bereans did—to see if these things are so.

Questions remain. There will always be questions. If we have no questions, then we're not looking hard enough. Some matters will remain unsolved until we have the opportunity to ask the Lord for ourselves. That should not disturb us. Indeed, it should motivate us to look harder.

In graduate school I had a teacher describe theology—by which he meant the study of God—as the greatest scientific pursuit. Scientific? That puzzled me until I understood what he meant. He was telling all of us fresh-faced students that Bible study is a reasoned pursuit, that it required thought and effort and work—and that it was worth every drop of sweat.

The Overall Goal

No matter how intriguing a passage, no matter how thrilling the pursuit of knowledge, it is all meaningless unless it leads us to the face of God. Talk of angels and demons, mysteries and conundrums are enlightening, but knowing God is eternity-changing.

So here's my challenge to you: Examine the Bible openly, without gullibility but also without cynicism. See if these things are true. Search, investigate, ask questions. Pray. Pray again.

There's a cliché that is making the rounds these days: "Don't sweat the small stuff. Everything is small stuff." I want to give the opposite advice. When it comes to Scripture, do sweat the small stuff. That's where the spiritual rewards are. Don't sacrifice the larger picture for a single dab of paint, but don't overlook the painter's technique and practiced brush strokes.

Our God is a mysterious God, and He truly works in mysterious ways. But He has enabled us to search out those unexpected activities.

The Bible is there for anyone to read, to examine, to study, to enjoy. It is my prayer that in the process, God will work in an unexpectedly wonderful way in your life.